THE
SIGNS
OF OUR
TIME

Semiotics:
The Hidden Messages of Environments,
Objects, and Cultural Images

Jack Solomon, Ph.D.

JEREMY P. TARCHER, INC.
Los Angeles

Library of Congress Cataloging in Publication Data

Solomon, Jack.
   The signs of our time: semiotics, the hidden messages of environments, objects, and
cultural images / Jack Solomon.
      p. cm.
1. Semiotics.   I. Title
P99.S57   1988
001.51–dc19
ISBN 0-87477-479-9   88-15928
ISBN 0-87477-480-2 (pbk.)   CIP

Jeremy P. Tarcher, Inc.
9110 Sunset Blvd.
Los Angeles, CA 90069

Distributed by St. Martin's Press

Design by Gary Hespenheide

Manufactured in the United States of America
10 9 8 7 6 5 4 3 2 1

First Edition

For Sonia, again,
and the cat pack: Susie, Charlie, and Pooh

Contents

In a book as sensitive to the significance of ordinary human gestures as this one is, the reader may well wonder just what an "acknowledgments" page signifies. Over the years, when reading other people's books, I have often had the (mistaken) impression that such pages were simply *pro forma* gestures of politeness. But having had the opportunity to write a few pages myself by now, I can say that an author's acknowledgments signify the real gratitude one feels to those who helped one along in the often lonely, and arduous, business of writing books. So let me extend my thanks, first, to my students at UCLA, who have patiently listened to me expatiate on the nature of signs, and in particular to Blake Ferris and Timothy Murphy, who have spoken back with keen semiotic insights of their own. I'm grateful to Arden Reed, who read portions of my manuscript and provided invaluable suggestions for improvement and equally invaluable encouragement and praise. I'd like to thank Michael North for his collegial willingness to share his broad knowledge of architecture with the semiotician down the hall, Ellen Pader for her stimulating remarks on the semiotics of space, and Felice Li for her insights into Chinese culture.

Michael Moore intervened at a crucial moment as I was puzzling out the causes of the mesmeric attractions of TV, while Simon Varey (whether he knew it or not) played the indispensable role of comradely confidant during those not infrequent moments when an author simply has to blow off a little steam.

I'd like to thank my editor, Hank Stine, for whipping my manuscript into a book, and Joan Leemhorst and Dianne Woo for their attentive copy editing of the manuscript. And I'd like to thank my parents, Robert and Helen Solomon, for their curiosity about my project and for providing examples for semiotic analysis. But most of all, I wish to thank my wife and in-house editor, Sonia Maasik, without whose always cheerful assistance as textual editor, researcher, and semiotic consultant this book might never have seen the light of day.

Cracking the Code: Discovering the Signs of American Culture

When I use a word . . . it means just what I choose it to mean—neither more nor less.

Humpty Dumpty
in *Through the Looking-Glass*

In the looking-glass world of Lewis Carroll's whimsical sequel to *Alice in Wonderland*, words do not always mean what they may appear to mean. Take Humpty Dumpty, whom Alice meets sitting high up on a wall, confident in his powers over both gravity and language. Humpty has a disconcerting habit of making words mean what he wants them to mean, constructing his own private linguistic codes and ignoring ordinary usage. In Humpty's dictionary, for example, the term *glory* means "there's a nice knock-down argument for you!" and the term *impenetrability* means "that we've had enough of that subject, and it would be just as well if you'd mention what you mean to do next, as I suppose you don't mean to stop here all the rest of your life." Understandably puzzled, Alice points out that "*glory* doesn't mean 'a nice knock-down argument,' " and that Humpty's definition of *impenetrability* seems to be "a great deal to make one word mean." Humpty simply replies, "When I make a word do a lot of work like that . . . I always pay it extra." But, Alice complains, "The question is . . . whether you *can* make words mean so many different things," to which Humpty retorts, "The question is . . . which is to be master—that's all."

Shortly after delivering *this* "nice knock-down argument," Humpty loses his balance and crashes to the ground, proving that one can't mess with gravity. But he was right about words. They *do* mean what we want them to mean. Although a word and its meaning may appear to be one and the same, the truth is that words are only *signs* of meaning, arbitrary symbols whose significance, like the dots and dashes of the Morse code, is determined by cultural beliefs and social convention. We are ordinarily so immersed in these conventions, however, that we do not see them *as* conventions. Rather, we look upon our languages as objective reflections of reality, when they are actually codified systems of signs.

This book is about codes and the way that ordinary words, objects, and activities can be signs that point to hidden systems of cultural belief. We usually think of codes as special signaling devices used by spies, secret societies, and ham radio operators. But the fact is that culture itself is a tissue of codes, a complex system of signs whose meanings may not always lie on the surface. If I say "Good morning" to you, I'm not really describing the weather; after all, it could be raining. Rather, I'm dipping into a store of phrases governed by the codes of social etiquette to express my desire to be civil or polite. A visitor from a foreign country who understands the words *good* and *morning* but does not know the code to which they belong will get the wrong message. Similarly, if I give my wife a heart-shaped greeting card on February 14, I'm not suggesting that she have a cardiovascular checkup: I'm sending a message according to the conventional code of St. Valentine. And when I approach a traffic intersection, it isn't enough for me to know that one light is red and the other green; I have to know the significance of these signs as they function in the code, or I'm likely to get into an awful smashup.

To understand a code is to be able to link its signs—like words or traffic signals—with their meanings. This doesn't happen automatically, however. Signs are not windows through which the light of meaning innocently shines. They are screens that let through only those meanings that belong to the code. Often the nature of this screen can be charged with ideological significance. Consider, for example, the meaning of the word *abortion*. The word is a linguistic sign that on one level simply refers to the voluntary termination of a pregnancy, but that certainly doesn't constitute its entire meaning. Ask a pro-lifer what "abortion" means, and he or she will instantly answer "murder." Ask the same of a pro-choice advocate, and he or she will refer to a woman's right to choose her own biological destiny. Each answer reflects the ideological code of the respondent. The meaning of "abortion" in the pro-life camp is determined by a religious code of values, while the meaning of the same term in the pro-choice movement reflects a more secular code that relates abortion to human rights issues, in this case women's rights. But rather than conceding the ideological nature of their interpretations, each side generally sees its answer as the "real" or objective meaning, and considers the "other" side guilty of clouding the issue with "ideology."

The ideological nature of signs is particularly marked in the political arena, where a battle over words may have much more than mere semantic significance. For example, were the Contra rebels in Nicaragua "freedom fighters" or "terrorists"? Throughout the 1980s, the President and Congress of the United States argued over such words, with the question of continued Contra funding hinging upon the outcome. To find the meanings of the words, however, one had to look at the codes to which they belonged. In the Reagan administration code, a "freedom fighter" was any U.S.-backed guerrilla who was fighting against a Soviet-supported regime. But one man's "freedom fighter" is another man's "terrorist," and in the world of international politics—where both East and West toss around the words *freedom fighter*, *liberation organization*, and *terrorist* according to the side the man with the gun serves—Humpty Dumpty always has the last laugh.

Of course, not all codes are ideologically motivated. There's nothing ideological about choosing the color green for a "go ahead" signal, although red does have its cultural connotations, as in "red flag" or "Reds." However, most of the codes we confront every day do bear political and social meanings that we may fail to understand because we don't recognize that they *are* codes. There are dress codes, traffic codes, legal codes, codes for eating and drinking, architectural codes, aesthetic codes, sexual codes . . . the list is nearly endless. Each belongs to that vast system of signs that we call "culture," a system whose influence is so pervasive that we often don't realize it exists, just as we don't notice the air we breathe.

We don't recognize the cultural codes that surround us because many of their most influential signs aren't words at all; they are objects and social practices with hidden meanings that we usually don't think to look for. From an advertising campaign to the food we eat to the way we define sexual identity, we are being secretly manipulated by our culture to believe certain things and to act in certain ways. Politicians aren't the only ones who speak in code: our entire society does, sending us a constant bombardment of signals that can shape our very consciousness and dictate our behavior and values.

An advertisement placed by Chevron in *Sierra* magazine, the official journal of the Sierra Club, is a good example of a sign that a major oil company has used to manipulate us. The ad fully occupies two facing pages. On the left, a color painting of an owl's face is superimposed over an image of Yosemite National Park's Half Dome. On the right is the headline "Now Disappearing in Yosemite." The ad copy tells us of the research being conducted to investigate why the great gray owl is vanishing.

This research, we are told, is partly supported by Chevron, who invites us to make monetary contributions to the project.

On the surface, the ad merely seems to refer to a certain environmental problem in Yosemite that Chevron is making efforts to solve. However, we have to see this advertisement as it relates to a number of other things. First, as a leading critic of Chevron's environmental record, the Sierra Club would seem to be an odd audience for such an ad. Even as the ad appeared, the two organizations were locked in a battle over the compliance of Chevron's Southern California refineries with the Clean Water Act. At the same time, the Sierra Club was challenging the Reagan administration's plan to lease offshore drilling rights along the California coast to companies like Chevron.

When we consider these facts, the ad appears to be a sign of Chevron's desire to outflank its critics. Similar versions of this ad have appeared in a number of magazines and on radio and television as well, but its appearance in the pages of *Sierra* lends it an added significance. The fact is that few members of the Sierra Club are likely to believe that Chevron is a true friend of conservation. The ad's appearance in *Sierra* is thus something of an anomaly. On the one hand, it may signify the editors' belief that it is better to accept the conciliatory gestures of an opponent than to reject them outright. But on the other hand, it may only be a sign of how badly the journal needs advertising dollars.

Advertisements can also be signs of general cultural trends. One of the most prominent developments in the 1980s, for example, has been the way that America's popular imagination shifted its attention from Woodstock, New York, to New York City, New York. The latter became the locus of American desire as communal "hippies" evolved into corporate "yuppies," drawing their inspiration more from Wall Street than from Walden. We can recognize this change by examining a number of related television commercials, such as the glitzy award-winning spots for Levi's jeans which first appeared during the 1984 Olympics. Set on the streets of New York, the ads showed us the culture of the alley and subway, a sort of urban theater of the city streets. Here's an old black man playing a harmonica. There's a hipster dancing to his own music. Gaggles of young women seductively breeze past. Most of them are wearing jeans.

We don't actually see what brand of jeans these people are wearing, however, nor are we directly told why we should choose Levi's over another brand. These commercials are not referring to a particular product but to a state of mind. Wearing Levi's jeans, the advertisers hope, is a sign that you belong to the "in" crowd of the eighties. By taking advantage of the fact that Levi's are already easily recognizable following their explosive success during the sixties, these commercials simply translate the rural imagery of the original jeans culture into the now-popular imagery of the city.

Such signs of our time can be found all around us—in the images on our television screens, on the billboards that line our streets, and in the clothing that we wear. In the early eighties, for example, formal evening dress and BMWs replaced the work-shirts and Volkswagens of the sixties, signaling a newfound pride in conspicuous consumption. Whereas affluent young Americans once symbolically concealed their wealth behind the patches of their jeans, today they seem more in tune with the slogan "You can't be too thin or too rich." Designer chocolates are signs of the new sensibility, as are the Hunt Club and St. John's Bay lines of apparel offered by the once-modest J. C. Penney department store chain. These signs are not simply waiting for us to interpret them; they actively work to convince us that the prestige of material well-being is both desirable and natural. Polo and Members Only sportswear capitalize on an elitist spirit that many yuppies would have been ashamed of ten years ago. The berets and army fatigues of "terrorist" fashions and "guerrilla chic" parody the revolutionary spirit of the sixties and trivialize the international violence of the eighties.

These signs will change with the times. The suspenders made popular by yuppie stockbrokers will go into decline, while a more realistic economic view may alter the culture of conspicuous consumption. As the 1980s wane, there are signs that the aging baby-boom generation, which has managed to set the popular cultural agenda for the past twenty years, is turning its attention to building families and dealing with mid-life crises. Three films released in 1987, *Baby Boom*, *Three Men and a Baby*, and *Raising Arizona,* indicated an emerging trend toward child-rearing, while *Fatal Attraction* signaled a violent pull away from the sexual revolution. In early 1988, advertisements for everything from life insurance to Pepto-Bismol began to depict men at their fortieth birthday parties expressing rueful surprise at the threshold they have crossed.

Through their characteristic self-involvement and generational narcissism, the baby boomers are almost certain to launch new cultural trends with each stage of life they enter. As they turned a nation on to the cult of youth in the 1960s, the baby boomers are almost certain to inaugurate an "old is bold" fashion revolution when they enter their golden years during the twenty-first century. Look for "sensible-shoe chic" and an overwhelming demand for cardigans in the 2020s.

In each chapter of this book, we will investigate a different cross section of the signs of our time, surveying everything from advertising to architecture to sexuality to clothing and even to the food we eat. Most of the signs we will look at will be of the nonverbal sort because these are ordinarily the most invisible to us. Did you know that a teddy bear is a sign that can be decoded? Or a business suit? Or a Cadillac? Where are you going to find what these things mean? What codes do they belong to? You can always go to a dictionary to find out the "official" definition of a word, but there are no standard reference books that will interpret the meanings of all the objects, images, and words you encounter every day.

Think of this book as a guide to the signs of contemporary American culture, one that will show you the powerful influence of signs in your life and how to spot, interpret, and ultimately control them. Because the signs that confront us most often belong to an economic system grounded in consumer capitalism, many of them will point to the same meaning, forming an interlocking network of related cultural phenomena. But to find a capitalist ideology underlying the system of American signs is not the same thing as judging that system. With a few exceptions, the interpretations you will read here are meant to be more descriptive than evaluative, and when I do criticize some of the semiotic aspects of American life, I don't mean to imply that there is anything especially wrong with our society. Every cultural system, East and West, First World and Third World, has its problems. No social construct is perfect, and as one looks at the world today one is tempted to agree with Douglas Adams's rueful observation in *The Restaurant at the End of the Universe*: "To summarize the summary of the summary: people are a problem."

As long as you are unable to decode the significance of ordinary things, and as long as you take the signs of your culture at face value, you will continue to be mastered by them and by those who have constructed them. But once you see behind the surface of a sign into its hidden cultural significance, you can free yourself from that sign and perhaps find a new way of looking at the world. You will control the signs of your culture rather than having them control you.

CHAPTER 1

Semiotics:
The Science of the Sign

Semiotics is concerned with everything that can be
taken *as a sign.*

Umberto Eco

I t is not an exaggeration to say that we are confronted by signs
everywhere we turn, but in spite of their ubiquity—or perhaps because of it—we are often unaware of them *as signs*, and
so are unaware of the significant network in which they move.
There is a science dedicated to the study of this network, but it
is not yet well known outside of the academic circles in which
it began. This science is called semiotics, an unfortunately fright-
ening-looking word that will be as familiar to you by the time
you finish reading this book as the much more common science
known as semantics. Both sciences are devoted to the study of
meaning, but the latter explores only the linguistic significance
of word-signs, while the former delves into their social and
political significance. Semanticists are concerned only with
words. Semioticians are concerned with *us*, and though they do

analyze words, their analyses also explore the ways that clothes, buildings, TV programs, toys, food, and other ordinary objects are signs of hidden cultural interests.

There is a single commanding reason why you should want to learn to think like a semiotician: so you won't get hoodwinked. For example, when you are made to feel inadequate because you don't have a lot of money, you have been duped by a culture that measures everything in monetary terms. When you are told that a "woman's place is in the home," your culture is trying to conceal a patriarchal interest behind the veil of "nature" and "common sense." You can find alternatives to such beliefs by employing what I call the Six Principles of Semiotics:

1. Always question the "commonsense" view of things, because "common sense" is really "communal sense": the habitual opinions and perspectives of the tribe.
2. The "commonsense" viewpoint is usually motivated by a cultural interest that manipulates our consciousness for ideological reasons.
3. Cultures tend to conceal their ideologies behind the veil of "nature," defining what they do as "natural" and condemning contrary cultural practices as "unnatural."
4. In evaluating any system of cultural practices, one must take into account the interests behind it.
5. We do not perceive our world directly but view it through the filter of a semiotic code or mythic frame.
6. A sign is a sort of cultural barometer, marking the dynamic movement of social history.

The first principle tells us to distrust what is called "common sense." To a semiotician, "common sense" is really *communal sense*, the set of beliefs that is shared by the members of a group or culture. Most Americans, for example, believe that it is only "common sense" to prepare themselves financially for the future, accumulating whatever stores they can against the advent of an accident or old age. We "save for a rainy day," hoard our resources, and generally conform to the materialistic slogan "You can't be too rich" rather than to the more spiritual "You can't take it with you." In orthodox Hindu society, by contrast, a man may give up all the security he has accumulated during the first three stages of his life—youth, manhood, and middle age—and become *sannyasa* in old age, abandoning his family and former ties to wander India with a begging bowl and staff in order to acquire religious merit. Let the rain fall, the orthodox Hindu believes, because no amount of wealth will free you from life's illusions and bring eternal peace.

A semiotician looks at these two different systems of belief and explores the cultural motivations behind them. He views saving money for retirement as "common sense" because Americans live in such a competitive environment. There is little comfort for the destitute in a country that equates one's quality of life with one's level of consumption. America's "commonsense" notions about retirement have been determined by an economic system that stresses material consumption rather than spiritual exploration. In the cultural codes of traditional Hindu society, where this ideology is lacking, a different set of values *can* motivate a man to abandon everything and throw himself upon the charity of his neighbors.

This doesn't mean that Leisure World is necessarily any better or any worse than *sannyasa*. What it does mean is that the "normal" attitude toward something as basic as retirement is actually only a social attitude; behind the "norm" lies a cultural interest, in this case, the interest a consumerist society has in encouraging its members to a lifetime of consumption.

According to the second principle of semiotics, a cultural interest lurks behind our most fundamental beliefs. However, if we were aware of this interest, we might not conform to it, so cultures tend to cover up their ideological investments by making them appear to be the only ones that conform to nature. For example, sexual activity is both "natural" and also governed by cultural interests. Of all the possible sexual acts that occur between men and women, men and men, and women and women, only those that take place between men and women are considered "natural" in mainstream American culture. Homosexual acts are labeled "unnatural" and are still forbidden by law in many states. Furthermore, some statutes declare the so-called "missionary position" as the only acceptable heterosexual practice.

To call one sexual act "natural" and another "unnatural" is to conceal what is in fact an ancient set of ideological interests that can be traced to the founders of Judeo-Christian culture. For the ancient Hebrews, the strident condemnation of homosexuality was one way to maintain their distinct cultural identity. Under Alexander the Great, Hellenic culture, which tolerated and even endorsed homosexuality, began spreading and threatened to engulf the indigenous cultures in the Middle East. Thus, the Hebrews were led to reject the new Hellenic social mores for the purposes of cultural survival. Other sexual prohibitions, such as those forbidding nonprocreative sexuality, have similar origins. Christianity began to rise during the decline and fall of ancient Rome. As Edward Gibbon writes in *The Decline and Fall of the Roman Empire*, the men and women of the early Church, reacting to Rome's notorious licentiousness, sought a purity beyond all measure. During the long Roman nights, they often tested themselves by lying naked side by side without touching. I can't help but say that if anything is "unnatural" it's that, but it's through these traditions that we have inherited many of our notions of sexual "naturalness."

Culture often conceals its own ideological interests behind the veil of "nature," naturalizing beliefs that are, in fact, only social and conventional. This is the third principle of semiotic thinking. The implications of this principle are not, as you might expect, that we must find some values that are truly "natural" and objective; on the contrary, what is implied is that no set of cultural beliefs can claim logical superiority over another set because all such beliefs are motivated by subjective interests. Of course, we *do* make moral distinctions between different cultural practices, but such judgments are not an ordinary part of semiotic analysis. The semiotician doesn't try to choose between cultural systems, he or she only demystifies them, revealing the ideological origins of human values. Hence, we come to the fourth principle of semiotics.

To a committed ideologue, the semiotician may look like a fence sitter, but that can't be helped. Semiotics never tells you *what* to think, only *how* to think and how to probe beneath the surface. This doesn't mean that you can't take a position of your own when thinking semiotically; it only means that to be consistent the semiotician should reveal and be aware of his or her own ideological stand before pursuing an analysis. My own stand in the analyses to follow is to take a fundamentally progressive line, venting occasional aggravation at the excesses of capitalism, suggesting a greater sensitivity to the rights of animals, and often taking a position that might be characterized as "soft-core" feminism. "Hard-core" feminists and committed Marxists—who, it should be added, are among the most distinguished of contemporary academic semioticians—may be disappointed by some of my analyses, but so be it. I'm not trying to peddle my beliefs beyond the one central semiotic belief that it is better to analyze what is going on around you than to take everything at face value, even if this means acknowledging the relativity of your own position.

There is something liberating in the semiotic rejection of the absolute, however. Once you open up to a plurality of possible perspectives, you can be free to choose those which are most suited to you. I don't mean to efface the distinction between good and evil, but I do mean to suggest that there are more ways of looking at things than our culture ordinarily admits.

THE CIRCLE OF SIGNS

The modern science of semiotics traces its descent to two late-nineteenth-century philosophers who, working independently of each other, first began to elaborate the conceptual framework on which contemporary semioticians rely. Charles Sanders Peirce, a logician and physicist by training, inaugurated the science of the sign in America, while Ferdinand de Saussure, a Swiss linguist and psychologist, worked on the Continent. Although they called their sciences by different names (Peirce coined the word *semiotics*, while Saussure called his science "semiology"), both men arrived at strikingly similar conclusions in strikingly similar ways.

It is rather poignant to note that semiotics, or semiology, is a posthumous science. Despite the close parallels between their research, neither Peirce nor Saussure ever learned of each other's work, for they both died in relative obscurity before the full range of their ideas appeared in print. Saussure died shortly after completing a series of lectures on linguistics, which he delivered between 1906 and 1911. It was this series on which the science of semiology was to be founded. We owe our knowledge of these lectures wholly to the devotion of his students, who together compiled their notes and published them in 1915 as the *Course in General Linguistics*.

Peirce's story is sadder still. He labored for more than forty years, producing page after page of largely unpublished speculations, but he could never collect his thoughts into a single, master text (if the complete collection of his papers is ever published, it may run to a hundred volumes). When he died in 1914, his work was still unfinished. Years later, editors began to sift through the mass and made portions of it available to scholars who are now energetically developing the science that Peirce did not live to see blossom.

Together Peirce and Saussure established the foundation for the fundamental semiotic conviction that the meaning of a sign is not to be found in the *object* to which it appears to refer but in a *concept* that functions within a culturally constituted system. For Saussure, the "signified" (or meaning) referred to by the "signifier" *dog*, for instance, is not a flesh-and-blood animal but a concept that can be distinguished from our concepts of, say, foxes, wolves, and even cats. The meaning of each concept—dog, wolf, cat—lies in its *difference* from every other concept in the system of English-language classification. Thus, a wolf is a wild, doglike animal that is neither a dog nor a fox, and a fox is a wild, doglike animal that is neither a dog nor a wolf. In each case, the semiotic definition of the concept lies not in some biological entity but in the coils of a conceptual system.

Similarly, when Ronald Reagan calls a soldier a "freedom fighter," the meaning of the sign belongs to a conceptual system that distinguishes between gunmen sponsored by the Soviet Union and gunmen backed by the United States. Reagan calls Afghan guerrillas and Contra rebels "freedom fighters" but does not put the same label on SWAPO guerrillas in South Africa who are presumably fighting for freedom too but who are not supported by America. The difference, then, between U.S.–backed and non-U.S.–backed forces provides the real meaning of the name. On the other side of the political spectrum, the Soviets call members of the Polish labor union Solidarity "hooligans," which really means "opponents of Soviet hegemony" in the conceptual system of the Soviet Union and has no intrinsic relation to the character of the union members themselves. The Soviets also label Russian dissidents "insane," a concept similarly defined by a conceptual system rather than by reality.

Semiotic systems, in other words, are self-enclosed codes in which meaning is determined by a movement from sign to concept rather than from sign to thing. Within the terms of this movement, the continuum of reality is divided up into the culturally defined categories of objects that we call "dogs," "wolves," and "foxes," or "freedom fighters," "liberation organizations," and "terrorists," depending on the interests behind the system (see chapter 2 for more on the ideology of classification). In this way, semiotic systems are closed off from any competing views, self-reflexively defining all things only in terms of their own conceptual and ideological beliefs. Think of these systems as labyrinths, or as those wooden Russian matrushka dolls that you open up only to find another doll, which you then open only to find another doll, and so forth. Or think of the way a Bible-thumping evangelist answers every challenge by referring back to the Bible. You never get out of the system.

The implications can be rather disconcerting. If the meanings of our signs reside in a closed system of concepts, then it seems that we can never break out of the circle to see our world as it "really is." Systems of signs always intervene between our perceptions and what we perceive. A sign system thus forms a kind of *frame* that determines the shape of our knowledge in advance. As the American anthropologist and linguist Edward Sapir said: "Human beings do not live in the objective world alone . . . but are very much at the mercy of the particular language which has become the medium of exchange for their society. . . . We see and hear and otherwise experience very largely as we do because the language habits of our community predispose certain choices of interpretation."

Semioticians refer to these interpretive frames as "myths." According to the fifth semiotic principle, a myth is not a fanciful story but a code that informs an entire structure of belief. There are gender myths that shape our conceptions of the relation between the sexes. The American presumption that free enterprise is an absolute necessity for a thriving economy is an example of an economic myth. Historical myths include the belief that all human history is progressive and is constantly moving upward toward better things. Such myths are not necessarily right or wrong, and they can be countered only with another myth, but it is only by recognizing them *as* myths that we can begin to consider how to interpret them.

Living within the terms of a cultural myth is like coming into the world with permanently attached violet-colored eyeglasses. We'd never know that the lavender-tinted world around us was really an artificial effect. The nature of the frame in which we live and move can accordingly be of the utmost importance in our lives, and it is one of the major tasks of semiotics to expose the ordinarily hidden contours of such frames.

Americans, for example, tend to conceive their relation to the natural environment according to one of the dominant cultural myths of the West. This myth predisposes us to view the world in the terms of an opposition between the natural world and the human world and to judge all things by virtue of their relation to human needs. The meaning of our own sign of *Homo sapiens* within this mythic code is determined by a hierarchical structure that defines humans as the earth's dominant and sole important species. All other creatures are defined only as they relate to us. This viewpoint stems from a biblical culture whose code tells us that the earth and everything on it are ours to control. Such a system can be and is being used to justify everything from industrial pollution to animal vivisection. But if we change frames and look at things from another perspective, we may see new ways of perceiving our relationship to the natural world, causing us to drop the hierarchical scheme of things and see ourselves on equal terms with other species, as dwellers on earth, not rulers.

Semiotics, then, can be of great practical use to those who wish to dislodge the ordinary way of viewing things. To a certain extent, it is a potentially subversive science in that it can enable you to challenge the status quo by revealing its systematic presuppositions. Almost any cultural object can be read as a sign whose significance can be traced to a larger social system. For example, what is the significance of a high-heeled shoe? To the women who wear them, they may be merely fashionable articles of dress, but to feminist decoders the shoes signify the desire of a male-dominated culture to disable its women physically, to keep them jacked up on heels that prevent them from running away. A less extreme interpretation is that high heels tend to make a woman look as if she were trying to attract sexual attention. This fact does, at any rate, point to a common gender myth that defines women as sexual objects and requires them to appear sexually attractive. Men are not subjected to the same pressures within the terms of the myth; rather, they are expected to appear sexually aggressive. This division of labor is not the outcome of nature; it is the result of a gender myth. The propagation of the species would still continue even if women were expected to be the sexual aggressors and men the sexual objects. In fact, in most animal species the males are the beautiful sex. Think of the difference between a drab brown peahen and her iridescent mate, the peacock.

Academic semioticians have been probing both linguistic and nonlinguistic sign systems for many years but have been doing so largely among themselves, publishing their findings in technical articles and books aimed primarily at professional audiences, thus writing *of* but not *to* the cultures in which they live. Although semiotics has not yet been made widely accessible, there is nothing inherently obscure about it. It is actually the most intimately familiar of all the sciences, focusing on what we do and say. You only need to be introduced to it to become a semiotician yourself.

WHAT THE APPLE SAID

Because the system to which a given cultural sign belongs is often an historical one, referring to a cross section of the life and times of the society that produces it, semiotics is a profoundly historical science. To be a semiotician one must have a keen awareness of the dynamics of popular culture. This brings us to semiotic principle number six.

Consider the significance of the Apple Computer logo. At one level, it simply signifies an American corporation, like the RCA dog ("His Master's Voice"), the Chrysler star, or McDonald's golden arches. In recognizing this sign, you have already performed a sophisticated act of semiotic analysis that has been made possible by the corporate trademark code. It's easy to take this act for granted, but a visitor from a foreign culture who is unacquainted with the system of symbols that informs the trademark code might see only a rainbow-colored, half-eaten apple. To read this symbol you must be versed in the code, just as centuries ago a medieval knight could identify the family of a strange knight by the heraldic symbols on his shield. Knowing this code was essential to a knight's survival. Although one might survive without knowing the meaning of the trademark code, life in a consumer society does require a certain facility in corporate signs, lest we confuse a Chrysler with a Mercedes-Benz.

The Apple Computer logo can tell us more than the mere identity of the corporation it symbolizes, however. To discover its entire message, we must see the logo in its original historical context. First, we might ask why a computer company emerging in the mid-seventies chose to represent itself with a rainbow-striped apple. The answer lies in the subculture to which the company's young founders belonged and in the market they envisioned.

Steven Jobs and Stephen Wozniak, along with the generation that responded to their product, were not comfortable with the impersonal artificiality of the unadorned machine. Machines were for the "Establishment," not for the newly emerging generation (eventually called "yuppies") who by the mid-seventies were abandoning the campus and commune for the corporate board-room but were feeling rather uneasy about it. The Woodstock generation was entering the Establishment at full speed but did not like to be reminded of it, as was dramatized in the film *The Big Chill*. This generation was thus perfectly primed to respond to a bearded and sandaled Jobs, whose appearance was in itself a sign of his belonging to the counterculture. Jobs offered not a mechanical Establishment computer with a cold, impersonal name like IBM but a mellow little "Apple" sporting a Peter Max rainbow. The yuppie market liked the way a machine could be associated with the natural world, as well as the sly irony of the bite taken out of the apple (shades of Eden here?). The Beatles' company, Apple Records, was another association. Colored a soothing, nonthreatening adobe gray, the Apple computer was calculated to appeal to the nostalgic sentimentality of its initial market, consumers who were fonder of rock 'n' roll than of technological wizardry but who needed that wizardry to get ahead.

The full meaning of the Apple logo emerges when we see it

in its social and historical context. It does not refer only to a computer (which could have just as easily been called a "Wozniak") but to a system of signs that expresses the consciousness of the mid-seventies, charting a trend that was among the most profound cultural movements of the era.

Not only social activists can benefit from semiotics. Businesspeople can also read their cultures to spot emerging trends that may either be exploited or ridden out. In a sense, Steven Jobs might be considered one of the premier semioticians of his generation—if only unconsciously so—because he was able to take the pulse of his time and determine which sort of signs best fit the system then emerging. Of course, by choosing an apple, Jobs was manipulating his market, which is why the semiotic sword can always be said to cut two ways. Semiotically astute businesspeople can use signs to manipulate consumers, but semiotically astute consumers can, in turn, read these signs to determine how much manipulation is going on.

By carefully reading cultural signs, we can see how much more sensitive they are to rapid changes in our popular sensibility than the more conservative linguistic signs that we are taught in school. Words can keep their meanings for centuries; cultural images can change their meanings overnight. When Peter Fonda painted an American flag on his motorcycle helmet in *Easy Rider*, for example, the flag signified the sixties' ironic attitude toward blind patriotism. When Sylvester Stallone wrapped himself in the same symbol in *Rocky IV*, its meaning had changed dramatically to an *approval* of the same patriotism that had been questioned in *Easy Rider*. What you do with this knowledge is up to you. Remember, semiotics doesn't tell you what to do, only what things signify.

MAKING WAVES

Let's look at one last example: the Coca-Cola Company's abandonment of Norman Rockwell for computer-generated Max Headroom, its use of Mr. T, and its "Catch the Wave" campaign.

All three of these signs relate to one another within a certain cultural code that has its own history. Mohawk haircuts made their first widespread appearance in England in the early 1970s as a symbol of a working-class rebellion against a recession-ridden country. When the punk culture came to America in the mid-1970s, it found a climate far different. The American economy had not been as battered as England's, and so the punk look instead became the latest fashion fad, following the path of the "Mod Look" that emigrated from England to America ten years earlier. However, since America was not quite prepared for the radical punk look, the results were a bit different. The trend that brought Sid Vicious to American shores also brought a "New Wave" look that often parodied fifties-era kitsch in a highly self-conscious but somehow chic manner. Back came horn-rimmed sunglasses and narrow-lapeled suits, beehive hairdos and leopard-skin skirts. Dan Aykroyd and John Belushi's "Blues Brothers" routines played their part, as did the deliberately over-done fifties-era music performed by such bands as the B-52's.

The fatuously grinning face of Max Headroom belongs to this suite of New Wave images. So does the aggressive mohawk of Mr. T. Far from representing a threat to middle-class America, Mr. T's mohawk signifies the ultimate domestication of one of the most violent symbols of the little-understood and now-forgotten punk rebellion. The mohawk has gone Hollywood, and so Mr. T fits perfectly into Coca-Cola's advertising strategy of packing its commercials with fleeting images of celebrities. Furthermore, the Coca-Cola Company wants you to accept its "Catch the Wave" campaign uncritically as the only way to go in the New Wave eighties.

We can see from these examples that there are no fixed meanings for many of the signs that surround us. In this sense, semiotics is a profoundly dynamic science, because the meanings of the objects that it interprets are forever changing with the tides of cultural history. To learn the science of the sign, then, is not to acquire a body of fixed information but instead to acquire a sensitivity to such changes. Once you do learn to read the signs that surround you, you can free yourself from their often hypnotic grasp. It is in the best interest of advertisers, fashion designers, politicians, television writers, and the like, that you receive their signals passively without probing beneath the surface for the hidden meanings. But is it in *your* best interest? To find these meanings, to decode the signs of your time, is to discover the pulse of our culture, enabling you to make your own cultural diagnoses and perhaps suggest your own solutions for what may appear to be going wrong.

...d chant together a phrase in their own language that in
...lation might run, "This is how a wise man would do this."
... anthropologists administering the test finally became exas-
...ed and asked the tribesmen "how a damned fool would do
... They immediately regrouped the knives with the forks and
...apples with the oranges.

... The moral of the story has partly to do with the different
...s that various cultures classify the same things and partly with
...cultural arrogance that causes one culture—ours—to judge
...intelligence of other cultures by its own standards. It happens
...be the case that our Western approach to classification is an
...ract one; we tend to group things together conceptually
...er than concretely. A knife, for instance, is a very concrete
...ect and so is a fork, but an "eating utensil" is a conceptual
...traction, a generalization rather than a thing. Our understand-
... of the actual knife and fork, in other words, is shaped by a
...tural code that groups objects conceptually and abstractly, and
...expect all other "intelligent" people to understand such things
...the same way.

... But can't we look at knives and forks differently? After all,
...u use a knife, not a fork, to cut an orange, and so there would
...m to be a perfectly good—and intelligent—reason for group-
...g the knife with the orange rather than with the fork. This, in
...ct, is precisely what the tribesmen in the story did: they classi-
...d the objects placed before them by virtue of their concrete
...lations to each other. A knife, in other words, is concretely
...lated to an orange because it is used for the physical act of
...tting. Within the terms of a cultural code constituted by
...oncrete rather than abstract perceptions, it is perfectly reasonable
...d only simple common sense to group the knife with the
...range.

... Even the most trivial of classifications can be seen sometimes
...o conceal a particular point of view. Several years ago, for
...xample, the Reagan administration created something of a flap
...when it decided to classify tomato ketchup as a "vegetable" in

What's in a Name? The Ideology of Cultural Classificatio

And out of the ground the Lord God formed ever
beast of the field, and every fowl of the air; and
brought them unto Adam to see what he would ca
them; and whatsoever Adam called every living
creature, that was the name thereof.

Gen. 2.19

There's a funny story that anthropologists tell
how many different ways the same things can
classified, depending on the culture doing the nam
of anthropologists were giving a sort of IQ test
aboriginal tribesmen. The purpose of the test (and
such a test) is to see how someone will group a
twenty different objects drawn from four classes:
cooking utensils, and clothes. The test predicts th
intelligent individual will, say, group knives and
"cooking utensils" and apples and oranges under "
  In this particular test, the tribesmen consistentl
"less intelligent" classification, however, grouping
oranges rather than with forks. After each classific

order to save money on school lunch programs. At the time, a feeble attempt was made to defend this reclassification of ketchup from "condiment" to "vegetable" on the grounds that since ketchup is made from tomatoes (which means, of course, that it is really derived from a "fruit," but that's another issue) it could be seen as belonging to one of the four major food groups (which, if you're old enough to remember, were once the seven major food groups: meat, fish, dairy, grains, green vegetables, yellow vegetables, and fruit). This attempt to change a classification was quickly abandoned, however, in the face of protests from parents and jeers from administration critics.

In the ketchup caper, we find the conflict of two political interests. One believes that it is not the role of government to subsidize nutritional programs, and one believes that it is. From the former perspective, it may seem expedient to reclassify ketchup, but the decision to do so is determined by political rather than natural reasons. Conversely, keeping ketchup in its place as a "sauce" can also be seen to be a political decision because there is nothing to prevent us from viewing it as "food." It does have *some* nutritional value. The question is simply where we draw the line, and where that line is drawn will be determined by our interests, not by some "natural" power outside those interests.

In fact, all the most basic distinctions represent some human interest. In the United States, for instance, we presume that there is an obvious difference between the "inside" and the "outside" of a house. "Inside," we take off our coats and turn on the heat. "Outside," we put on "outerwear." It seems to be a perfectly natural distinction. Yet a friend of mine in the People's Republic of China tells me that the Chinese do not make quite the same distinction that we do between the inside and the outside of a house. When the temperature drops, the Chinese simply put on more underclothing rather than turn on the heat. Because outdoor and indoor temperatures are similar, there is no need to make a sharp distinction between indoor and outdoor clothing.

Thus, where my friend would take off her overcoat when going indoors, and then shiver until she put it on again to go outside, her hosts were equally comfortable indoors and out. That's not because they wore their overcoats indoors and out, for as far as my friend could see they did not even have overcoats. Instead, the Chinese bundle up in winter underneath the jackets they wear in warmer weather.

The interest served by this lack of a clear distinction between indoors and out is not difficult to find: it conserves fuel in a country where fuel is scarce. But this does not mean that the Chinese can't differ among themselves on how to classify things. My friend also tells me, for instance, that even though it is technically illegal to do so, Chinese peasants strew their un-threshed grain onto roadways in order to benefit from the thresh-ing action that automobile traffic accomplishes for them. What the authorities see as a "road," built solely to bear traffic, the peasants see as a "threshing floor." The interest behind this reclas-sification of roadways is also easy to spot. There isn't much space to spare for threshing purposes in a typical Chinese village. So a little-used road may be redefined to satisfy a specific need.

Americans also disagree on where to draw the line. Is a one-minute pause in a school classroom a "moment of silence" or a constitutionally forbidden "prayer"? Is an abortion an act of "murder" or an act of "privacy" protected by the Fifth Amend-ment? Is a fifteen-year-old killer an "adult" or a "juvenile"? Is a nuclear warhead an "offensive weapon" or a "peacekeeper"? In each of these controversies you will find two sides equally certain that their designation is the right one, that they alone have drawn the line strictly according to the "truth." It would be nice if the truth were that easy to find, but in each of these cases the line we draw is only ideologically true.

The interests served by a classification scheme can sometimes be harmlessly personal. I was once told the story of a certain retired Harvard professor who, somewhat against his own more indolent inclinations, had been persuaded by his wife to take up the fashionable hobby of bird-watching. Wishing to avoid the labor of having to distinguish among, and remember the names of, too many species, he drastically simplified the usual scheme by employing only four basic names for the classes of birds he was able (or willing) to recognize. These four classes included "crows," "gulls and robins," "small brown birds," and "other." That simplified things. Crows, gulls, and robins are easy to spot. So are small brown birds. Anything more complicated—say, a scarlet ibis—can be effortlessly tucked away into the class of "other."

But even this harmless approach to classifying animals harbors ideological implications. As long as we are only talking about recreational bird-watchers, there's no problem at all. But if the question of where to draw the line appears in the context of a controversy over environmental protection, it can be quite another matter.

In the mid-1970s, for instance, the Tennessee Valley Authority's plan to build a dam on the Little Tennessee River was halted when it was discovered that the dam would threaten the survival of several local species, including the snail darter and the Anthony's River snail. Proponents of the dam, known as the Tellico project, argued that the snail darter was not an endangered species since there were plenty of closely related darter species scattered throughout the region. Opponents of the dam argued conversely that the snail darter was an irreplaceable component of the biological diversity of the earth and was accordingly covered by the Endangered Species Act of 1973. The differing political interests of each camp were reflected in the way each chose to classify the darter. The pro-dam forces took a more general approach—once you've seen one darter you've seen them all—while the anti-dam forces insisted on detail. The whole issue depended on where you chose to draw the line. The line was finally drawn, and the snail darter was saved.

One reason we disagree so often on where to draw the line is because there are so many different ways to categorize objects and images. Thus, we usually classify them in terms of how they affect and serve our individual or cultural interest. An individual horse, for example, can be classified in quite a number of ways that are not all necessarily biologically based. There's nothing to stop us from seeing a horse as a rather oversized, short-eared donkey—after all, with a little help from a breeder, horses and donkeys can interbreed—but that would drive down the value of horseflesh, which would hardly be in the interest of the horse-breeding industry.

But what about the horse's potential to end up on your dinner plate? We eat cattle, after all, and horses, like cattle, are herbivores, a group of animals generally classed as edible within the terms of our culinary code. This is the way the French draw the line to include the horse in the class of edible meats, and if you were a horsemeat-peddling entrepreneur with an interest in cracking the U.S. market with "le fillet de cheval," you'd want to get Americans to think this way too.

How we choose to classify things may seem to be a trivial matter, but its implications can be deadly. For when one powerful group of people classifies another less powerful group as either inferior or, even worse, not quite human at all, the result can be genocidal. We only need to look at what happened to the American Indians in the nineteenth century, or to European Jewry in the twentieth century to see what the stakes can be in the matter of human classification.

THE SEMIOTICS OF RACE

Before commencing his extermination of European Jewry, Hitler first set his Nazi biologists to work on "proving" the "natural" racial inferiority of the Jews. He then had others come up with a definition of just what constituted a Jew in the first place. To create as large a net as possible, it was decided that anyone with at least one Jewish grandparent was a Jew, regardless of his or her actual religion or parentage. It was one short step from the creation of this taxonomic myth to behaving as if the Jews weren't people at all, turning them effectively into cattle who could be slaughtered at will. It is bloodcurdling to realize that the eventual boiling down of human beings into soap was first sanctioned by ideologically motivated biologists and genealogists who shifted at will the crucial boundary line between the human and the nonhuman.

The point here is not that there is such a thing as an absolute racial classification scheme, which the Nazis perverted. After all, Jewish scholars have themselves struggled for centuries over the definition of a Jew in the Diaspora. In the scheme they have devised, any child whose parents are Jewish is, of course, Jewish, but so too is a child of mixed parentage if his or her mother is Jewish. The child of a Jewish father and non-Jewish mother, however, is not considered Jewish.

Hitler's racial taxonomy was motivated purely by a murderous interest. One might say that the entire code was genocidal in intent. That is not to say there is no interest behind the Jewish manner of self-definition, but the interest here is a peaceful one, motivated by the Jewish desire for cultural survival. Believing that our life essence is contained in our blood, Orthodox rabbis have made a distinction between the male and female role in procreation. The ancient rabbinical teaching reasons that since a fetus is generated in the body of its mother, it must inherit her blood, not the blood of its father. If that blood is Jewish, the child has Jewish blood in its veins. To preserve the blood-identity of the Jewish people, the rabbis have insisted on the maternal descent of the racial essence.

In these cases, we can distinguish between two different classification schemes on the basis of their different motivations. It doesn't matter whether you classify someone as a Jew or not when the issue is considered taxonomically, but when one definition is motivated by a murderous ideology and the other by a desire for survival, it is easy to say which is the morally superior scheme. In fact, we can say that the moral value of a classification can be judged not by its form but by its motivation and by its effects.

The Afrikaners of South Africa have not gone so far as the

Nazis, but their political ideology is equally apparent in their racial classification schemes. There are "whites," "coloreds," "blacks," "Malays," "Indians," "Chinese," "Griquas," other "Asians," and a special category for Japanese businessmen called "honorary whites" (the interests involved in this final category are almost comically obvious: the South Africans do a good deal of business with the Japanese, and they would have a hard time maintaining this commerce if visiting Japanese businessmen were subjected to the rules of apartheid).

The purpose of the Afrikaner's scheme is, in essence, to divide and conquer. If they simply divided up the country into a "white" ruling class and a "non-white" class of politically impotent subjects (which would express what is indeed the status quo in South Africa), the Afrikaners would face a seamless front of political opposition. This would make the overthrow of the Afrikaner regime a great deal easier than it is now, because the "non-white" population would all share an identical set of interests with respect to the ruling power. But as matters stand, Asians and Indians, for instance, enjoy certain privileges that are denied to blacks and coloreds. Even coloreds are better off than blacks (who have virtually no privileges at all), and to keep the interests of the two groups at odds, the regulations of apartheid make it possible for an occasional black to have his position "upgraded" to colored.

By investing each "non-white" group with privileges denied to other groups, the Afrikaner system of apartheid creates interests that divide each class from the others. When Indians were granted a degree of parliamentary representation in the South African parliament, blacks rioted against them in Durban. It wasn't the Indians' fault that they were given these rights, but by granting them, the Afrikaners succeeded in deflecting onto Indian shopkeepers the resentment that should have been directed at them. That is why it is so important to the resistance in South Africa that the many nonwhite groups in the country see themselves as "non-white" rather than as Asian or Indian or Griqua or whatever. The motivation for such a reorganization of the South African racial code, of course, would not come from any sort of biological discovery: its purpose would be purely political, just like the purpose of the code it would mean to overthrow.

Things are subtler in America, but not necessarily less pernicious. In the stories of William Faulkner, you can see just how sensitive the South has been to the classificatory challenges created by racial admixture. For instance, Charles Bon, the hero of Faulkner's novel *Absalom, Absalom!*, has a fair-skinned mistress who is just one-eighth Negro—hence, an "octoroon"—but that slim one-eighth is enough to cast her among the slaves. At the end of the novel, we discover that Bon, who is an officer in the Confederate Army, has a trace of "black blood" in his veins as well, which is enough to cause his all-white half-brother to murder him.

Just one drop of Negro blood in America, it seems, is enough to make you "black"—and not only in fiction. My father, who is a physician, has told me a story of how once during World War II he was called in to diagnose the illness of a civilian child who lived near his southern boot camp. The child was blonde, blue-eyed, and, as my father informed his thunderstruck parents, suffering from sickle-cell anemia. "But he can't have *that*!" the child's parents insisted. I'm afraid that I don't know what became of the child, but given the racial situation in the South in the 1940s, it can only have been tragic.

HUMAN OR ANIMAL

We not only draw lines between races, of course, but between species as well, and here, too, cultural interests may be at work. Take the way that the aboriginal Dalabon tribesmen of northern Australia name and classify the flora and fauna of their environment. As traditional hunter-gatherers, the Dalabon must have a keen awareness of their natural surroundings in order to survive. And yet, when we look at their classifications, we may be in for a surprise. For rather than identifying the hundreds of species that a European zoologist or botanist would be able to identify in their territory, the Dalabon give names to only four major groups: *djen* (fish); *du:l* (trees); *guin* (large marsupials); and *ma:n* (which includes small marsupials, lizards, snakes, insects, dogs, and birds). Where we might distinguish "lizards" from "birds," then, the Dalabon see two related animals that can be called by the same name. For those of us trained in the Western scheme of taxonomic classification, which groups animals according to biological and evolutionary traits, the Dalabon taxonomy may look rather "primitive" and "unintelligent."

But it is nothing of the sort. For if you, like the Dalabon, spent your entire life hunting and gathering, you'd be more interested in the number of meals a given animal could provide than in its biological similarity to another species. You'd accordingly be likely to distinguish between small marsupials and large ones too, even though they're biologically related. Similarly, if your interest in fish did not extend beyond their potential for a meal, you wouldn't need to distinguish among their many kinds. All you'd need to know was that fish are found in water, and the Dalabon carefully distinguish between those animals which are found exclusively in water and those which are not.

Seen from a Dalabon perspective, then, a fourfold natural order makes perfect sense because it serves a concrete interest. This leads us to a related question: "What interest is served by *our* way of classifying natural species?" This isn't an easy question to answer, much less to ask, because it ordinarily doesn't occur to us to ask it. The way we classify and name things seems to be the only way that it can be done. Ask a Dalabon tribesman why he calls both dogs and birds by the same name (*ma:n*), and he is likely to respond, "because they are *ma:n*." If he asked us why we call one *ma:n* a "dog" and another a "bird," we are likely to say, "because that *is* a 'dog' and that *is* a 'bird.' "

Only recently in the history of the West has it been possible to ask the semiotic question, "What interests do our classification of natural species serve?" It would have been unintelligible to the founders of Western culture. To answer this question, we must begin, as semiotic analysis often does, by examining history. For the writers of the Bible, the names that Adam gave to the beasts of the field were the only names that could be given. Cows were "cows" and camels were "camels," and that was the end of it.

For the ancient Greeks the situation was somewhat different, but their taxonomic outlook was essentially the same. Aristotle, writing in the fourth century B.C., believed that while various peoples might give different names to things (in the Greek language or in the Persian, for example), these names ultimately referred to the same classes of things. Various peoples may name their world differently, use different signs, but their names all refer to the same reality.

Aristotle's attitude is probably the one most of us hold today. It seems to be only common sense. But as the first of our fundamental semiotic precepts tells us, "common sense" is really "communal sense," the set of concepts shared by a group. For the Western community, for instance, it is only common sense that cows were put on earth for us to eat. But that isn't common sense in India.

Let's look more closely now at the interests behind our Western way of classifying animals. Our first clue as to the nature of this interest comes from the Bible itself, in which the West has encoded its belief that all Creation has been turned over to humanity for its own use. God gives Adam dominion over all the species of the earth, as well as the right to name them. This act of naming symbolizes the control that we have over the earth, for to name a thing, as we have seen, is to define its uses. It is to gain power over it.

The "myth" of Genesis (and I use the term *myth* in its semiotic sense) reflects the interests of a people whose relation to nature was an embattled one. Life on the Mesopotamian plain, where the Semitic "myths" that eventually culminated in the Bible originated, was not easy. Disastrous floods, murderous heat, and wild beasts all threatened the lives of the forefathers of

Western culture. Animal rights and environmental considerations had no significance for a people at war with a natural environment that appeared to be at war with them.

The fact that Adam names the species of the earth also symbolizes the ancient Hebrews' sense of separation from their environment. By exercising his power to name every other species, Adam places himself in a special category above them. Adam never names himself, for no one except God stands above him. Adam also never attempts to speak with the animals, as happens so often in what we call "primitive" mythology, because there is simply no dialogue between Adam and the rest of Creation, and little sense of creaturely community. Adam just tells the animals what their names are and accordingly exercises his dominion over them, thus symbolizing the Western belief that animals are just things, soulless objects over which humans have absolute control.

Our Western heritage thus bequeaths to us a sense of a profound division between humanity and the rest of nature. Nature is there to be subdued, to be forced to conform to the needs of human culture. This attitude serves a clear interest that our culture has concealed by "naturalizing" it. To us, it seems only natural to divide up the animate world into the broad classes of "animals" and "humans," with the covert assumption that it is equally "natural" for the one class to dominate the other.

The results of the West's conceptual division between nature and culture are all too apparent today. The massive extinction of species, the pollution of our land, air, and water, the crowding out of other forms of life can all be traced, semiotically speaking, to our own isolation of ourselves from nature.

The current controversy over the linguistic capabilities of such animals as great apes and whales involves a similar set of clashing interests in the question of where to draw the line. From the time of the ancient Greeks, who defined man as the animal with the "logos"—that is, the only animal with a capacity for rational speech—to the present, philosophers have believed that it is our ability to use language that separates us from the lower animals. If it could be proved that at least some animal species share our capacity to use language, then we might be compelled to redraw the line between the human and animal kingdoms. A number of long-term experiments have been conducted accordingly to see whether an animal can be taught a human language, the most famous involving a chimpanzee named Washoe and a gorilla named Koko. But the results of these experiments have been controversial, because the ways they are interpreted reflect the particular interests of the interpreters.

Take Francine (Penny) Patterson's Koko, a gorilla who now has her own pet cat, her own line of stuffed toys, and even her own research foundation. Recognizing that gorillas are not physiologically equipped to utter actual words, Patterson has attempted to teach Koko a language of the deaf: American Sign Language. Koko, as Patterson tries to demonstrate in her *National Geographic* article, "Conversations with a Gorilla," can apparently use scores of abstract symbols as we do—that is, conceptually and spontaneously. "Soft good cat cat," Koko says (in sign language) of her kitten Smoky, thus apparently mastering such abstract concepts as "cat" and "good" and spontaneously attributing them to her particular cat. Koko has also "told" Patterson the "story" of how she was captured in Africa, signing a chilling tale of the destruction of her entire band. It's hard not to be convinced by Patterson's many videotaped demonstrations of Koko's abilities. Perhaps, like Doctor Doolittle, she has finally learned to "talk to the animals."

Thomas Sebeok, a leading figure in academic semiotic circles, is not convinced, however. In an article pointedly entitled "Smart Simians: Self-Fulfilling Prophecy and Kindred Methodological Pitfalls," he voices his opinion that Patterson, consciously or unconsciously, actually cues Koko to use the signs that she does. For example, in one photograph from her *National Geographic* article, Patterson shows Koko signing "teeth." Koko does this by pointing to her own teeth with her index finger—in response to an image of a grinning chimpanzee and a request from Patterson to make the sign for teeth. If this were a spontaneous response to the picture of the chimp, it would be proof that Koko had mastered the abstract concept of "teeth" and had learned its appropriate sign. But Sebeok points out that in the same photograph in which we see Koko pointing to her teeth, we can see Patterson touching the teeth of the pictured chimpanzee with her own index finger. If Koko were simply imitating Patterson, this would be a case of monkey see, monkey do, not a genuine use of a human language.

The debate over Koko's linguistic capabilities involves some critical interests. If it could be proved that Koko really can communicate with us, and if, more generally, we really could learn to "talk to the animals," then our ordinary way of treating them would be profoundly shaken. For if animals could talk, they would seem a lot closer to humans than they seem now. What we now call poaching or hunting would then be seen as simply murder—like the way the late naturalist Dian Fossey viewed the poaching of her gorillas or the way the poisoning of your dog would appear to you. Eating your next roast beef dinner might be viewed as an act of cannibalism. And not only our pets but all animals would merit their own proper names.

The interests at stake here are clear. On the one side we find the interests of the beef and poultry industry, or anyone who profits (if only in a culinary way) from the assumption that animals are something less than human beings. On the other side, we find those who believe animals deserve the same rights that we assume are "natural" to human society.

Another example of this division is the raging battle over where the line should be drawn in animal experimentation. On the one side, we find cosmetics firms, drug companies, cigarette manufacturers, medical researchers, universities . . . almost the whole gamut of corporate and institutional America. On the other side, we find such antivivisectionist groups as the People for the Ethical Treatment of Animals, In Defense of Animals, and the Humane Society. The former camp attempts to conceal its economic and professional interests by emphasizing the benefits to humans that accrue from animal research and seeks to draw the line as broadly as possible to include everything from fruit flies to chimpanzees in the class of "experimental animals." The latter camp would like to see the class abolished and bring an end to animal vivisection. Both sides see their position as the more natural and moral, but though it is not easy to judge between them, one can say that the antivivisectionists have less of an economic stake in the outcome of the debate and thus may be said to be less in danger of being motivated by selfish interests.

THE HOPI VIEW

The Hopi Indians view their world as a complex network of interrelated species. Rather than absolutely separating animals from plants, and both of these from other natural phenomena as well as from human beings, the Hopi taxonomy groups these things together into a number of interrelated "totems" that together form a unified natural system. In the north–west totem, for instance, we find grouped together the color yellow, pumas, orioles, Douglas firs, green rabbit-brush, mariposa lilies, yellow corn, and French beans. Similarly, in the south–west totem we find the colors blue and green, bears, bluebirds, white pines, sagebrush, larkspur, blue corn, and butterbeans.

Such a totemic organization of species brings human beings directly into the natural order, for humans also belong to totemic classes by virtue of their clan relation to some other member of the totem. A man belonging to the Bear clan, for example, feels himself to be related to an ancestral, if mythological, Bear who is the father of those bears and people who belong to the same totemic group. In this scheme nature and culture enjoy a certain harmony. Because every Hopi Indian belongs to some totem or other, all the natural species of the earth can find a point of correspondence within the human order.

In this way totemism reverses the mythology of the Adamic

scheme of things, for where Adam dictates to the animals in the founding cultural myth of the West, an ancestral animal totem speaks from the past to its human "descendants." Far from seeing themselves in cultural opposition to a natural world that they must subdue, the Hopi see themselves in intimate relation with their world, as being parts of a vast web of universal correspondences.

A belief in such correspondences has occasionally surfaced in Western thought, though not often. There is a relation, for instance, between totemic thinking and the astrology of prescientific Europe, for the astrologer, too, believes in an essential correspondence between one natural object—a constellation, star, or planet—and the human being who is born under it. Even today, people check their daily horoscopes, and Nancy Reagan made headlines in 1988 when her faith in this nonscientific "science" was revealed. I do not mean to imply that we should abandon our scientific way of classifying species and adopt a totemic or astrological worldview, however. The semiotic lesson that we can draw from the difference between our way of looking at things and the Hopi's is simply that we *can* look at things differently. Indeed, we don't even have to give up our biological approach to classifying animals, for the fundamental lesson of the Darwinian revolution is not that humankind sits on the top of the evolutionary heap but rather that our history is governed by the same laws that govern the histories of other species. We're all in this together, modern science tells us. There is no binding reason we should see ourselves in opposition to the natural world.

In addition, it's not always necessary for us to be conscious of the motives behind our ways of naming and classifying things. But sometimes our ignorance of the original interests served by our taxonomic schemes can impel us to act in ways that are no longer in our interest at all. At such times, it can be useful indeed to know just how and why we classify things as we do; such knowledge might enable us to think of some other way of perceiving our world.

Here is where semiotics can help us. For it is one of the tasks of semiotics to explore the different ways in which various cultures classify and name things. In this enterprise, semiotics often joins hands with anthropology, seeking to get to the heart of a culture by uncovering the hidden interests or, we might say, the ideologies that cause a culture to classify things as it does.

To look at our organization of the world as a reflection of our interests can help us to change our views when some change becomes necessary. When we know that we are not required to see the world in any particular way, we are free to choose new ways that can better serve our changing interests. We do not have to see ourselves in opposition to nature. As we face an increasingly polluted world, it is no small matter to learn that we might look at things differently. It's all in a name.

CHAPTER 3

Of Myths and Men: Culture's Hidden Frames

A mythology reflects its region.
Wallace Stevens

As I stared at the cover of the January 26, 1987, issue of *Time* magazine, three battered G.I.'s stared back at me beneath a bold headline. "*PLATOON*," it read, "Viet Nam as It Really Was."

And so *Time*, in a feature story on Oliver Stone's Oscar-winning film, charted yet another cinematic contribution to the ever-unfolding mythology of Vietnam—a mythology that has included *Apocalypse Now*, *The Deer Hunter*, *The Hanoi Hilton*, *Full Metal Jacket*, the "Rambo" films, and even *The Green Berets*. More such films will appear in the years to come as Americans continue to tell and retell the story of Vietnam, weaving a mythic web that future generations may well compare with Homer's epic tales of the Trojan War.

You may be surprised that I call the stories of the Vietnam War a "mythology," comparing them with the legends of the ancient Greeks. Surely fifty thousand American dead and over a million Vietnamese casualties are hardly the stuff of fiction and fantasy. No, such a war was no myth. It was an all too real national and international catastrophe from which we are still recovering. And yet, when we look at the Vietnam War from a semiotic perspective, seeking to understand the many interpretations that it has endured, we find the clear outline of history blurring into the gray depths of mythology. Here, the objective clarity of events yields to ideology; combat slips into code; and the "truth" of experience—"Viet Nam as it really was"— becomes hostage to the teller of the tale.

But whose myth should we believe? John Wayne's or Francis Ford Coppola's? Oliver Stone's or Sylvester Stallone's? Believe Wayne, and Vietnam appears as Lyndon Johnson wanted it to appear: a war against totalitarianism, a noble-minded defense of freedom. Believe Coppola, and the war was a moral fiasco that corrupted America just as the Belgian Congo corrupted Kurtz, the fallen missionary in Joseph Conrad's *Heart of Darkness*. For Stallone, Vietnam has all the moral complexity of a "He-Man" cartoon, while in Oliver Stone's *Platoon*, the war is reframed as a myth of male initiation, the story of a young soldier coming to manhood in a contest between surrogate fathers. Is this, finally, what Vietnam was all about?

Certainly not to a Vietnamese peasant. Nor to the women who waited at home while their sons and lovers fought it out in a distant jungle. Nor even to many of the men who were there. The same events take on a very different appearance depending on who is looking at them. In this sense, the war can be viewed as a sign, as an experience surrounded by a mythology whose meaning refers more to the values of its interpreters than to the actual conflict. To put this another way, *Time*'s headline is misleading: no single version of the war can represent "Viet Nam as it really was." There are only versions, stories erected within a mythic frame.

The myths of Vietnam have been particularly visible in the

photographic imagery that the war produced. In the late 1960s, when American revulsion to the war began to reach its peak, the iconic image of a naked child running away from her napalmed village, or of a Vietcong guerrilla grimacing as a bullet shatters his brains, told a story of American brutality and callousness that literally and figuratively left Hanoi's brutality and callousness out of the picture. But in the 1980s, as Americans forgot the moral ambiguities of the war amid a general patriotic revival spearheaded by the Reagan presidency, the picture was reversed. Images of middle-aged men running their trembling hands over the black marble walls of the Vietnam War Memorial tell the tale of American suffering in Vietnam, but leave Vietnamese suffering outside the frame. Meanwhile, the "Rambo" films propagate a mythology of betrayal, blaming the American failure in Vietnam on the antiwar movement, and offering the figure of a machine gun–wielding Sylvester Stallone as a symbol of vicarious revenge for battles lost.

For the French semiotician Roland Barthes, photographs do an especially good job of propagating cultural myths. That's because we assume they mirror reality; a photographic image presents itself to us as an absolutely neutral representation of its subject. A camera, supposedly, never lies. In fact, however, any photograph—whether taken by a photojournalist in the Vietnam jungles or by Dad with his Kodak in the backyard—can be stage-managed. Just look at your family photo album. How many pictures show the family gathered round, smiling brightly, despite the quarrel that broke out only moments before? By telling, or sometimes forcing, Mom, Dad, and Junior to say "cheese," we manufacture images of the happy families we want to believe in, even if that's not what our family is like at all.

Similarly, when you look at the photographic image of a fashion model, you're not really seeing the natural representation of a human being. Through the careful orchestration of light, camera angle, background, airbrush, and so on, a fashion photographer doesn't so much capture as *manufacture* an image—an image that represents not the model but a cultural ideal of human beauty. Just think of the way that Cheryl Tiegs and Christie Brinkley have become figures symbolic of a particular "look" that our culture admires. The finished photograph covers all this up by pretending to represent its subject as she "really" looks, but this is a myth. The *Cosmo* Girl, for instance, and the model who portrays her, are not really one and the same. The model is the fashion photographer's raw material for the myth, but while the model is real, the image manufactured for the cover of *Cosmopolitan* is not.

Photographs don't create myths by accident, however. In a book appropriately titled *Mythologies*, Barthes explores the way that photographs produce a "reality effect" that conceals the ideological motives of the culture behind them. Probing beneath the surface of a *Paris-Match* cover photo featuring a black African soldier devotedly saluting the French flag, for example, Barthes sees more than an innocent image of a man dressed in a French uniform. Instead, he decodes the way in which a colonial power naturalizes its own ideology. The editors of *Paris-Match* picked this photograph because they wanted their readers to believe "here is the image of a devoted French soldier." But the picture was not so innocent as that because, in presenting the apparent equality of devotion among all those who serve under the French flag, it distracted its viewer from noticing the fact that the African soldier was really serving in the army of his conquerors. His apparent contentment belied the simmering resentment that would eventually lead to violent uprisings against French rule. For Barthes, the photograph was simply part of a cultural mythology, actually a sort of propaganda, in which colonial power was framed so as to appear to be both natural and necessary, part of the proper order of things.

Barthes intended his essays in *Mythologies* to be subversive, and (in the semiotic sense) they were, for each was intended to jolt the French out of their cultural complacency and force them to confront their own ideological presuppositions. What Barthes

meant to do was compel his readers to look under the surface of
the ordinary images and objects of their daily lives in order to
see the cultural forces that were producing them. To understand
those forces, French readers would have to know the historical
circumstances that brought them into being. They couldn't
"read" the photograph on the *Paris-Match* cover, for example,
without knowing the history of the French colonial experience
in Africa. Semiotic understanding, in other words, requires historical understanding, and one of the major tasks of semiotics is to
reveal the histories behind our perceptions.

Indeed, you might look at *The Signs of Our Time* as a sort
of American "Mythologies," a probing into the histories and
meanings of some of the most common objects, images, and
beliefs of American culture. For American society, too, is per-
meated through and through with cultural myths that present
themselves as realities, as "life as it really is." But life, as the
semiotician sees it, never presents itself to us in such a straightforward manner. Between our perceptions and the realities we perceive there always lies a cultural myth. Let's take five classic
cultural "myths," which appear as inseparable parts of the natural
world to most people, and look at them the way a semiotician
would see them.

THE MYTH OF CHILDHOOD

Consider, for example, our perception of childhood. For most of
us, childhood is a stage of life separate from adulthood, a time
of innocence set off against the experience of grown-up life. It
seems only natural to view childhood this way. How else *could*
we look at it? "Quite otherwise," history answers, for as Roger
Sale explains in his book *Fairy Tales and After: From Snow White
to E. B. White*:

> In our sense, children and childhood did not exist
> until recent centuries. . . . If there were any stages in
> the growth of children, they were simply before and

after infancy. This is easily seen in medieval and early
Renaissance depictions of the Seven Ages of Man and
in portraits of royal and noble children in that period.
There are no children there, at least not as we think
of them, but babes in arms . . . and then people of
varying sizes all of whom have adult faces. People we
think of as children look like midgets.

Our perception of the child has changed owing to a major
shift in the way families make their livings. Before the Industrial
Revolution of the eighteenth and nineteenth centuries, most
European families lived on the land. Farm life necessitated the
full participation of everyone in the economic life of the family,
and so youngsters whom we would now regard as being barely
out of infancy were expected to do their share of the work. With
little distinction between an "adult's" and a "child's" responsibilities, few distinctions were made between children and adults.
Children were thus seen *as* adults, albeit smaller and weaker ones.

The distinctions that we now make between childhood and
adulthood began to emerge once the Industrial Revolution
shifted the center of economic activity from the farm to the
factory and office. During the eighteenth and nineteenth centuries, the majority of Europe's population moved from the country to the city and, consequently, the children of the new
economic order generally had less work to do. You don't have
to feed the pigs or plough any fields when you live in an urban
setting. Father earned the family's wages and mother took care
of the house, but the kids were left with few responsibilities of
their own. In response, a new myth of childhood emerged, declaring that children shouldn't have to work or bear adult responsibilities at all, but should be free to play and to learn.

By the end of the eighteenth century, child labor thus began
to be viewed for the first time as a kind of violation of nature,
an evil intrusion into the lives of innocent children. We can catch
an early glimpse of the emerging sensibility by reading William

Blake's *Songs of Innocence*, poems in which he often depicts the plight of exploited children sent to work before they even had a chance to *be* children. In the poem "The Chimney Sweeper," for example, a young London chimney sweep tells us his story:

> *When my mother died I was very young,*
> *And my father sold me while yet my tongue*
> *Could scarcely cry " 'weep! 'weep! 'weep! 'weep!"*
> *So your chimneys I sweep, and in soot I sleep.*

Blake's chimney sweeps dream of an angel who will set them free and take them to heaven, but they wake to cold days and hard work. By the early nineteenth century, however, children began to appear *as* angels, or at least as superior beings, in the poetry of William Wordsworth, who perhaps did more to construct the myth of childhood than anyone else. In his great "Ode on Intimations of Immortality from Recollections of Early Childhood," Wordsworth addresses the child as a kind of infant philosopher, a "Mighty Prophet" and "Seer blest," whose "exterior semblance doth belie/Thy soul's immensity." No one could have written that in the middle ages, when children were regarded as being born in the wrath of original sin, saved only by the rituals of the Church.

By the mid-nineteenth century, the myth of childhood as we know it today was pretty much in place. That was the period in which child-labor laws first began to reform the exploitation of young children in the workplace, and public education made schooling a reality for more European youngsters than ever before. Protected from the corrupting pressures of the working world, the child began to assume an aura of innocence that continues into the present day.

The myth of childhood innocence has all the sentimental attractiveness of a tale written by A. A. Milne or Kenneth Grahame, but it is still only a myth. At present, it appears that a new myth may be emerging, one not of childhood innocence but of childhood experience. The fact that teachers are now being asked to educate students about the danger of AIDS, for example, is a sign that adults now suspect—or fear—that their children are sexually active and must be warned and protected. Birth-control clinics and subtance-abuse treatment on grade-school campuses are a far cry from the world of *Winnie the Pooh* or *The Wind in the Willows.*

In short, the myth of childhood innocence is weakening all around us, but it's not going down without a fight. The resurgence of interest in stuffed toys, particularly Edwardian-style teddy bears, signals a nostalgic desire for the innocent icons of a bygone era. The appearance of elaborate rocking horses in the more expensive toy stores is another sign of this nostalgia for the icons of the Victorian-Edwardian nursery. However, the self-conscious revival of such emblems of mythical childhood suggests that this is a last-ditch effort, and that the children of the future will be seen differently from the way they are seen now. (See chapter 5 for more on the semiotics of toys and the myth of childhood.)

MYTHS OF GENDER

Perhaps the most naturalized of all the cultural myths that frame our perceptions of reality are the myths of gender and sexual identity. We normally assume that sexual traits are something determined by nature rather than by culture, by sheer biology, not ideology, but that's not entirely the case. The ideological motivations behind our perceptions of the sexes can be revealed by semiotic analysis.

You'll recognize the myths of gender as sets of opposite psychological and social traits: "men are rational," "women are intuitive"; "men are active," "women are passive"; "men are ambitious," "women are nurturing"; "a man's place is in the office," "a woman's place is in the home." The belief that a man can find fulfillment in his career but that a woman's happiness lies at home and with her family was a particularly potent cultural

myth in the 1950s and 1960s, but though we now live in an era
of feminist myth and consciousness, the old myth is still going
strong. We don't have to look at Phyllis Schlafly's attacks on the
Equal Rights Amendment to find signs of the continuing authority of the myth. A glance at a simple advertisement can tell us
all we need to know, particularly when it pretends to be challenging what we might call the "myth of the happy housewife."

In a recent Whirlpool magazine ad, a woman chats happily
on her kitchen telephone, waiting for the dishwasher to finish.
The scene's relative darkness indicates it's evening, suggesting that
the woman has probably come home from work, eaten dinner,
and changed into jeans, a sweater, and flats before seeing to the
dishes. In other words, the setting implies that this is no
housecoat-and-apron drudge of the 1950s; this is a modern liberated woman. But even though she has shed her apron and has
apparently gotten a job of her own, she's still associated with the
kitchen and the telephone. We don't see a man in the kitchen,
and we don't see the woman doing any office "homework"—as
we commonly see men doing in advertisements featuring products (such as computers) aimed at male audiences. Furthermore,
a televised version of the same ad reveals that the woman on the
phone is talking to her mother about dishwasher noise. According
to the myth of the happy housewife, this is the sort of thing that
women discuss with one another.

Although the ad pretends to adapt itself to the liberated
1980s, it has actually only updated the myth of the happy housewife. The modern woman in the ad doesn't look like a fifties-era
housewife but, like her earlier counterpart, she is associated with
the kitchen, the telephone, and her mother. Even in an age of
feminist consciousness, we can still find the American Housewife
in an advertisement that appears to say one thing—"Whirlpool
announces the end of the noisy dishwasher"—but is really a sign
of the enduring patriarchal vision of American womanhood, the
traditional belief that "a woman's place is in the home."

A more subtle gender myth lurks behind our belief that

women are the more beautiful sex. "Men see," the myth says, "but women are to be seen." "Men are voyeurs," as Freud put it, "women are exhibitionists." There is a long history behind this myth that the English art critic John Berger explores in his book *Ways of Seeing.* Berger analyzes the history of the nude in Western art, pointing out how nude portraiture has always assumed a male viewer gazing upon a female subject. Such paintings, he insists, are created *by* men, *of* women, *for* men. The modern version of this genre is, of course, the *Playboy* centerfold. Even though the famous *Cosmopolitan* centerfold of Burt Reynolds proved that women like to look at men too, the predominant cultural myth still holds that ogling is a male prerogative. Women have been taught to turn their gazes inward, to watch themselves being watched, conscious of being forever on display. Men are accordingly associated with binoculars and telescopes, women with mirrors.

In attempting to subvert the myths of gender that have so long dominated American consciousness, feminists have developed their own myths. During the 1970s women disregarded the passive, nurturing housewife and invented the superwoman—iconically represented by the comic-book character of Wonder Woman—who can have it all: career, family, and sex appeal. But this myth put so much pressure on women that some began to crack under the strain in the 1980s, abandoning their careers to return to the haven of the home. A mythic compromise is slowly emerging that puts less pressure on women and allows more latitude to their desires, requiring them to be neither housewives nor superwomen. In the new myth, sex roles will be less strictly defined, leaving more room for "house husbands" and female breadwinners, but allowing women to be just wives and mothers if they so desire. (See chapter 10 for more on the semiotics of gender.)

THE MONEY MYTH

So, there are myths of childhood and myths of gender, fundamental frames within which we define our sense of self-identity. But what about the ordinary *objects* in our lives? They too are defined mythologically. Take the money in your wallet, or the change in your purse. Have you ever asked yourself what money really is? Paper and metal and marks on your banker's balance sheet? Of course not. These are just the *signs* by which we represent wealth, tokens for the purposes of economic exchange. But what do these tokens represent? What myths surround them?

In semiotic terms, the ultimate significance of money is purely mythological. I'm not referring to the fact that our paper currency is no longer backed by an equivalent quantity of gold at Fort Knox, or that our so-called "silver" coins are really silver, copper, and nickel sandwiches. Even if the dollar were still backed up by gold, or if pure silver coins were still in general circulation, this would still not explain why gold and silver are so precious to us. These metals are of no strategic value. They are too soft to be fashioned into weapons or tools or into anything useful. Yet their value is legendary, and the origin of that value lies in a myth, not in the metals themselves.

Often an object becomes valuable because it is rare, and gold and silver indeed owe part of their value to their scarcity. But that is not the ultimate cause of their preciousness. Rather, gold and silver became precious in the ancient world because of their *resemblance* to other precious things: gold, to the brightness of the sun that rises every morning and returns with renewed strength every spring to begin a new season of growth; and silver, to the brightness of the moon that waxes and wanes through the months, associated in the ancient world with feminine fertility. More importantly, gold, which neither rusts nor tarnishes, resembles unchanging, incorruptible immortality itself. Year after year, century after century, gold remains unchanged, like that most precious mythical possession of all, eternal life. When the medieval alchemists searched for the key to transforming base metals into gold, they were not looking for a way to make a fast buck; they were seeking immortality. They believed if they could find the secret of gold, they could unlock the secrets of eternity.

Although we are no longer conscious of the original mythical significance of gold, it still retains the aura it has always held. We still purchase it in times of economic uncertainty as a kind of talismanic protection against inflation and international catastrophe. Prophets of impending doom commonly counsel their flocks to store food, stock weapons, and buy gold—even though in a real crisis I doubt that anyone would stop to barter for ingots. Food and weapons are the essentials, not symbolic bits of precious metal. Interestingly enough, though, it is gold that costs over $400 an ounce.

Even something as solid and enduring as the value of gold is grounded in mythological belief. Gold, finally, is also a sign, an icon of all that we desire as mortals in a dangerous world. Gold can grant us neither immortality nor permanent economic security. But it is divine insofar as it resembles immortal things, and its divinity has lost none of its mythic luster even in an age that has substituted science for superstition, an age that believes it has finally transcended the myths of the past to see the world in the clear light of scientific knowledge.

SCIENCE OR MYTH?

Is science the answer to mythology, the one way to see things as they really are? Can we escape from cultural myth by adopting a purely scientific attitude? Not exactly, according to the semiotician, for science is also a kind of mythology.

To say that science is mythological, however, is not at all the same as saying that it is untrue or that it is in any sort of real competition with religious mythologies. Religious myths frame the invisible world of the spirit, the realm of belief and desire; scientific myths frame the world of the senses, the material reality that we see and experience. Scientific theory demands empirical testing and support; religion requires only faith. The fact that scientists cannot explain everything in the universe is not a valid reason for rejecting science in favor of religion. The two mythologies are simply incommensurate and should not be compared with each other as competing views of the world. Many scientists are religious, but this does not mean that their science is in any way undermined by belief. Einstein believed in God—whom he called the Old One—but this didn't make him believe in the geocentric universe presupposed by the myth of Creation.

There are two ways in which science is mythological. First, like any myth, it causes us to look at the world through a frame. Nonscientists commonly believe that the scientist merely observes things and objectively describes their behavior for the sake of knowledge alone, but that is not the way science works. First, a scientist doesn't investigate something unless he or she has a reason for looking at it. Sometimes this interest is sheer ambition, sometimes it is political; for example, German phycisists in the 1930s sought to discredit Einstein's work because Einstein was a Jew—they called his theories "Jewish physics." Most of the time, however, a scientist does something because that is what his or her peers are doing. To put this another way, there is an *historical* component to scientific investigation that scientists and non-scientists alike often ignore.

In his groundbreaking study of the history of science, *The Structure of Scientific Revolutions*, Thomas Kuhn argues that most scientists engage in what he calls "normal science"; that is, they conduct the research projects that are accepted by the scientific establishments in which they work. Astronomical investigation, for example, is a part of the normal science of the twentieth century, while astrology, which was an acceptable part of medie-val science, is not. Psychologists and psychiatrists are accredited by modern scientific institutions, but students of the paranormal and of ESP are still relegated to the margins of scientific inquiry. Phrenology, or the tracing of specific character traits back to the shape of one's skull, was a popular tool for nineteenth-century criminology, but is entirely discredited in twentieth-century sci-ence.

The paradigms of normal science can differ from place to place as well as from time to time. In modern China, for example, the theory and practice of acupuncture is not just a part of the normal training of a Chinese physician, it may be the only treatment he or she is taught to use. If on a business trip to Peking you have a toothache, an eye problem, or even appendicitis, expect acupuncture to be a part of your treatment. But don't expect it in New York or Boston, for while American physicians are allowed to dabble in acupuncture, it is still not an accepted part of the American medical community. What is normal in China is met in America with amusement and sometimes incredulity. In Kuhn's terms, American and Chinese physicians each operate within different "paradigms," or within different frameworks, of medical practice—what a semiotician would call different "myths."

There is a second sense in which modern science is mythological. Consider how often you are exhorted to buy something because it contains "beta carotene," or because "nine out of ten doctors agree" about it, or because it will end your pain with "ibuprofen." Advertisers seek to dazzle us with technical or scientific terms because science and technology have become the dominant mythology of our times. The language of science has become an almost sacred tongue today, a discourse known only to the initiated which the rest of us must accept from the scientist on faith. Compare the sacred Latinity of the Catholic priesthood with the language on a medical prescription. Physicians, too, have their own Latinate jargon that divides them from the nonmedical laity.

Indeed, scientists have become the "priests" of a new kind of materialistic religion, the religion of scientific expertise. Where we once consulted oracles and priests about the nature of the universe and of the future, we now go to scientific experts, even when their expertise is more limited than their pronouncements would suggest. When Linus Pauling published his opinion that vitamin C could cure the common cold, for example, thousands of Americans began to gobble down vitamin supplements, even though Pauling's two Nobel Prizes do not include one in medicine. Scientific celebrities like Carl Sagan and Stephen Jay Gould

are consulted on everything from "nuclear winter" to race relations in South Africa. And Isaac Asimov is sure to be found on
any panel delegated to predict what our lives will be like in the
twenty-first century.

Like any religion, however, science can fall victim to its own
promises if those promises are not borne out. Having replaced the
soothsayers and witch doctors of the past, scientists today are
expected to foresee the future, and when they fail in their predic-
tions they must often endure public criticism. Consider the beating the U.S. Geological Survey took when it failed to predict the
magnitude of the Mount St. Helens explosion. Or the mounting
impatience of many Californians who want to know precisely
when "the Big One" (the great quake everyone is predicting will
occur within the next quarter century) will occur. Government
agencies consult the scientific community to learn what effect
industrial air pollution will have on future weather patterns and
are given two conflicting answers: either there will be a "green-
house effect," which will heat up the earth, or there will be a
cooling trend due to the blockage of solar heat by dust particles
in the air. Scientists are not dismayed by such uncertainty, but
the nonscientists who consult them certainly are.

Perhaps more seriously, we have come to believe in a scientific myth that science is capable of curing every human ill, and
blame the scientist when the cure is not forthcoming. You know
the old complaint: "We can put a man on the moon, why can't
we cure the common cold?" Gay activists accuse the medical
establishment of deliberate betrayal as years pass without a cure
for AIDS. Cancer patients thumb their noses at the medical
experts and head south for laetrile clinics in Tijuana. And faith
healers move in with their prescientific treatments when science
fails to provide relief.

Whenever the myth of science fails, myths of religion re-
emerge with renewed strength. It is probably no accident that in
the 1980s America experienced a resurgence of orthodox religious fervor at a time when science and technology no longer

seemed to be providing satisfactory answers to our deepest questions about our place in the universe. Nonscientists tend to confuse the scientist's search for physical origins—the Big Bang, the beginnings of life on earth—with religion's search for the Absolute. Reputable scientists, however, don't pretend to deliver absolute knowledge, and are perfectly aware that their theories are often incomplete. Evolutionary theory, for example, which isn't really a theory anymore but an established fact of the normal science of twentieth-century biology, is still itself in a process of evolution. Scientists disagree among themselves about the precise mechanisms of evolution, but few doubt the overall truth of the theory. Confident of their own absolute and unchanging knowledge, however, religious Creationists leap in with a triumphant "I told you so" every time biologists differ among themselves, but this simply misses the point. The myth of science presupposes theoretical uncertainty and approximation. It expects its framing paradigms to change as scientific knowledge changes. Science grows through a dynamic process of theoretical conjecture and experimental verification; religion cites preestablished textual authorities. You simply can't compare the two.

THE MYTH OF PROGRESS

Everyone knows the old adage "you can't stop progress," which usually means that you shouldn't oppose some technological invention or industrial development scheme. But the belief in progress is older than modern technology. It first made its appearance during the eighteenth-century Enlightenment, when philosophers like Voltaire saw the rise of rational thought and the decline of the Catholic Church as a sign of social progress. By the early nineteenth century, the German philosopher G. W. F. Hegel had declared that all human history is necessarily progressive, that society becomes freer and more rational with every passing epoch of civilization. And so there emerged a general "myth of progress," which held that social progress was an inevitable product of history, and optimistically looked to the future for better and better things.

The astounding technological advances of the twentieth century—the way we have gone from the Wright brothers to the moon in but half a century—have often been taken as proof of the inevitability of human progress. Equating technological progress with social and moral progress, the defenders and exponents of the virtues of technology often accuse their opponents of being against progress itself. But the myth of progress, both social and technological, is beginning to weaken in the face of Auschwitz, Hiroshima, and Chernobyl. The population explosion and the worldwide pollution of the earth point to a dismal, not promising, future. Plenty of optimists are still around who denounce the prophets of "gloom and doom," but the certainty of future improvement and perfection promised by the myth of progress is being sorely tested.

The myths that frame our perceptions and beliefs are generally invisible to us *as myths* so long as they seem to correspond to reality. Once the frame begins to appear, the myth's authority weakens and a new myth takes its place. The authority, for example, of the Creation myth found in the Bible was shattered by mid-nineteenth-century discoveries in geology and biology, and with it the authority of traditional religion itself. Similarly, the myth of progress is now being exposed and undermined at a moment when human events seem more irrational and violent than ever before. The myth of progress is accordingly being replaced today by a "myth of uncertainty" in an uncertain age.

We can discover the traces of an emerging myth of uncertainty by looking at some of the changes in attitude that have occurred within the scientific community in recent years. For example, when Darwin formulated his theory of evolution, he assumed—believing in the myth of progress as he did—that species evolved into higher and more progressive forms as the years went by, eventually culminating in man. But modern evolutionary scientists, like Stephen Jay Gould, who have rejected the myth of progress now argue that evolution is a more or less random process, a history of accidents leading neither to "higher" nor to "improved" species. Evolutionary change, the new myth suggests, is just a dice throw.

Similarly, whereas Sir Isaac Newton invented the calculus to predict with certainty the motion of any object in space, contemporary physicists now believe in a general "uncertainty principle." First formulated in the 1920s by the German physicist Werner Heisenberg, it holds that a physicist can never be certain of the position of an atomic particle in space. All that he or she can calculate is the *probable* behavior of the atom. The old deterministic certainty is gone.

Of course, scientists like Gould or Heisenberg don't regard their observations as the product of a myth; they view them as discoveries and truths, and at the moment, they *are* truths, because they have not been challenged by any contrary evidence. The myth of uncertainty itself is still quite young and has not yet been falsified by experience. Nor has it been contradicted by history. Living in the shadow of nuclear weapons, the population explosion, and the unchecked destruction of our environment, we face an uncertain future indeed. No wonder everything appears chancy to us. And I expect that the myth of uncertainty will only grow in authority as long as the world hovers on the brink of destruction.

This doesn't mean, however, that the myth of uncertainty is the final word on the nature of the universe. It's just another way of viewing things. Will there someday be a final myth that we can settle on as the "truth" of things at last? How fine it would be to be able to answer this question in the affirmative, but, as a semiotician, I'm afraid I must demur. If the last frame ever crumbles and reality shines on us in its pure unmediated being, semiotics itself will vanish and will perhaps be the last myth to fall.

CHAPTER 4

Masters of Desire: The Culture of American Advertising

Amongst democratic nations, men easily attain a certain equality of condition; but they can never attain as much as they desire.
Alexis de Tocqueville

On May 10, 1831, a young French aristocrat named Alexis de Tocqueville arrived in New York City at the start of what would become one of the most famous visits to America in our history. He had come to observe firsthand the institutions of the freest, most egalitarian society of the age, but what he found was a paradox. For behind America's mythic promise of equal opportunity, Tocqueville discovered a desire for *unequal* social rewards, a ferocious competition for privilege and distinction. As he wrote in his monumental study, *Democracy in America*:

> When all privileges of birth and fortune are
> abolished, when all professions are accessible to all,
> and a man's own energies may place him at the top

of any of one them, an easy and unbounded career
seems open to his ambition . . . But this is an
erroneous notion, which is corrected by daily
experience. [For when] men are nearly alike, and all
follow the same track, it is very difficult for any one
individual to walk quick and cleave a way through
the same throng which surrounds and presses him.

Yet walking quick and cleaving a way is precisely what
Americans dream of. We Americans dream of rising above the
crowd, of attaining a social summit beyond the reach of ordinary
citizens. And therein lies the paradox.

The American dream, in other words, has two faces: the one
communally egalitarian and the other competitively elitist. This
contradiction is no accident; it is fundamental to the structure of
American society. Even as America's great myth of equality
celebrates the virtues of mom, apple pie, and the girl or boy next
door, it also lures us to achieve social distinction, to rise above
the crowd and bask alone in the glory. This land is your land and
this land is my land, Woody Guthrie's populist anthem tells us,
but we keep trying to increase the "my" at the expense of the
"your." Rather than fostering contentment, the American dream
breeds desire, a longing for a greater share of the pie. It is as if
our society were a vast high-school football game, with the bulk
of the participants noisily rooting in the stands while, deep down,
each of them is wishing he or she could be the star quarterback
or head cheerleader.

For the semiotician, the contradictory nature of the American
myth of equality is nowhere written so clearly as in the signs that
American advertisers use to manipulate us into buying their
wares. "Manipulate" is the word here, not "persuade"; for advertising campaigns are not sources of product information, they are
exercises in behavior modification. Appealing to our subconscious emotions rather than to our conscious intellects, advertisements are designed to exploit the discontentments fostered by

the American dream, the constant desire for social success and the material rewards that accompany it. America's consumer economy runs on desire, and advertising stokes the engines by transforming common objects—from peanut butter to political candidates—into signs of all the things that Americans covet most.

But by semiotically reading the signs that advertising agencies manufacture to stimulate consumption, we can plot the precise state of desire in the audiences to which they are addressed. In this chapter, we'll look at a representative sample of ads and what they say about the emotional climate of the country and the fast-changing trends of American life. Because ours is a highly diverse, pluralistic society, various advertisements may say different things depending on their intended audiences, but in every case they say something about America, about the status of our hopes, fears, desires, and beliefs.

Let's begin with two ad campaigns conducted by the same company that bear out Alexis de Tocqueville's observations about the contradictory nature of American society: General Motors' campaigns for its Cadillac and Chevrolet lines. First, consider an early magazine ad for the Cadillac Allanté. Appearing as a full-color, four-page insert in *Time*, the ad seems to say "I'm special —and so is this car" even before we've begun to read it. Rather than being printed on the ordinary, flimsy pages of the magazine, the Allanté spread appears on glossy coated stock. The unwritten message here is that an extraordinary car deserves an extraordinary advertisement, and that both car and ad are aimed at an extraordinary consumer, or at least one who wishes to appear extraordinary compared to his more ordinary fellow citizens.

Ads of this kind work by creating symbolic associations between their product and what is most coveted by the consumers to whom they are addressed. It is significant, then, that this ad insists that the Allanté is virtually an Italian rather than an American car, an automobile, as its copy runs, "Conceived and Commissioned by America's Luxury Car Leader—Cadillac" but

"Designed and Handcrafted by Europe's Renowned Design Leader—Pininfarina, SpA, of Turin, Italy." This is not simply a piece of product information, it's a sign of the prestige that European luxury cars enjoy in today's automotive marketplace. Once the luxury car of choice for America's status drivers, Cadillac has fallen far behind its European competitors in the race for the prestige market. So the Allanté essentially represents Cadillac's decision, after years of resisting the trend toward European cars, to introduce its own European import—whose high cost is clearly printed on the last page of the ad. Although $54,700 is a lot of money to pay for a Cadillac, it's about what you'd expect to pay for a top-of-the-line Mercedes-Benz. That's precisely the point the ad is trying to make: the Allanté is no mere car. It's a potent status symbol you can associate with the other major status symbols of the 1980s.

American companies manufacture status symbols because American consumers want them. As Alexis de Tocqueville recognized a century and a half ago, the competitive nature of democratic societies breeds a desire for social distinction, a yearning to rise above the crowd. But given the fact that those who do make it to the top in socially mobile societies have often risen from the lower ranks, they still look like everyone else. In the socially immobile societies of aristocratic Europe, generations of fixed social conditions produced subtle class signals. The accent of one's voice, the shape of one's nose, or even the set of one's chin, immediately communicated social status. Aside from the nasal bray and uptilted head of the Boston Brahmin, Americans do not have any native sets of personal status signals. If it weren't for his Mercedes-Benz and Manhattan townhouse, the parvenu Wall Street millionaire often couldn't be distinguished from the man who tailors his suits. Hence, the demand for status symbols, for the objects that mark one off as a social success, is particularly strong in democratic nations—stronger even than in aristocratic societies, where the aristocrat so often looks and sounds different from everyone else.

Status symbols, then, are signs that identify their possessors' place in a social hierarchy, markers of rank and prestige. We can all think of any number of status symbols—Rolls-Royces, Beverly Hills mansions, even Shar Pei puppies (whose rareness and expense has rocketed them beyond Russian wolfhounds as status pets and has even inspired whole lines of wrinkle-faced stuffed toys)—but how do we know that something *is* a status symbol? The explanation is quite simple: when an object (or puppy!) either costs a lot of money or requires influential connections to possess, anyone who possesses it must also possess the necessary means and influence to acquire it. The object itself really doesn't matter, since it ultimately disappears behind the presumed social potency of its owner. Semiotically, what matters is the signal it sends, its value as a sign of power. One traditional sign of social distinction is owning a country estate and enjoying the peace and privacy that attend it. Advertisements for Mercedes-Benz, Jaguar, and Audi automobiles thus frequently feature drivers motoring quietly along a country road, presumably on their way to or from their country houses.

Advertisers have been quick to exploit the status signals that belong to body language as well. As Hegel observed in the early nineteenth century, it is an ancient aristocratic prerogative to be seen by the lower orders without having to look at them in return. Tilting his chin high in the air and gazing down at the world under hooded eyelids, the aristocrat invites observation while refusing to look back. We can find such a pose exploited in an advertisement for Cadillac Seville in which we see an elegantly dressed woman out for a drive with her husband in their new Cadillac. If we look closely at the woman's body language, we can see her glance inwardly with a satisfied smile on her face but not outward toward the camera that represents our gaze. She is glad to be seen by us in her Seville, but she isn't interested in looking at *us*!

Ads that are aimed at a broader market take the opposite approach. If the American dream encourages the desire to "arrive," to vault above the mass, it also fosters a desire to be popular, to "belong." Populist commercials accordingly transform products into signs of belonging, utilizing such common icons as country music, small-town life, family picnics, and farmyards. All of these icons are incorporated in GM's "Heartbeat of America" campaign for its Chevrolet line. Unlike the Seville commercial, the faces in the Chevy ads look straight at us and smile. Dress is casual; the mood upbeat. Quick camera cuts take us from rustic to suburban to urban scenes, creating an American montage filmed from sea to shining sea. We all "belong" in a Chevy.

Where price alone doesn't determine the market for a product, advertisers can go either way. Both Johnnie Walker and Jack Daniel's are better-grade whiskies, but where a Johnnie Walker ad appeals to the buyer who wants a mark of aristocratic distinction in his liquor, a Jack Daniel's ad emphasizes the down-home, egalitarian folksiness of its product. Johnnie Walker associates itself with such conventional status symbols as sable coats, Rolls-Royces, and black gold; Jack Daniel's gives us a Good Ol' Boy in overalls. In fact, Jack Daniel's Good Ol' Boy is an icon of backwoods independence, recalling the days of the moonshiner and the Whisky Rebellion of 1794. Evoking emotions quite at odds with those stimulated in Johnnie Walker ads, the advertisers of Jack Daniel's have chosen to transform their product into a sign of America's populist tradition. The fact that both ads successfully sell whisky is itself a sign of the dual nature of the American dream.

Beer is also pitched on two levels. Consider the difference between the ways Budweiser and Michelob market their light beers. Bud Light and Michelob Light cost and taste about the same, but Budweiser tends to target the working class while Michelob has gone after the upscale market. Bud commercials are set in working-class bars that contrast with the sophisticated nightclubs and yuppie watering holes of the Michelob campaign. "You're one of the guys," Budweiser assures the assembly-line worker and the truck driver, "this Bud's for you." Michelob, on the other hand, makes no such appeal to the democratic instinct of sharing and belonging. You don't share, you take, grabbing what you can in a competitive dash to "have it all."

Populist advertising is particularly effective in the face of foreign competition. When Americans feel threatened from the outside, they tend to circle the wagons and temporarily forget their class differences. In the face of the Japanese automotive "invasion," Chrysler runs populist commercials in which Lee Iacocca joins the simple folk who buy his cars as the jingle "Born in America" blares in the background. Seeking to capitalize on the popularity of Bruce Springsteen's *Born in the USA* album, these ads gloss over Springsteen's ironic lyrics in a vast display of flag-waving. Chevrolet's "Heartbeat of America" campaign similarly attempts to woo American motorists away from Japanese automobiles by appealing to their patriotic sentiments.

The patriotic iconography of these campaigns also reflects the general cultural mood of the early- to mid-1980s. After a period of national anguish in the wake of the Vietnam War and the Iran hostage crisis, America went on a patriotic binge. American athletic triumphs in the Lake Placid and Los Angeles Olympics introduced a sporting tone into the national celebration, often making international affairs appear like one great Olympiad in which America was always going for the gold. In response, advertisers began to do their own flag-waving.

The mood of advertising during this period was definitely upbeat. Even deodorant commercials, which traditionally work on our self-doubts and fears of social rejection, jumped on the bandwagon. In the guilty sixties, we had ads like the "Ice Blue Secret" campaign with its connotations of guilt and shame. In the feel-good Reagan eighties, "Sure" deodorant commercials featured images of triumphant Americans throwing up their arms in victory to reveal—no wet marks! Deodorant commercials once had the moral echo of Nathaniel Hawthorne's guilt-ridden *The Scarlet Letter*; in the early eighties they had all the moral subtlety of *Rocky IV*, reflecting the emotions of a Vietnam-weary nation eager to embrace the imagery of America Triumphant.

The commercials for Worlds of Wonder's Lazer Tag game featured the futuristic finals of some Soviet-American Lazer Tag shootout ("Practice hard, America!") and carried the emotions of patriotism into an even more aggressive arena. Exploiting the hoopla that surrounded the victory over the Soviets in the hockey finals of the 1980 Olympics, the Lazer Tag ads pandered to an American desire for the sort of clear-cut nationalistic triumphs that the nuclear age has rendered almost impossible. Creating a fantasy setting where patriotic dreams are substituted for complicated realities, the Lazer Tag commercials sought to capture the imaginations of children caught up in the patriotic fervor of the early 1980s.

LIVE THE FANTASY

By reading the signs of American advertising, we can conclude that America is a nation of fantasizers, often preferring the sign to the substance and easily enthralled by a veritable Fantasy Island of commercial illusions. Critics of Madison Avenue often complain that advertisers create consumer desire, but semioticians don't think the situation is that simple. Advertisers may give shape to consumer fantasies, but they need raw material to work with, the subconscious dreams and desires of the marketplace. As long as these desires remain unconscious, advertisers will be able to exploit them. But by bringing the fantasies to the surface, you can free yourself from advertising's often hypnotic grasp.

I can think of no company that has more successfully seized upon the subconscious fantasies of the American marketplace—indeed the world marketplace—than McDonald's. By no means the first nor the only hamburger chain in the United States, McDonald's emerged victorious in the "burger wars" by transforming hamburgers into signs of all that was desirable in American life. Other chains like Wendy's, Burger King, and Jack-In-The-Box continue to advertise and sell widely, but no company approaches McDonald's transformation of itself into a symbol of American culture.

McDonald's success can be traced to the precision of its advertising. Instead of broadcasting a single "one-size-fits-all" campaign at a time, McDonald's pitches its burgers simultaneously at different age groups, different classes, even different races (Budweiser beer, incidentally, has succeeded in the same way). For children, there is the Ronald McDonald campaign, which presents a fantasy world that has little to do with hamburgers in any rational sense but a great deal to do with the emotional desires of kids. Ronald McDonald and his friends are signs that recall the Muppets, "Sesame Street," the circus, toys, storybook illustrations, even *Alice in Wonderland.* Such signs do not signify hamburgers. Rather, they are displayed in order to prompt in the child's mind an automatic association of fantasy, fun, and McDonald's.

The same approach is taken in ads aimed at older audiences —teens, adults, and senior citizens. In the teen-oriented ads we may catch a fleeting glimpse of a hamburger or two, but what we are really shown is a teenage fantasy: groups of hip and happy adolescents singing, dancing, and cavorting together. Fearing loneliness more than anything else, adolescents quickly respond to the group appeal of such commercials. "Eat a Big Mac," these ads say, "and you won't be stuck home alone on Saturday night."

To appeal to an older and more sophisticated audience no longer so afraid of not belonging and more concerned with finding a place to go out to at night, McDonald's has designed the elaborate "Mac Tonight" commercials, which have for their backdrop a nightlit urban skyline and at their center a cabaret pianist with a moon-shaped head, a glad manner, and Blues Brothers shades. Such signs prompt an association of McDonald's with nightclubs and urban sophistication, persuading us that McDonald's is a place not only for breakfast or lunch but for dinner too, as if it were a popular off-Broadway nightspot, a place to see and be seen. Even the parody of Kurt Weill's "Mack the

Knife" theme song that Mac the Pianist performs is a sign, a subtle signal to the sophisticated hamburger eater able to recognize the origin of the tune in Bertolt Brecht's *Threepenny Opera.*

For yet older customers, McDonald's has designed a commercial around the fact that it employs a large number of retirees and seniors. In one such ad, we see an elderly man leaving his pretty little cottage early in the morning to start work as "the new kid" at McDonald's, and then we watch him during his first day on the job. Of course he is a great success, outdoing everyone else with his energy and efficiency, and he returns home in the evening to a loving wife and happy home. One would almost think that the ad was a kind of moving "help wanted" sign (indeed, McDonald's *was* hiring elderly employees at the time), but it's really just directed at consumers. Older viewers can see themselves wanted and appreciated in the ad—and perhaps be distracted from the rationally uncomfortable fact that many senior citizens take such jobs because of financial need and thus may be unlikely to own the sort of home that one sees in the commercial. But realism isn't the point here. This is fantasyland, a dream world promising instant gratification no matter what the facts of the matter may be.

Practically the only fantasy that McDonald's doesn't exploit is the fantasy of sex. This is understandable, given McDonald's desire to present itself as a family restaurant. But everywhere else, sexual fantasies, which have always had an important place in American advertising, are beginning to dominate the advertising scene. You expect sexual come-ons in ads for perfume or cosmetics or jewelry—after all, that's what they're selling—but for room deodorizers? In a magazine ad for Claire Burke home fragrances, for example, we see a well-dressed couple cavorting about their bedroom in what looks like a cheery preparation for sadomasochistic exercises. Jordache and Calvin Klein pitch blue jeans as props for teenage sexuality. The phallic appeal of automobiles, traditionally an implicit feature in automotive advertising, becomes quite explicit in a Dodge commercial that shifts back and forth from shots of a young man in an automobile to teasing glimpses of a woman—his date—as she dresses in her apartment.

The very language of today's advertisements is charged with sexuality. Products in the more innocent fifties were "new and improved," but everything in the eighties is "hot!"—as in "hot woman," or sexual heat. Cars are "hot." Movies are "hot." An ad for Valvoline pulses to the rhythm of a "heat wave, burning in my car." Sneakers get red hot in a magazine ad for Travel Fox athletic shoes in which we see male and female figures, clad only in Travel Fox shoes, apparently in the act of copulation—an ad that earned one of *Adweek's* annual "badvertising" awards for shoddy advertising.

The sexual explicitness of contemporary advertising is a sign not so much of American sexual fantasies as of the lengths to which advertisers will go to get attention. Sex never fails as an attention-getter, and in a particularly competitive, and expensive, era for American marketing, advertisers like to bet on a sure thing. Ad people refer to the proliferation of TV, radio, newspaper, magazine, and billboard ads as "clutter," and nothing cuts through the clutter like sex.

By showing the flesh, advertisers work on the deepest, most coercive human emotions of all. Much sexual coercion in advertising, however, is a sign of a desperate need to make certain that clients are getting their money's worth. The appearance of advertisements that refer directly to the prefabricated fantasies of Hollywood is a sign of a different sort of desperation: a desperation for ideas. With the rapid turnover of advertising campaigns mandated by the need to cut through the "clutter," advertisers may be hard pressed for new ad concepts, and so they are more and more frequently turning to already-established models. In the early 1980s, for instance, Pepsi-Cola ran a series of ads broadly alluding to Steven Spielberg's *E.T.* In one such ad, we see a young boy who, like the hero of *E.T.*, witnesses an extraterrestrial visit. The boy is led to a soft-drink machine where he pauses to drink a can of Pepsi as the spaceship he's spotted flies off into the universe. The relationship between the ad and the movie, accordingly, is a parasitical one, with the ad taking its life from the creative body of the film.

Pepsi did something similar in 1987 when it arranged with the producers of the movie *Top Gun* to promote the film's video release in Pepsi's television advertisements in exchange for the right to append a Pepsi ad to the video itself. This time, however, the parasitical relationship between ad and film was made explicit. Pepsi sales benefited from the video, and the video's sales benefited from Pepsi. It was a marriage made in corporate heaven.

The fact that Pepsi believed that it could stimulate consumption by appealing to the militaristic fantasies dramatized in *Top Gun* reflects similar fantasies in the "Pepsi generation." Earlier generations saw Pepsi associated with high-school courtship rituals, with couples sipping sodas together at the corner drugstore. When the draft was on, young men fantasized about Peggy Sue, not Air Force Flight School. Military service was all too real a possibility to fantasize about. But in an era when military service is not a reality for most young Americans, Pepsi commercials featuring hotshot fly-boys drinking Pepsi while streaking about in their Air Force jets contribute to a youth culture that has forgotten what military service means. It all looks like such fun in the Pepsi ads, but what they conceal is the fact that military jets are weapons, not high-tech recreational vehicles.

For less militaristic dreamers, Madison Avenue has framed ad campaigns around the cultural prestige of high-tech machinery in its own right. This is especially the case with sports cars, whose high-tech appeal is so powerful that some people apparently fantasize about *being* sports cars. At least, this is the conclusion one might draw from a Porsche commercial that asked its audience, "If you were a car, what kind of car would you be?" As a candy-red Porsche speeds along a rain-slick forest road, the ad's voice-over describes all the specifications you'd want to have if you *were* a sports car. "If you were a car," the commercial concludes, "you'd be a Porsche."

In his essay "Car Commercials and 'Miami Vice,' " Todd Gitlin explains the semiotic appeal of such ads as those in the Porsche campaign. Aired at the height of what may be called America's "myth of the entrepreneur," these commercials were aimed at young corporate managers who imaginatively identified with the "lone wolf" image of a Porsche speeding through the woods. Gitlin points out that such images cater to the fantasies of faceless corporate men who dream of entrepreneurial glory, of striking out on their own like John DeLorean and telling the boss to take his job and shove it. But as DeLorean's spectacular failure demonstrates, the life of the entrepreneur can be extremely risky. So rather than having to go it alone and take the risks that accompany entrepreneurial independence, the young executive can substitute fantasy for reality by climbing into his Porsche— or at least that's what Porsche's advertisers wanted him to believe.

But there is more at work in the Porsche ads than the fantasies of corporate America. Ever since Arthur C. Clarke and Stanley Kubrick teamed up to present us with HAL 9000, the demented computer of *2001: A Space Odyssey,* the American imagination has been obsessed with the melding of man and machine. First there was television's "Six Million Dollar Man," and then movie-land's *Star Wars*, *Blade Runner,* and *Robocop*, fantasy visions of a future dominated by machines. Androids haunt our imaginations as machines seize the initiative. *Time* magazine's "Man of the Year" for 1982 was a computer. Robot-built automobiles appeal to drivers who spend their days in front of computer screens— perhaps designing robots. When so much power and prestige is being given to high-tech machines, wouldn't you rather be a Porsche?

In short, the Porsche campaign is a sign of a new mythology that is emerging before our eyes, a myth of the machine, which is replacing the myth of the human. The iconic figure of the little tramp caught up in the cogs of industrial production in Charlie Chaplin's *Modern Times* signified a humanistic revulsion to the age of the machine. Human beings, such icons said, were superior to machines. Human values should come first in the moral order of things. But as Edith Milton suggests in her essay "The Track of the Mutant," we are now coming to believe that machines are superior to human beings, that mechanical nature is superior to human nature. Rather than being threatened by machines, we long to merge with them. "The Six Million Dollar Man" is one iconic figure in the new mythology; Harrison Ford's sexual coupling with an android is another. In such an age it should come as little wonder that computer-synthesized Max Headroom should be a commercial spokesman for Coca-Cola, or that Federal Express should design a series of TV ads featuring mechanical-looking human beings revolving around strange and powerful machines.

FEAR AND TREMBLING IN THE MARKETPLACE

While advertisers play on and reflect back at us our fantasies about everything from fighter pilots to robots, they also play on darker imaginings. If dream and desire can be exploited in the quest for sales, so can nightmare and fear.

The nightmare equivalent of America's populist desire to "belong," for example, is the fear of not belonging, of social rejection, of being different. Advertisements for dandruff shampoos, mouthwashes, deodorants, and laundry detergents ("Ring Around the Collar!") accordingly exploit such fears, bullying us into consumption. Although ads of this type are still around in the 1980s, they were particularly common in the fifties and early sixties, reflecting a society still reeling from the witch-hunts of the McCarthy years. When any sort of social eccentricity or difference could result in a public denunciation and the loss of one's job or even liberty, Americans were keen to conform and be like everyone else. No one wanted to be "guilty" of smelling bad or of having a dirty collar.

"Guilt" ads characteristically work by creating narrative situations in which someone is "accused" of some social "transgression," pronounced guilty, and then offered the sponsor's product as a means of returning to "innocence." Such ads, in essence, are parodies of ancient religious rituals of guilt and atonement, whereby sinning humanity is offered salvation through the agency of priest and church. In the world of advertising, a product takes the place of the priest, but the logic of the situation is quite similar.

In commercials for Wisk detergent, for example, we witness the drama of a hapless housewife and her husband as they are mocked by the jeering voices of children shouting "Ring Around the Collar!" "Oh, those dirty rings!" the housewife groans in despair. It's as if she and her husband were being stoned by an angry crowd. But there's hope, there's help, there's Wisk. Cleansing her soul of sin as well as her husband's, the housewife launders his shirts with Wisk, and behold, his collars are clean. Product salvation is only as far as the supermarket.

The recent appearance of advertisements for hospitals treating drug and alcohol addiction have raised the old genre of the guilt ad to new heights (or lows, depending on your perspective). In such ads, we see wives on the verge of leaving their husbands if they don't do something about their drinking, and salesmen about to lose their jobs. The man is guilty; he has sinned; but he upholds the ritual of guilt and atonement by "confessing" to his wife or boss and agreeing to go to the hospital the ad is pitching.

If guilt looks backward in time to past transgressions, fear, like desire, faces forward, trembling before the future. In the late 1980s, a new kind of fear commercial appeared, one whose narrative played on the worries of young corporate managers struggling up the ladder of success. Representing the nightmare equivalent of the elitist desire to "arrive," ads of this sort created images of failure, storylines of corporate defeat. In one ad for Apple computers, for example, a group of junior executives sits around a table with the boss as he asks each executive how long it will take his or her department to complete some publishing jobs. "Two or three days," answers one nervous executive. "A week, on overtime," a tight-lipped woman responds. But one young up-and-comer can have everything ready tomorrow, today, or yesterday, because his department uses a Macintosh desktop publishing system. Guess who'll get the next promotion?

Fear stalks an ad for AT&T computer systems too. A boss and four junior executives are dining in a posh restaurant. Icons of corporate power and prestige flood the screen—from the executives' formal evening wear to the fancy table setting—but there's tension in the air. It seems that the junior managers have chosen a computer system that's incompatible with the firm's sales and marketing departments. A whole new system will have to be purchased, but the tone of the meeting suggests that it will be handled by a new group of managers. These guys are on the way out. They no longer "belong." Indeed, it's probably no accident that the ad takes place in a restaurant, given the joke that went around in the aftermath of the 1987 market crash. "What do you call a yuppie stockbroker?" the joke ran. "Hey, waiter!" Is the ad trying subtly to suggest that junior executives who choose the wrong computer systems are doomed to suffer the same fate?

For other markets, there are other fears. If McDonald's presents senior citizens with bright fantasies of being useful and appreciated beyond retirement, companies like Secure Horizons dramatize senior citizens' fears of being caught short by a major illness. Running its ads in the wake of budgetary cuts in the Medicare system, Secure Horizons designed a series of commercials featuring a pleasant old man named Harry—who looks and sounds rather like Carroll O'Connor—who tells us the story of the scare he got during his wife's recent illness. Fearing that next time Medicare won't cover the bills, he has purchased supplemental health insurance from Secure Horizons and now securely tends his rooftop garden.

Among all the fears advertisers have exploited over the years, I find the fear of not having a posh enough burial site the most arresting. Advertisers usually avoid any mention of death—who wants to associate a product with the grave?—but mortuary advertisers haven't much choice. Generally, they solve their problem by framing cemeteries as timeless parks presided over by priestly morticians, appealing to our desires for dignity and comfort in the face of bereavement. But in one television commercial for Forest Lawn we find a different approach. In this ad we are presented with the ghost of an old man telling us how he might have found a much nicer resting place than the run-down cemetery in which we find him had his wife only known that Forest Lawn was so "affordable." I presume the ad was supposed to be funny, but it's been pulled off the air. There are some fears that just won't bear joking about, some nightmares too dark to dramatize.

THE FUTURE OF AN ILLUSION

There are some signs in the advertising world that Americans are getting fed up with fantasy advertisements and want to hear some straight talk. Weary of extravagant product claims and irrelevant associations, consumers trained by years of advertising to distrust what they hear seem to be developing an immunity to commercials. At least, this is the semiotic message I read in the "new realism" advertisements of the eighties, ads that attempt to convince you that what you're seeing is the real thing, that the ad is giving you the straight dope, not advertising hype.

You can recognize the "new realism" by its camera techniques. The lighting is usually subdued to give the ad the effect of being filmed without studio lighting or special filters. The scene looks gray, as if the blinds were drawn. The camera shots are jerky and off-angle, often zooming in for sudden unflattering close-ups, as if the cameraman was an amateur with a home video recorder. In a "realistic" ad for AT&T, for example, we are treated to a monologue by a plump stockbroker—his plumpness intended as a sign that he's for real and not just another actor—who tells us about the problems he's had with his phone system (not AT&T's) as the camera jerks around, generally filming him from below as if the cameraman couldn't quite fit his equipment into the crammed office and had to film the scene on his knees. "This is no fancy advertisement," the ad tries to convince us, "this is sincere."

An ad for Miller draft beer tries the same approach, re-creating the effect of an amateur videotape of a wedding celebration. Camera shots shift suddenly from group to group. The picture jumps. Bodies are poorly framed. The color is washed out. Like the beer it is pushing, the ad is supposed to strike us as being "as real as it gets."

Such ads reflect a desire for reality in the marketplace, a weariness with Madison Avenue illusions. But there's no illusion like the illusion of reality. Every special technique that advertisers use to create their "reality effects" is, in fact, more unrealistic than the techniques of "illusory" ads. The world, in reality, doesn't jump around when you look at it. It doesn't appear in subdued gray tones. Our eyes don't have zoom lenses, and we don't look at things with our heads cocked to one side. The irony of the "new realism" is that it is more unrealistic, more artificial, than the ordinary run of television advertising.

But don't expect any truly realistic ads in the future, because a realistic advertisement is a contradiction in terms. The logic of advertising is entirely semiotic: it substitutes signs for things, framed visions of consumer desire for the thing itself. The success of modern advertising, its penetration into every corner of American life, reflects a culture that has itself chosen illusion over reality. At a time when political candidates all have professional image-makers attached to their staffs, and the President of the United States is an actor who once sold shirt collars, all the cultural signs are pointing to more illusions in our lives rather than fewer—a fecund breeding ground for the world of the advertiser.

CHAPTER 5

Action Toys and Teddy Bears: Or Does Every Girl and Boy Want a Rambo Toy?

Toys "Я" Us
   American toy store chain

Once upon a time there was a baby girl named Cornela Lenora. Cornela was an orphan, but she had plenty of friends who wanted to bring her home and adopt her as a child of their own. Thousands of friends, in fact; so many that soon there weren't enough baby Cornelas to go around. No one minded that Cornela was a rather homely child as babies go, with her puffy cheeks, pudgy limbs, and snub nose. Nor did they seem to mind the high cost, both in dollars and energy, necessary for her adoption. For Cornela Lenora was a Cabbage Patch doll, and in the Christmas shopping season of 1983 hordes of frantic parents were willing to pay almost anything to bring Cornela, or one of her many brothers and sisters, into their homes.

The Cabbage Patch fever of 1983—those giddy months when shoppers stampeded toy counters around the country for a chance to purchase the undersupplied dolls—is now over. No longer do scalpers offer Cabbage Patch Kids (boxed or unboxed) through the classified ads for $100 or more. There are no more battles in department-store aisles, no more broken limbs, no more media hype. But though the fever has passed, we can still ask what it all means. What is the semiotic significance of this wild scramble for a doll whose appearance reminded some observers of Nikita Khrushchev? Clearly, Cornela Lenora is more than a doll. As many culture critics recognized at the height of the Cabbage Patch craze, Cornela and her friends are signs as well as toys. But signs of what?

To some, Cornela Lenora's astonishing success signifies, quite simply, the mesmeric power of the modern marketplace, the seemingly irresistible hold that corporate America has on the imaginations of our children and ourselves. For such interpreters, the Cabbage Patch Kids are not so much toys as consumer fetishes, icons of a materialist society whose high priests dwell in the temples of Madison Avenue. To other observers, however, the secret lies in the dolls themselves. As Dr. Joyce Brothers suggested in a *Newsweek* cover story on the Kids, the key to Coleco's success rests in the primitive homeliness of the dolls. Children accustomed to the adorable Rainbow Brite and Strawberry Shortcake dolls recognized something of themselves in the ordinary and relatively individualized faces of Cornela Lenora and her friends. The Kids seemed to say, "It's all right to be plain; homely children are lovable, too."

Not all psychological readings of the dolls have been quite so positive. For example, Dr. Ralph Wittenberg, a psychiatrist from George Washington University, draws dark analogies between the fury of the Cabbage Patch mobs and the hysteria of the Nuremberg rallies of the 1930s. For Wittenberg, the irrational violence displayed by thousands of desperate parents caught between their children's desires and a short supply of dolls seems to hint at more dangerous passions lurking in the American soul, a suppressed hysteria waiting to explode.

Everyone seems to have a theory about the Cabbage Patch

Kids. But while the various interpretations differ in their conclusions, each begins with the same basic question: Why did the dolls become such a national sensation? A semiotician, on the other hand, whose interest lies in the entire social system to which the Cabbage Patch Kids belong, would begin by asking even more fundamental questions. Why do we give toys to our children at all? Have our motives changed over time? What sorts of toys do we give our children today, and why?

In this chapter, we will answer these questions by looking at two major groups of American toys: soft, humanoid dolls such as the Cabbage Patch Kids, and action toys such as the Transformers and the Rambo or G.I. Joe set. Of course, there are many other sorts of toys in the American marketplace today, ranging from Nintendo video games to educational toys to traditional toys like tricycles and sports equipment, but the soft toy/action toy dichotomy represents such a crucial contradiction in the toy world that we can profitably limit our semiotic exploration to these two groups. I will leave it to you to interpret the many new toys that will inevitably appear before and after this book reaches the book stores.

The semiotician begins with the question of why we give toys to our children in the first place. As is so often the case with semiotics, we have to be wary of the commonsense answers that will immediately occur to us: "because we want them to have fun"; "because we want them to be happy"; "because we want them to know that we love them." But while these may be among the conscious reasons we have for giving toys to our children, there is a far more fundamental, and much less reassuring, rationale for toy giving that lies just beneath the surface.

Consider what you ordinarily do when you give your child toys. It will probably be Christmas or a birthday—festive days on which the vast majority of toys are given in America. The day begins in a state of shared excitement as the whole family gathers round for the ritual moment when the packages are unwrapped. "Oh look! Susie's found her Care Bear! Charlie's got his

Puffalumps!" For a brief time, all the rules of the ordinary workweek are suspended, as the family lingers together in robes and pajamas, sharing a moment of bonding and love.

But then look at what happens. The instant passes. The scene splits up. Mom and Dad have other things to do. If it's a birthday, they have to go to work. If it's Christmas, it's likely that preparations have to be made for adult entertainment in which the kids can't participate. At any rate, the room has to be cleared. "Susie, Charlie, why don't you go play with your new toys somewhere?" And off they go, outside or to their rooms, as the momentary bonding between parent and child shifts to a much more common scene: the solitary play enacted every day between a child and his or her toys.

That's what our conscious understanding of toys conceals: we give toys to our children not only to make them happy or to show them that we love them but to *separate* them from us, to give them something to do in our absence, indeed often just to get them out of our hair. We tuck our children away in their own bedrooms and play areas and expect them to play there, alone or with other children, but generally out of our sight and hearing. To make certain that they aren't at a loss for things to do, we give our kids lots of toys (that is, if we can afford them), and so assuage any guilt we may feel for leaving them so much on their own.

Whatever conscious or subconscious guilt modern American parents may feel for the relative lack of time they have to spend with their children, they usually have little choice in the matter. The maintenance of a middle-class household in the 1980s commonly requires two wage earners, and so large numbers of America's new parents find that much of their time must be spent working away from the home. Their long hours and commutes also leave them exhausted by the time they come home in the evening, making them grateful for stimulating toys that can occupy their children while they recuperate and prepare themselves for another day at the office. Modern toys, we might say, are things we give our children because we cannot give ourselves. They are people substitutes, surrogates for absent or exhausted parents.

Interestingly, though, toys have not always had this meaning in American society. As Brian Sutton-Smith explains in his book *Toys As Culture*, the modern toy is a product of the peculiar economic conditions of the industrial era, conditions that almost overnight changed traditional patterns of family behavior dating back thousands of years.

Before the Industrial Revolution, most people lived in agrarian households (they still do in the Third World, which is one reason children in developing countries haven't either the time or the economic wherewithal for many toys). Such homes had relatively little need for toys. For one thing, children didn't have much time for them. Working from sunup to sundown with their fathers in the fields and with their mothers around the house, they had little time for leisure play. What leisure they did have could be taken up with exploring their natural surroundings, or playing with the sorts of toys—like toy weapons or dolls—that have traditionally prepared children for their adult roles.

Children in the preindustrial world didn't have much need for adult substitutes either, because they were less often separated from parental or adult company. With everyone going to bed shortly after nightfall, there was little parental need for objects that might keep restless children occupied until bedtime. With the whole family participating in the economic support of the household, there just wasn't much time left over at the end of the day for noneconomic activities like play. There also wasn't much time for childhood. Children in the preindustrial era went to work soon after they ceased to be toddlers, married in their teens, and could expect to have children of their own by their twentieth birthdays. You had to grow up fast under such conditions, and this left little time for fantasizing or for imaginative play.

All this changed with the advent of the Industrial Revolution in the late eighteenth century. For the first time in history, the majority of the population in Europe and America shifted from the country to the city, a move that radically altered the traditional design of family life. Where agrarian families once shared the burden of economic survival, the factory system shifted that responsibility to wage-earning fathers who were compelled to leave their homes to support their families. Mother was still responsible for the management of the household, but her children, shut up in urban or, later on, in suburban houses, were relieved of the endless chores of farm life and consequently had much less to do. With the important exception of the children of the working classes, who were thrust willy-nilly into the mines and factories of the early Industrial Revolution, many children found themselves in need of occupation.

Their need was answered in two ways. First, they were sent to school. Children of the preindustrial period didn't have much time for formal education. They also didn't have much need. Expecting to do what their parents had done, they were generally taught at home how to be farmers, or smiths, or homemakers. But the son of a nineteenth-century clerk or accountant did need a formal education, whether he planned to follow in the footsteps of his father or to pursue one of the many new careers that the industrial age was opening up for middle-class children. (It should be noted that these opportunities were not equally open to girls and were generally out of reach of working-class boys until the twentieth century.) The new economy created a need for literate citizens who could read, write, and cipher, and that need was filled by the creation of the sort of public education systems that we simply take for granted today.

But when a child comes home from school, he or she still needs something to do. So nineteenth-century parents began to give their children more toys to play with than they had ever had before. Many of these toys—like the stereopticon viewers popular during the period—were purely recreational, designed to appeal to a child's imagination rather than to train him or her for adult responsibilities. Eventually, the new toys became part of the "myth of childhood," the idea that childhood is a special time of life ideally reserved for learning and for play, an almost magical realm set apart from the rigors of adulthood.

The myth of childhood may have reached its peak of influence in the years immediately following World War II, when Dad came home from the war and Mom abandoned her job riveting bombers, and they moved to the newly emerging suburbs—like Levittown—to raise a family. These children of the Great Depression, who had to face the rigors of adulthood very early in life, yearned for a world in which their own children could enjoy to the full the special privileges promised by the myth of childhood. Indeed, their entire lives often came to revolve around homes in which the myth appeared to be so completely fulfilled.

The children of the 1950s, then, had plenty of toys. Living in the suburbs, they lacked the natural playgrounds that their agrarian predecessors enjoyed and so required artificial playthings. Their parents supplied these objects in historically unprecedented numbers. But they also supplied themselves. If Dad was away for most of the day, Mom could be expected to be on hand. And when Dad came home—I remember this to be the case in my childhood—he often carried inexpensive presents that brought his children running to the door. Were they bribes to win his children's affection? Perhaps not, but even if they were, in semiotic terms they signified a father's desire to play a central role in the lives of his children, and the central role that his children played in his.

The purchase of a $100 talking Cabbage Patch doll, however, has a rather different semiotic significance. For one thing, you can't bring one of these toys home every day—special occasions are required. But the meaning of such a present is more profound than this, finally touching on the dramatic changes in the lives of American families that are now taking place as we move through the 1980s. The most obvious change is the fact that many, if not most, middle-class families need two wage earners today to make ends meet. More and more children, accordingly, are growing up without an adult in the house during the day, and even the middle-classes, in the face of a shortage of affordable day-care centers, are now raising their own "latchkey" kids. Two-career families also have less time to give to childbearing, which has meant that an increasing number of children are growing up without brothers or sisters.

Enter Cornela Lenora. She struck both parent and child alike as a little person who could take the place of an absent parent or sibling. Her one-of-a-kind uniqueness, certified by clever sets of "adoption papers," enhanced this effect, and before you knew it, Cornela was answering the needs of children who craved human company. The doll gave the children, at least symbolically, the human contact the parents didn't always have time to give.

Cornela Lenora didn't have to shoulder this burden alone, of course. The Care Bears, psychologically designed teddy bears created to invite a child to express his or her most intimate emotions, burst on the scene right alongside the Cabbage Patch Kids. Certainly the toy manufacturers have recognized the potency of marketing toys as people surrogates. By the Christmas shopping season of 1987, parents could choose from an almost endless variety of talking people–substitutes, including Teddy Ruxpin and Julie by Worlds of Wonder, and Playmates' Jill, who, as her makers describe her, is "an animated doll with speech recognition" that "acts like you."

Toys, it appears, are assuming a greater role in the nurturing of our young. But is this good for us or our children? The results of the Christmas shopping season of 1987 suggest that many of us don't think so. Worlds of Wonder went into bankruptcy that year, and toy companies took a much worse-than-average beating in the October 19 stock market crash. For many parents, high-tech toys had simply become too expensive, but for many others the importance of the home began to outweigh that of the office. Perhaps the 1990s will be a period of resurgence in parent-child interaction and characterized by a reluctance to buy expensive people–substitutes.

ALL DRESSED UP AND NO BEAR TO GO

But adults in the 1980s were not only lavishing toys on their children, they were giving themselves toys as well—real toys—as if play had become part of their "work," too. I don't mean things like fishing rods, or expensive cars, or jewels, or new clothes. I mean toys like Paddington Bear, or Douglas Bearbanks, or Humphrey Beargart, or Lauren Bearcall. Bears in evening dress, bears in fisherman's knit sweaters, bears in police uniforms, bears in any costume you might dream of—and at grown-up prices. Unlike those other bears of the eighties—the Teddy Ruxpins and the Care Bears, for example—these bears were not really designed for children, and you don't often see them in children's toy stores. You can find them instead in specialty stores—that is, in pricey stuffed-toy boutiques (such as The Very Very Beast) and floral shops where bears, dressed in formal evening wear ("all dressed up and no bear to go") and velvet smoking jackets, look right at home. I don't think that an ordinary child would respond to these rather formal creatures, nor catch the joke behind "Lauren Bearcall." But an adult would, especially a sophisticated single adult of the sort who would be likely to have a busy, high-paying career and no children of his or her own.

The wide sales of such toys signify a shift in adult self-awareness in the 1980s. Today's adults seem to be more playful than their parents, less afraid of acting like children. And the fact is that the grown-ups of the 1980s have been able to *be* children much longer than their parents could. Children of the Great Depression and the war years that followed had to face adult realities very early in life; but for those middle-class baby boomers who managed to avoid military service in Vietnam—and most of them did—adult realities were often deferred by years of college and professional or graduate school. Extending their school years well into their twenties, the children of the 1950s effectively extended their childhoods. No wonder they're still interested in toys past their thirtieth birthdays.

The new teddy bears for adults are sending all sorts of messages. To a semiotic gaze, they can appear not as toys at all but as children, as child substitutes for busy adults whose careers have prevented—or distracted—them from raising families of their own. You may have noticed how they are often packaged and sold as if they were cuddly babies who have to be tucked in at night, dressed in nightshirts, and generally loved and coddled. Paddington Bear, we could say, is as much a surrogate for absent children as Cornela Lenora is a compensation for absent parents.

There are other absences to be compensated for in today's households. With more and more families forced by the high cost of housing to live in pet-restricted apartments and condominiums, many of us are turning to realistic stuffed pets to replace the real animals we are forbidden to have. Thus, from Dakin, Avanti, and Gund come astonishingly lifelike German shepherd puppies, Persian cats, Doberman pinschers, Afghan hounds . . . just about any breed you like. For children living in pet-restricted apartments, there are Pound Puppies, Pound Pur-r-ries, and Junk Yard Dogs. All these new toys are signs of the deep need we still have for pets at a time when owning a dog or cat has become very difficult.

The fact that we manufacture Pound Puppies or Dakin German shepherds testifies to the enduring place that animals play in our emotional lives. Living in an industrial world, we have been cut off from direct contact with the natural environment. We no longer have much opportunity to observe wild deer or dairy cows, hedgehogs or horses, foxes or raccoons. To compensate for that loss, we often fill our homes with domestic species—the dogs and cats that are "work" animals on the farm, not pets—which supply the necessary contact with nature that urban and suburban life denies. But when we are denied contact with even these animals, we must find some substitute for them and, once again, the American toy industry has responded.

For Brian Sutton-Smith, there is a direct link between the need we have for soft humanoid toys and the emotional appeal of domestic animals. Animals and toys alike provide us with cute and cuddly companions who make none of the emotional demands of human beings. Our pets love us unreservedly, which is not always the case with our families; our pets make no demands on us, and neither do our toys. And while neither our animals nor our toys can really talk to us, we can talk to them, and with just a little imaginative effort, we can "hear" them talk back.

I speak from experience. Four years ago I rather self-consciously plunked down $35 for a Dakin German shepherd when my wife's (and my own) desire for a dog was simply getting out of hand after years of apartment living. Purchased on impulse during a visit to the San Diego Zoo's gift center, Woofie soon took the place of the live dog that we had wanted. Since then, we've moved into a house of our own and keep three lively cats, but even now we think of our stuffed dog as a "real" part of the family.

I've felt rather embarrassed by this—by the importance this toy has assumed in my house, by the small collection of stuffed animals that we are accumulating. But a little research has shown me that I am not alone. Many of my own friends, professionals in their thirties, have similar menageries. The explanation is not hard to find: with more and more men and women postponing marriage and children, many adults find themselves in need of the emotional stimulation of children. To satisfy the cravings of their parental instincts, many of today's childless singles and couples keep zoofuls of stuffed toys that have their own names and personalities.

Somehow, our stuffed toys come to have minds of their own, distinct selves that we project upon them as if we were still children ourselves. But while a child may bruise and batter a doll to relieve his or her frustrations, adults may use them in more subtle ways. My wife and I, for example, like to pretend that Woofie can talk, but he only "talks" when we're both around. I realize that he has become a part of our intimacy with each other, a stuffed version of the baby talk that loving couples have engaged in throughout the ages. After all, the severe and satiric

Jonathan Swift wrote a massive *Journal to Stella* (Stella being a young girl with whom he had apparently fallen in love) that is entirely couched in a childish code. Virginia Woolf devised her own baby talk for a somewhat older woman with whom she had become infatuated, referring to herself in her letters as "Roo," the kangaroo "baby" of her beloved correspondent. James Joyce's uncensored letters to his wife, Nora, are frankly embarrassing to read for all their erotic baby talk. I suppose talking to a toy animal with one's beloved is the semiotic equivalent of calling a portly old chairman of the board "Bunny."

Finally, the plethora of teddy bears in today's adult toy market is a sign of a disturbingly new emotional need prompted by the anxieties of the nuclear age. For teddy bears are not only surrogate children; they are also icons of a bygone era. Along with a new generation of wooden rocking horses, the teddy bears of the 1980s recall a world that, at least from today's perspective, looks a great deal safer and more innocent than our own. Teddy bears first appeared around the turn of the century—they get their name from Teddy Roosevelt—and they still carry with them an aura of that relatively quiet epoch before the world wars.

We have become so beguiled by that aura that genuine survivors from the period have become not only collector's items but status symbols as well (an antique Steiff teddy bear was auctioned off for $8,237 in 1987). Belonging to the era of A. A. Milne rather than to the post-Freudian world of Maurice Sendak, the teddy bear imaginatively takes us back to an ideal Edwardian utopia. Ideally ensconced within the nursery of a newly refurbished Victorian townhouse, surrounded by wooden rocking horses, cradles, and Laura Ashley wallpaper, teddy looks out on the timeless twilight of an era that has been forever lost but whose shadow can be captured by anyone who can afford the right props. He has survived both the nuclear and the space age, remaining as a talisman of genteel stability and tradition, a full-fledged, if modest, testimony to the mythic power of nostalgia.

RAMBO TO THE RESCUE

But there is a second face to the American toy industry, one that is neither cute nor consolatory and that appears to contradict the interpretation of toys which we have pursued so far. I can think of no better way to begin analyzing this second side to modern toys than by quoting this description of some Mattel action figures that I found in a Toys "R" Us advertisement: "GUTS! SOLDIER PACKS," the ad reads, "War specialists with the best technology! Ages 5-up."

Leaving the toys themselves aside for a moment, let's just look at the words describing them. The fact that they insist that the Guts! Soldiers are "war specialists with the best technology" suggests that there has been a major change in our cultural attitude toward soldiering. Traditionally, Americans have taken pride in the amateur, not professional or specialized, status of their armies. From the Minutemen of the Revolution to the dogfaces of World War II, American soldiers have been civilians called upon to fight for a cause they believe in. But ads like Mattel's suggest that the image of the professional warrior is now more appealing than the traditional figure of the citizen soldier. The new professional, it seems, is more interested in his equipment—"the best technology"—than he is in any particular cause.

Many interpreters of the toy industry have gone so far as to argue that the new assortment of militaristic action toys signifies a sharp turn toward militarism in the country at large. By supplying our children with such toys, the argument runs, we are projecting that militarism on them. While this may be true, I think that the military appeal of these toys masks a deeper cultural emotion, one that is very close to frustration and despair.

Consider the large line of Rambo action toys. Rambo began his life in the American imagination as a man obsessed with the U.S. failure in Vietnam. Glorified on the silver screen, he fought and won fantasy encounters with the North Vietnamese, cathartically providing the victories that some Americans so missed during the Vietnam War. As an action toy, however, Rambo has been devoted to the destruction of a group of international thugs and terrorists called S.A.V.A.G.E. With this move, Rambo joins Chuck Norris—who is also a movie hero and action toy devoted to counterterrorist warfare—and G.I. Joe, who is now a play figure in the murky war against international terrorism as well.

All this counterterrorist play is a sure sign of the deep sense of frustration that Americans feel in the face of international terrorism. Ronald Reagan himself once quipped during a hijacking episode in Lebanon that he sure knew what Rambo would do about it. This sort of fantasizing has not been lost on our children. Reflecting the frustrations and desires of their parents, they too desire "real American heroes" who will restore America to the power and prestige it enjoyed in international affairs before the Vietnam War upset our military confidence. Imitating adults who elected a president who promised to make their country "walk tall" again in the world by initiating the greatest peacetime military buildup in history, American children are being treated to a military buildup of their own. Just look at a toy catalogue, and you can find things like the G.I. Joe Tomahawk 'Copter, Cobra Maggot (a combination attack tank and tactical command center), and Persuader (a ten-wheel high-speed attack vehicle with a top-mounted laser cannon), not to mention all the Uzi submachine guns and laser pistols.

In our children's action toys, then, we find a make-believe reflection of an adult fantasy. The Pentagon's antiterrorist Delta Force has yet to go into action, but Rambo's "Force of Freedom" and G.I. Joe's "Real American Heroes" can get to work every day in the hands of our children. Unfettered by the complications of international diplomacy, our toy heroes accomplish what our real forces cannot.

We can also find in our children's toys a reflection of our national fascination with military technology. It is not surprising that a country bent on the multibillion-dollar development of a laser- and nuclear-powered arsenal of strategic defense weapons should also be manufacturing toys like Hasbro's "Decepticon," which is a "weapon-loaded defense bay [that] transforms into [a] stinging scorpion and robot and back!"

If you're not sure how such a contraption works, ask one of your children. Or better yet, tune in to Saturday-morning TV and watch it in action on "Transformers," where for 30 minutes you can see opposing squadrons of robotic-weapons systems attempting to annihilate each other with a laser-powered arsenal that would make the Strategic Defense Initiative scientists green with envy. In fact, since the whole purpose of the show is to promote the sales of the toys, we can learn a good deal about the cultural significance of Hasbro's high-tech playthings by looking at some cartoons.

I must say that I was especially intrigued by one episode of "Transformers" in which the explicit "moral" was peculiarly out of joint with the semiotic message that was being sent. The writers of this episode, I am sure, thought that they were concocting a "Star Trek"-like fable about the futility of war. But when you look at the cartoon closely, a far different message emerges. The story revolved around some interplanetary peace negotiations conducted between gigantic representatives from two warring worlds that have been trying to destroy each other for centuries. Of course, the talks haven't been going very well, and we are treated to a good deal of slapstick battling between the negotiators as a few human and humanoid arbiters struggle to keep them apart. Meanwhile, a group of Autobots—the good guys in the "Transformers" cartoons—have gone in search of a mysterious spaceship filled with creatures who look rather like a cross between the faces painted on the tombs of Egyptian pharaohs and robotic death-heads. These are the Quintesons, and they've been supplying both sides in the interplanetary war with weapons all this time, separately counseling each party in the conflict to stall the peace negotiations until they can receive delivery of a new, obviously nuclear, superweapon. The Autobots are out to stop the delivery, but are hampered by a gang of Decepticons, the bad guys in the series (like the original "Star

Trek's" Klingons), who seem to want to hinder them just for the hell of it, because they don't appear to be otherwise concerned in the Quinteson affair.

I watched this episode during the Iranscam hearings and was interested in seeing how it would turn out. Would the double-dealing arms merchants be shown up? Would the planets destroy each other? Interestingly enough, though the program itself was not only sponsored but created by the "weapons division" at Hasbro, it was the arms merchants who lost out. But they are not simply shown up. True to the uncomplicated, black-and-white solutions of kidvid today, the Quintesons are simply annihilated, their spaceship blown to smithereens in a glorious nuclear fireball. The warring negotiators are told how their planets have been duped by the Quintesons all these years, and the whole affair concludes with someone's rather pious declaration: "It's sad, all those centuries of war, and the only winners were the Quintesons."

This episode was almost certainly designed in response to the criticism of such groups as Action for Children's Television who have criticized the rampant violence on children's TV. The Quinteson affair seems to send a "pro-social" message to the children watching it and so seems to satisfy kidvid's critics. But in semiotic terms the real message is different. We see mostly weapons technology and plenty of Zap, Bam, and Crunch, which is where all the fun is. Only a sober voice-over at the end, which the kids are likely to miss while heading for the kitchen, makes any suggestion that there might be something amiss with all this violence.

What I particularly noted in this cartoon was how the nuclear destruction of the Quintesons is so calmly taken for granted. Such calm can be read as a sign of the way that the Bomb has been neutralized in the minds of our children and transformed into just another weapon. This neutralization may well have begun with the first *Star Wars* film in which a child could see an entire world destroyed without any noticeable disruption in the lives of the story's heroes. Children who grew up in the 1950s and early 1960s were not likely to take such a dispassionate attitude toward nuclear destruction. Having heard their parents debating whether or not to build bomb shelters during the Cuban Missile Crisis, they knew that nuclear warfare wasn't the sort of thing one can expect to survive.

Here the semiotician finds the crucial contradiction at the heart of the American toy industry. On the one hand, we find a growing host of soft, cuddly toys that signify our need for humanity and loving consolation, and on the other hand we find an army of war toys that signify a cultural acceptance of almost cosmic violence. Teddy bears recall for us the innocence of the world of Winnie-the-Pooh, while the "Transformers" take us into a fantasy future of glamorous, high-tech warfare. Or is it a contradiction after all? Do Cabbage Patch dolls console us for the violent world in which we live? Do soft, cuddly toys distract us from the dangers of the nuclear age? We have matched fantasy war with fantasy peace, and the two exist side by side on our toy shelves. "Hush, hush, whisper, who dares, Christopher Robin is saying his prayers." But he may be praying for a G.I. Joe Transportable Tactical Battle Platform. Well, why not? Toys are us.

CHAPTER 6

The Architectural Sign: Semiotics and the Human Landscape

Man was not made so large limbed and robust but that he must seek to narrow his world, and wall in a space such as fitted him.
Henry David Thoreau

In *Great Expectations*, Charles Dickens's story of the life and times of a mid-Victorian gentleman, the hero meets a London law clerk named Wemmick whose personality has an odd way of changing with the scenery. By day, Wemmick is a taciturn, almost surly man, his demeanor clearly reflecting the dehumanizing environment of London's criminal court district. But at night, Wemmick returns home to a suburban cottage that he has fashioned into a miniature fortress—complete with drawbridge, moat, and turreted tower—where this urban Mr. Hyde is transformed into a suburban Dr. Jekyll, a genial, generous, and even romantic fellow whose home is, quite literally, his castle.

There's a lesson in Wemmick's story for the architectural semiotician, a piquant reminder that the built environment is not simply a space "*in* which people act," as Barrie Greenbie has written in *Spaces: Dimensions of the Human Landscape*, but is also a space "*to* which they react." A building is not simply a pile of brick and stone and mortar; it is a sign system charged with significance. Empty space is usually meaningless, but put up a building or lay down a road and what was once an uncircumscribed and messageless landscape becomes a bounded *territory*, a human habitat that comes complete with its own written and unwritten codes of permitted and unpermitted behavior. The rules that govern the shared territory of a public space are familiar to all of us. We know, for example, that you needn't knock before walking through the door of a retail store, and that you shouldn't neglect to knock when entering a private office. You may handle the merchandise in a department store, but not the displays in a museum. Try to keep to the right when walking in a crowd or ascending a public stairway, but for heaven's sake don't stand still in the middle of a sidewalk. Written signs may tell you to "Keep Off the Grass" or "No Smoking." We know the difference between a door that says "Ladies" and one that says "Gentlemen." We know as well all those do's and don't's of the street: don't smile at strangers, don't talk to yourself in public, and do try to stand patiently in line like everybody else. Be streetwise and, above all, don't play by your own rules.

With so many written and unwritten rules and regulations to be learned and obeyed in order to survive in the public world, it's little wonder that it's such a relief to get home at night. Think for a moment of what your home means to you. It's much more than a shelter, it's *your* territory, a private space whose boundaries mark the line where the rules for public behavior yield to those that govern the home. Indeed, we may all be just a little like Wemmick as we shuttle back and forth between the public territory of the working world and the private territory of our homes, relaxing our guard as we enter those spaces which are under our own control.

When human beings are denied this sense of personal territorial control—something that often happens in public housing projects and that almost always happens in jails and prisons—they tend to lose their desire (or even ability) to respect the behavioral codes that govern society at large. Indeed, the crime, vandalism, and graffiti that plague the de-territorialized spaces of today's cities seem to confirm Robert Ardrey's suggestion in *The Territorial Imperative* that we may well require our own privately bounded territories in order to "preserve our biological sanity."

But while your home may appear to be entirely under your own control, it too is a codified space governed by unwritten sets of rules. To a certain extent, you're free to determine some of those rules for yourself, but generally the codes that govern the home are written by the culture in which it is built. As a language preexists those who are born to speak it, so too does the semiotic structure of the home preexist its inhabitants. In other words, what we often take to be natural or commonsense patterns of at-home behavior are really dictated to us by culture, just as culture determines the rules for the use of public territory. When we view them from a semiotic perspective, the buildings in which we live and work can be seen to reflect the desires and perspectives of the culture that builds them, and by "reading" the codes that are invisibly inscribed in both public and private territories, we can often uncover the fundamental values of the society in which we live.

In this chapter, we'll explore the semiotic significance of both the public and the private dimensions of the built environment, focusing on the private spaces defined by apartment buildings and single-family houses and on the public spaces of shopping malls, hotels, and office towers. Of course, other sorts of structures— like the hot-dog stands that iconically resemble the hot dogs they sell—have semiotic meanings as well, but the buildings I have chosen to interpret seem to carry the most enduring messages about the nature of modern American society. In interpreting these structures, I will often draw upon insights from the semiotically related field of *proxemics*, which specializes in interpreting the cultural significance of spatial organization, as well as from architectural history, which can illuminate the ideological intentions behind the most common building styles in the modern city. But in every case, we will look at architectural structures as *languages*, as systems of signs that have a great deal to say to anyone who takes the time to read them.

HOME SWEET HOME

Let's begin with the semiotic complex that you call your home. The most obvious signs at work here are territorial in nature, for whether you live in a detached single-family house of your own or rent a room in an apartment block, a semiotic perimeter marks the line between "outside" and "inside": the public territory outside your home and the private territory within. If you live in a secured apartment building, for instance, a locked front door guarded by a uniformed doorman or by an electronic monitoring device marks the first line of territorial division. Only the inhabitants of such a building are free to enter without permission. Even if your building is unsecured, the exterior doors and windows of the complex still serve as signs that define the line between public and private space. To cross that line without permission is to knowingly violate a spatial code.

Once you enter an apartment complex, the nature of the territory in which you find yourself is somewhat equivocal, for the distance between the public entrance to your building and your own front door operates as a *transitional* space that is at once public and private. On the one hand, it belongs to everyone who lives in the building, but on the other, it is accessible to outsiders if they have some good reason for being there—for example, if they're repairmen or guests. In essence, the transitional spaces of an apartment complex constitute a *neighborhood*, or group territory, and as we shall see shortly, when this territory is perceived as alien or unshared space, the result can be environmental anarchy.

The doorway to your apartment, in contrast, constitutes an

absolute territorial marker that should not be crossed without your permission. It's not only a physical barrier, it's a sign that marks the place where the neighborhood ends and personal territory begins. You may actively underscore this semiotic meaning of your front door by the way you decorate it. "Welcome" mats and potted plants can communicate the sense of territorial wellbeing felt by those who dwell within, while peepholes and "Neighborhood Watch" stickers tell a tale of suspicion and unease. Empty beer bottles left to lie around say that no one feels that this space is part of his or her "neighborhood" and can be a clear sign of a community at odds with itself. A glance down the hallway of an apartment building is usually sufficient to tell you what sort of neighborhood it is.

In the average American suburb, the signs that say "this is my territory" begin at the frontier where street and sidewalk touch the front yard of a house. Here, too, there are transitional and absolute spaces. Your driveway, for example, is a transitional space, much like the halls of an apartment complex. Strangers may use my driveway to turn around in, but they can't park there. The front yard is also a transitional space. If the kids walking home from school traipse over the street edge of my front lawn without damaging anything, I can keep my cool about it. But some signs of our territory—the exterior walls, windows, and doors of our homes—are absolute markers of private space. So are the side- and backyards. If anyone shows up in my backyard without my permission, I'll call the cops. Although the street is free to all, I have certain rights over the portion of it that immediately abuts on my front yard, for while my request may not have much legal force, I can usually succeed in preventing my neighbors from parking there if I make an effort to ask.

We generally take for granted the territorial codes that govern our homes and don't think much about them until they are violated. If you've ever been the victim of a burglary, you know only too well the vulnerability and outrage that one feels when one's territory has been invaded. Even if little is actually stolen, or if your insurance takes care of the loss, the knowledge that someone has been inside your territory can be overwhelming. This feeling is probably universal. No society is without its territorial codes. The nomadic !Kung Bushmen of South-West Africa, for example, often don't bother to build private shelters at all but will still mark off the sleeping space of each family with two ceremonial sticks placed in the ground to symbolize the "entrance" of the "home." So though various cultures may define public and private space differently, the urge to establish personal territories, as Robert Ardrey argues, most likely has a natural rather than a cultural origin.

Still, while the need for personal space may be biologically motivated, the kinds of personal territories we want reflect cultural values rather than natural necessities. Consider what we prefer to call "home." Middle-class Europeans have traditionally been content to rent their living spaces, and most live in apartments. But Americans prefer to own single-family houses, and a certain social stigma is attached to renting and apartment dwelling. Public policy, especially as written into tax codes, openly encourages home ownership while penalizing renters. To purchase your own home in America is not simply to escape the tyranny of a landlord or to increase your personal wealth and comfort, it is to signify your arrival in mainstream culture. Indeed, buying your first home is like passing through a rite of initiation, in which you cross the final line between childhood dependence and adult independence and maturity.

It's no secret that the "American dream" is one of land ownership, of buying your own little piece of earth. The dream reflects the consciousness of a nation whose frontier history once held out the promise of unlimited land to anyone who would go out and claim it, and its modern symbol is the detached, single-family suburban home. Like Thomas Jefferson, many contemporary Americans harbor a nostalgic belief in the moral superiority of the independent "homesteader" over the Old World-style city slicker. Although the frontier conditions that encouraged Jefferson's hopes for a nation of small farmers have long since vanished, Americans continue to hold to his values, seeking out their own suburban "homesteads" as soon as they can afford them.

Our preference for single-family houses over rented apartments thus reflects the values of a nation founded on the principles of frontier individualism. Henry David Thoreau, that archindividualist of the American tradition, couldn't bear the idea of living in an apartment building. The notion of all those other lives stacked around him made him suffocate, and we still find something restrictive in the relatively communal life of an apartment block. The kitschy wall hanging that my father once placed on the wall of his own suburban living room rather sentimentally sums up the characteristic American attitude toward space: "Sweet Clean Air from East to West," it read, "And Room to Go and Come, I Loved My Fellow Man the Best When He Was Scattered Some."

But all the individualism in the world couldn't have overcome the spatial limitations of the postfrontier landscape without a big help from technology. By the end of the nineteenth century, the American frontier had vanished and an increasing number of people had to earn their livings in the city, where there was precious little space for private home plots. There was room in the countryside surrounding the city, but until the advent of the commuter train and, a little later, the automobile, such space was unusable. The suburban sprawl with which we are so familiar today only began in the late nineteenth century, when America's great urban centers began to send tramlines into the surrounding countryside. The arrival of the automobile increased the available space for suburban development, and today commuters willingly endure drives of 50 or 100 miles and more per day in order to enjoy their little piece of the American dream.

Although among Europe's apartment-dwelling urbanites the automobile is generally regarded as a vehicle for holiday journeys, in America it has become an essential part of suburban economic survival. Though Americans also use their cars for vacation travel, the primary role of our automobiles is to transport us to and from work. In this sense, the suburban home is a sign not only of an individualistic ideology but of a national destiny that has been tied to the machine. And if the fuel ever runs out, if the engines ever stop running, we are going to have to rethink our domestic architectural preferences and perhaps surrender some of our individualistic zeal.

Behind Closed Doors

The design of our homes equally reflects cultural realities. Though we rarely stop to think of it, we territorialize the interior as well as the exterior of a house or apartment. To begin with, a home's interior is divided into its own public, private, and transitional spaces. The front door of an American house, for example, usually opens onto a foyer or entranceway that signals the shift from outside to inside. When a salesman comes to your door, you stand in the foyer so that the rest of the house remains invisible. For those whom you invite into your home, the foyer generally leads to a public room: the living room or drawing room where guests are entertained. The family room, den, library, and kitchen are more private spaces, but they are generally open to guests. Bedrooms, however, are usually off limits, and guests ordinarily enter them only to drop their coats or when on a "tour" of the house.

Not all homes, of course, have foyers or formal entrances (or dens or libraries or living rooms), but most of us usually try to arrange things so that the front door leads into some kind of semipublic space. No conventionally organized home with more than one room, at any rate, has its front entrance open onto a bedroom. When we can, we consign our bedrooms to the second story or set them off to the side where they can be reached only through hallways that lead from the more public areas of the house. This tendency to conceal the sleeping areas of our homes is not entirely culturally determined, however. After all, there's a very good natural reason for concealing a bedroom: we're most vulnerable when we're sleeping, and so it is only prudent to put our sleeping areas out of the way of intruders. Excavations of ancient Egyptian and Minoan houses reveal floor plans that similarly conceal the family sleeping space either at the back or sides of the home, and so there seems to be an ancient precedent for the spatial location of the modern bedroom. Still, we are a great deal more concerned about the separation of our bedrooms from the rest of the house than were our medieval ancestors (whose lives were no safer than our own), so there must be a cultural factor at work here as well. Medieval families were content to sleep together in the kitchen because that's where the fire was, and simply didn't make much fuss about their bedrooms. So why do we?

Our concern with the absolute privacy of the bedroom again reflects the cultural individualism that leads us to prefer single-family homes. Whenever space allows, each member of an American family stakes out his or her own private territory within the walls of his or her "room" (this is especially true of American teenagers, who often guard their "turf" with ferocity). This desire for privacy contrasts with the less individualistically motivated behavior of Mexican families, for example, whose children may prefer to share a bedroom even when the family is affluent enough to afford one for each member of the household. The codes of Mexican culture are much more communally oriented than are American values of privacy. Thus, well-to-do Mexicans may sacrifice bedroom space in their homes to make room for such public areas as a central patio, whereas Americans tie the value of a house directly to the number of private bedrooms it contains.

Individualism alone doesn't account for the American attitude toward the bedroom, however. Behind our desire for strictly segregated sleeping rooms we may find lingering traces of the sexual reticence of our Victorian forebears. Before the Victorian era, European children commonly shared the sleeping space not only of their brothers and sisters but of their parents as well. This, of course, would hardly do among the sexually self-conscious Victorians, and so when they could afford it they carefully re-designed their homes to separate the parental bedchamber from the children's bedrooms. Though they tended to have enormous families, the Victorians liked to pretend that they didn't know where babies came from—at least, they didn't want their children to know. Thus, we owe to the Victorians the perfection of the nursery, which enabled them to move their children far away from the sexually charged master bedroom into their own pro-tected spaces, where no hint of sexual realities could bring a blush to the cheek of a young lad or lass.

The tendency of American home designers in the 1980s to design master bedrooms that are as much playrooms as sleeping areas seems to signal the end of the Victorian era. Fitted out with entertainment centers, wet bars, spas, and bathrooms that you can go bowling in, the new master suites answer the demands of uninhibited—and well-heeled—young couples who are eager to enhance the sensual comforts of the bedroom. Having fewer children than their more Victorian-minded parents, such home buyers are freed to devote more space to their own bedrooms, and the master suite is growing in proportion.

Our homes are further territorialized into the spaces in which we find it appropriate to prepare food, to eat, to bathe, and to clean our clothes. As Joan Kron writes in her book *Home-Psych*, the spaces we define for such purposes are "dictated by one's definition of clean and dirty," definitions that "vary tremen-dously among cultures." The English, for example, "regard the kitchen as a dirt removal place," Kron reports, so "they will do laundry there, wash dishes there, even bathe in the kitchen, but they don't like eating in the kitchen." Americans, on the other hand, have never had any qualms about eating in the kitchen—indeed, we prize the "breakfast nook"—but we generally don't bathe or do our laundry there. Except for washing the dishes, we tend to regard the kitchen as a "clean" space. In fact, with more and more middle-class Americans discovering the joys of gourmet cooking, the American kitchen is going from "clean" to "dazzling." Designed to open onto living and dining room areas, it is a showcase of gleaming tile, well-stocked food preparation "islands," and shining copper pots and pans—so clean that it almost seems a shame to mess it up by cooking there.

The recent renaissance of American interest in the kitchen reflects a major shift in our social attitude toward cooking. In the past, middle- and upper-class Americans didn't think quite so highly of kitchens as they do today. Cooking was considered servants' work, and so the kitchen was set out of the way where a hired cook did the cooking. If you couldn't afford a cook, you tried to fill your kitchen with labor-saving devices that took the place of servants. Cooking just seemed to be an unpleasant chore that anyone who could afford to avoided. But by the 1970s, servants, even "hired girls," had disappeared from the scene. The middle class had to do their own cooking, so cooking became fashionable, even chic. Reflecting a generational disenchantment with what had come to be perceived as the sterile, "plastic" cookery of the fifties and sixties, the new attitude toward cooking impelled middle-class men and women to learn how to cook, and prompted home designers to create houses with prominent, showcase kitchens in which to do it. Thanks to Julia Child, one might say, owners of older houses with small, hidden kitchens are now tearing out the walls to integrate newly refurbished cooking areas with the rest of the house. Indeed, next to the master bedroom, a fancy kitchen is becoming one of the domestic features contemporary home buyers most covet.

It's not only the kitchen that's opening up in the houses of the eighties. The walls are going down and the ceilings are coming out in more and more American houses to enhance their spatial feel. The open-plan house, first pioneered in the beginning of the century by Frank Lloyd Wright, is coming back, and for a very good reason. For as Joan Kron reports, since the 1970s the average living space of a typical starter home has shrunk from about 2000–2500 square feet to 850–1400 square feet—a drastic reduction that directly reflects the dramatic rise in housing costs that occurred over the same period. To compensate for this loss of space, contemporary home designers favor cathedral ceilings, open floor plans, skylights, transoms, bay and clerestory windows, and atriums to take advantage of every cubic foot of space that today's smaller houses contain and to fill them with as much exterior light as possible.

Shared Territory

The quality of a home's interior space is not independent of the quality of its immediate exterior, however. If your sense of territorial proprietorship and responsibility starts and stops with the outer envelope of your house, it isn't going to be much of a home. Territorial well-being requires a sense of shared as well as of private space, a feeling of community or neighborhood in a space that is neither "mine" nor "yours" but "ours." Thus, there is a semiotic code of the neighborhood as well as of the private home, a signaling system by which private householders communicate to each other their sense of community—or lack of it.

When Americans still lived in towns and villages rather than in urban apartment blocks and suburban tracts, neighborhood cohesion was much more easily achieved. As in the long-vanished world represented in Thornton Wilder's *Our Town*, the members of the community tended to know the family histories of most of the people in town, and though this could often lead to the sort of small-town tyrannies ridiculed in the novels of Sinclair Lewis, it also fostered a sense of community identity.

The front porch is something of an architectural emblem of such times. Set squarely at the front of the house, the front porch was an area where neighbors could meet informally and spontaneously. Both private property and public stage, the porch was a space in which one could talk to people in the street, admit casual visitors, or court the girl or boy next door.

The fact that few modern houses have front porches is thus a sign of social change. First, the population of a typical suburban neighborhood is far more mobile than the population of a traditional town or village. Many of us live thousands of miles away from the places of our birth, and we may have lived in our current neighborhoods for too short a time to really get to know the neighbors. Commuting in our automobiles to distant workplaces, we tend to derive our sense of group identity more from our professional than from our neighborhood contacts, and the social geometry of our homes has adjusted accordingly. Where we once informally interacted with our neighbors from the public space of a front porch, we now more formally invite our guests—usually co-workers and colleagues rather than neighborhood friends—into the privacy of our backyards, where patios, swimming pools, spas, and barbecue pits have replaced the utilitarian garden sheds and garages we used to put there. The front yard is no longer much of a meeting area. More ornamental than social, it serves a different purpose in the neighborhood semiotic code.

For the front yard now serves as a signaling system by which we communicate to our neighbors, whether we know them or not, our willingness to maintain the physical integrity of the neighborhood. Lawns and gardens are not simply tokens of suburbia; they are signs with which private-home owners communicate their sense of neighborhood cooperation. This communication certainly has its competitive aspects, but the value of a well-kept front yard goes beyond the price of keeping up with the Joneses. It will do you no good to have the best front yard on the block if all the other yards are overgrown with weeds. That's because weeds do not simply run down property values; they also signify a neighborhood at odds with itself, a community of strangers withdrawn into their own private shells.

It is a rather fashionable cliché among social planners that suburbia promotes conformist rather than creative values, that the pressure for neighborhood consistency tyrannizes over our need for self-expression. But it is still important to consider the difference between the absolute privacy of a home interior and the modified privacy of its exterior. For though your yard legally belongs to you, in a certain sense it also belongs to the neighborhood. Forever on public view, it is part of your neighbors' prospect, what they must look at day after day. Even the toniest of neighborhoods can have problems in this direction. When an Iránian millionaire, for example, painted the statuary in the front of his Beverly Hills mansion, coloring in faces, nipples, and even pubic hair, the neighbors were understandably offended, both by the sight itself and by the hordes of tourists who came to gawk (the mansion, along with its statues, has since been demolished). The statues may have expressed something quite creatively individual about its inhabitants, but to design a yard that is so uncompromisingly "me" as to disrupt the public "we" of the neighborhood can be read as a sign of territorial withdrawal, a refusal to contribute to the kind of community semiotic code that solidifies a neighborhood into a mutually beneficial territory— a place that is "home" just as much as the house in which you live.

Where all feeling of community territory is lacking, the home becomes a fortress and the neighborhood a battleground. This frequently occurs in publicly subsidized apartment projects that sacrifice communal architectural values in the name of utility and cost-effectiveness. The worst of such projects tend to be high-rise apartment blocks where the residents are segregated by floor and further alienated from each other by miles of sterile and forbidding hallways. Such buildings lack the kind of public meeting areas that foster the creation of community feeling, and so isolate each family in its own isolated cell. The same thing is true in luxury high rises, of course, but the residents there have enough money and social power to establish their sense of proxemic well-being in other ways. In the high rises of the poor, the inhabitants have no alternative psychological resources, and the usual result is social anarchy.

The most infamous failure in the history of public housing is the notorious Pruitt-Igoe project, which was designed in 1951 to meet the housing needs of St. Louis's urban poor. Charles Jencks describes the project in his book *The Language of Post-Modern Architecture* as a series of "elegant slab blocks fourteen stories high with rational 'streets in the air' (which were safe from cars, but as it turned out, not safe from crime); [and] 'sun, space and greenery,' which Le Corbusier called the 'three essential joys of urbanism' (instead of conventional streets, gardens, and semi-private space, which he banished)." Designed to reflect the values of architectural theorists who preferred spare geometrical lines to the proxemic complexities of a traditional urban neighborhood, Pruitt-Igoe failed to provide its inhabitants with any sense of community identity. Brownstone tenements teeming with the life of the street can foster strong bonds of community feeling despite their squalid conditions, but the clean concrete slabs of the Pruitt-Igoe project felt impersonal and forbidding. Its "rational streets in the air" felt like dark alleys, and the residents of the project, instead of looking after each other as they often do in brownstone neighborhoods, retreated behind locked doors. With no buffer zone between the coldly threatening halls and their rows of blank doorways, with no effective transitional space between the outside of the complex and its semiprivate inside, with no gardens or community walkways or residential meeting areas, the inhabitants of Pruitt-Igoe developed no sense of community responsibility, and the place was vandalized at will. Eventually, Pruitt-Igoe became unlivable. The city of St. Louis finally had to give up on it and demolished part of the project in 1972 at the request of its own inhabitants.

In the Pruitt-Igoe project, the architectural sterility of the buildings failed to foster any sense of shared, mutually defensible territory. Ideally, an apartment building or neighborhood street should be like a coral reef: a complex of individual territories harmoniously integrated into a common structure. Unfortunately, public housing projects are all too often more like prison blocks: private cells connected only by mutual suspicion and fear. Their inhabitants thus often behave like the criminals their environment appears to be suited for. Like Dickens's Wemmick, they too reflect their surroundings.

BORN TO SHOP

For many middle-class Americans, particularly, but by no means exclusively, for teenagers, the local shopping mall has taken the place of the neighborhood as a space for communal gathering. We go to the mall not only to buy things but to see other people, to entertain ourselves, to have something to do. We can dine out at the mall, watch a movie, ice-skate, or just stroll down tree-lined avenues complete with park benches, fountains, and greenery. But while a neighborhood constitutes a territory that is at once public and private, the mall is entirely public, and it is designed to stimulate consumption, not neighborly feeling.

The shopping mall may be America's most characteristic, and influential, contribution to the language of world architecture, and it reflects the commercial values and history of the nation that developed it. As Peter Gibian writes in his article "The Art of Being Off Center: Shopping Center Spaces and Spectacles," the shopping center "came out of the car culture of 1920s-1930s California, when people discovered the simple 'one-stop' attraction of putting several small stores (with maybe a grocery store as base) near a single parking area." From this modest beginning, the shopping center has come a long way in a relatively short time, evolving from the great suburban shopping centers of the 1950s, through the enclosed malls of the 1960s, to the vertical "bird cage" malls of the 1970s and 1980s. But in each of its variations, the American shopping center has always functioned as a kind of consumer-stimulation machine, its architectural designs carefully tuned to the psychology of the consumers they mean to serve.

The first shopping centers only had to play on the novelty of the automobile in order to lure people in. Built to suit an automotive culture still enjoying a honeymoon with the internal combustion engine, they made no attempt to conceal their essen-

tial partnership with the road. Set down on the bordering highway strips that were replacing the Main Street shopping districts
of town-and-village America, they reflected the emerging consciousness of an expansive, mobile society that had come to view
village life as restrictive and provincial. To just get into one's car
and drive away from town was a liberating experience that the
shopping center could take advantage of, for it not only placed
itself on the main highways where the drivers were, it also gave
them a place to stop.

With the new mobility made possible by the automobile
came architectural standardization. In the postwar era, the interstate highways that enabled America to expand outward from its
traditional urban centers fostered an architectural style that could
be recognized by a national clientele. The great successes of such
roadside businesses as Howard Johnson's, Holiday Inn, and
McDonald's are testimony to the power of standardization in an
automotive culture, and shopping center design was no exception. Thus, the first large shopping centers basically looked alike.
Built at a time when there was still plenty of cheap land for
commercial development on the outskirts of America's cities and
towns, each had a single-level parking lot directly abutting a long
blocklike row of shops and department stores. Assuming that
automobile-age consumers were primarily concerned with convenience, the designers of these centers were concerned only with
moving cars as close as possible to the stores.

One might say that the succeeding steps in the evolution of
the American shopping center constituted refinements of rather
than drastic changes in the original pattern. In all cases, the goal
of the design was to facilitate and stimulate consumption. But
whereas the first shopping centers could rely on the novelty of
automotive convenience to move their goods (all your shopping
needs provided by a single parking lot!), their later incarnations
required some subtlety once the glow of the automobile had
begun to fade. Thus, to keep the customers coming, a few innova-
tive designers in the 1950s created a new sort of shopping center

that substituted an illusion of town-and-village serenity for the suburban realities of the automotive age.

Peter Gibian describes one such center in Skokie, Illinois. Called the Old Orchard Mall, this "market town" shopping area contains "streams, bridges, finely gardened courtyards and shop squares of various dimensions" that are all designed "to suggest the atmosphere of a country village." The point of the design is to make the customer feel that he or she has been transported to a more aesthetically pleasing time and place. To stroll the walkways of such a mall is to feel that one is on vacation, which is a very effective stimulus to the spending of money, because spending money while on vacation seems different from spending money while merely shopping. Vacation dollars don't just buy *things*, they buy *souvenirs*. It's simply a lot easier to part with your money while on holiday than when running errands, and the designers of the Old Orchard Mall knew this. The architectural structure of the place, then, was intended to stimulate impulse buying by making its visitors feel like tourists. In the semiotic sense, that is what all those streams, bridges, and courtyards *mean*.

These "market town" malls still remain, as do the "highway strip" shopping centers of the earlier phase, but they have been superseded by the giant mall enclosures that began to appear in significant numbers in the late 1960s and 1970s. Several stories high, arranged around a central pedestrian core with arcaded shops arranged on each side, these suburban malls partially re-create the ambience of a nineteenth-century *urban* shopping district. And this is no accident, since the prototype for such malls is the Galleria Vittorio Emanuele, a nineteenth-century shopping mall in Milan, Italy, which "combines the cool and quiet arcades that can still be seen in central Milan . . . with the city's monumental architecture," as William Kowinski writes in *The Malling of America*.

As with the market town malls, the enclosed malls cater to disenchanted motorists who would just as soon forget about their automobiles for a while. But their appeal is different. For one thing, they are a sign of a consumer desire for greater personal comfort. Market town malls are pleasant places when the weather's right, but they don't protect you from the heat of summer or the snow of winter. The enclosed malls, like the automobiles that are contemporaneous with them, are climate-controlled.

What is more, the market town malls were designed to simulate the iconic imagery of village life, thus reflecting the rural fantasies of suburban shoppers who had only recently fled the city for the suburbs. The idealized urban shopping environments simulated in the enclosed malls, on the other hand, reflect the fantasies of consumers returning to the city both for convenience and because they prefer it to the suburbs. This is especially true of the so-called "bird cage" malls, like Toronto's Eaton Centre, Houston's Galleria, and Chicago's Water Tower Place, which have sprung up in the nation's urban centers both to serve the large number of urban professionals who live and work there and to attract suburbanites back into the central shopping districts that they fled years ago.

What is architecturally most striking about the bird-cage malls is their height. This is partly a sign of necessity. The first shopping centers were free to sprawl across the apparently unlimited spaces of the 1940s and 1950s; the vertical bird-cage malls have been built to suit the more restricted environments of the city and even of the contemporary suburbs, where ever-rising land values prohibit the lavish horizontal developments of the past. Towering stories high into a sky revealed through glass skylights reminiscent of London's Crystal Palace, the new malls make up in volume for what they must give back in surface acreage.

But that's not the whole reason for the architectural style of the bird-cage mall. Again, the design is intended to stimulate impulse buying. With their cascading waterfalls and fountains, aerial walkways and open escalators, sidewalk cafés and park benches, these malls have become the urban tourist attractions of the 1980s. Indeed, Toronto's Eaton Centre, as Peter Gibian reports, "attracts many more visitors per year than Niagara Falls." It's difficult to enter such places and not remain for a few hours, even if you're only looking for a pair of shoes.

You can find lots of shoes in the new malls—countless stores full of them—but you can find a good many other goods and services that you never could have found in earlier shopping marts. Woolworth's has always had its modest cafeterias, but the new malls have set aside entire dining plazas offering international foods of every description. You can spend a dollar on a pretzel, or stroll into a luxury coffee and tea emporium and pick up a pound of decaffeinated chocolate fudge coffee for $9.95. The products too have changed, as expensive mail-order outfits like Eddie Bauer, The Nature Company, and Williams-Sonoma have moved in to lure upscale consumers from their living rooms into dazzling showrooms full of hard-to-find luxuries.

The effect is dizzying, as is the effect of the mall space itself. Pedestrian traffic runs up, down, and across without any trace of right-angled symmetry. Walkways lead you around and around in spirals of intoxicating displays. The effect resembles that of an amusement park, where every turn in the road reveals a new attraction. Oddly enough, such architectural extravagance is less a sign of prosperity than of the shaky consumer economy of the 1980s. With real or anticipated recessions to cope with, American consumers are nervous about parting with their dollars. The carnival atmosphere of the most up-to-date malls assuages that nervousness by transporting shoppers into a fantasy realm in which their real-world cares can be suspended and their purse strings relaxed.

This has rather raised the ante on mall construction, causing older-style malls to fall quickly into decline as newer, more spectacular shopping palaces are raised. The contrast between the old and the new is particularly striking in Santa Monica, California, where a brand-new atrium mall has gone up right next to an older, uncovered pedestrian mall built in the "Spanish Mission" style which comprises three blocks of shops and old-style department stores facing each other from either side of a pedestrian plaza. This older shopping area, the Santa Monica Mall, is almost entirely given over to poor and elderly shoppers, who pore over displays of cut-rate footwear, cheap toys, and unfashionable clothing.

Towering next door is Santa Monica Place. A glassed-in atrium with three stories of shops, vaulting skylights, and a hublike courtyard complete with fountain and sidewalk café, the mall is filled almost entirely with middle-class and upper-class shoppers. Even their age is homogeneous, with most appearing to be about 25 to 45 years old—excluding the ubiquitous bands of teenagers. No one, of course, actively tries to keep out the lower-class shoppers from next door, but they don't seem to want to enter. It's not their sort of territory. The prices, for one thing, are too high, and the glittering ambience of well-dressed shoppers, who animate the clothing to be found in the high-fashion shops, can make a poorly dressed customer feel conspicuously out of place. So they stay next door, enabling the old mall to survive in its shabby way as an emporium for the ever-increasing number of urban poor who now live side by side with upscale America without ever really crossing paths.

This juxtaposition of the old mall and the new can be taken as a symbol of yet another paradox of American society in the 1980s—the decade, we might say, of the excluded middle. For there now seem to be two broad patterns of American consumption: upscale and downscale, each with its own characteristic stores and shopping centers. You won't find K Mart or Pic 'N' Save in an atrium mall; they tend to congregate in "highway strip" shopping centers of their own that are thronged with working- and lower-middle-class shoppers. But upscale shoppers scarcely notice any of this, for though the centers devoted to their needs may often be constructed in the very midst of these newly poor populations—particularly when erected in downtown shopping districts—they are "protected" from demographic reality by the spectacular architecture of their atrium malls, like birds comfortably trapped inside a gilded cage.

BACK TO THE CITY

It is no mere coincidence that the design of modern atrium malls resembles that of some of the most spectacular urban hotels of the 1980s. For hotel designers, too, have been forced to create specially insulated artificial environments to lure wealthy customers back into America's decaying urban core. As Barrie Greenbie puts it in his book *Spaces: Dimensions of the Human Landscape*, "Our tendency to turn our backs on the outdoor environment in central cities as it gets more confused and ugly, more polluted and congested . . . has affected the evolution of another type of contemporary public social space, the large convention hotel."

Let's take a semiotic look at L.A.'s Bonaventure Hotel. Looming a few blocks away from Pershing Square—a once rundown park that has recently been renewed—the Bonaventure typifies the new generation of inward-looking urban architecture. Designed by architect-developer John Portman, who also designed the Westin Hotel in Detroit's Renaissance Center, Atlanta's Peachtree Plaza, and the chain of Hyatt Regency atrium hotels, the Bonaventure thrusts five mirrored-glass cylinders into the L.A. sky. But though the views of the city from the top are breathtaking, there are no such views from the bottom. As you sit by one of the three pools on the ground floor, or in one of the many concrete "pods" that hang above them, you see nothing of the street. Glass skylighting illuminates indoor "sidewalk cafés" that seem to belong to an idealized Parisian boulevard, while the careful concealment of the Bonaventure's entrances and exits completes the illusion of a utopian public park with clear vertical views to the sky but no horizontal views to the less than utopian conditions outside.

You can't see the entrances to the Bonaventure from the street, either, only the gleaming, inaccessible towers of the hotel complex. The whole forms an island of light and air amid the grimy inner city. You can look down from this island from a revolving restaurant thirty-five stories up, or from glass-walled elevators that shoot up the sides of the cylindrical towers like rocket ships; but from up there everything looks sanitized and remote.

By comparing the Bonaventure with its near neighbor, the Biltmore Hotel, we can see how each is an emblem of the era in which it was built. Constructed in 1923 while the downtown district was thriving, the Biltmore proudly faces Pershing Square, which served as a promenade for its wealthy patrons. The hotel's main entrances are easily accessible, and grandly visible, from the street. In its almost haughty relationship with its immediate environment, the Biltmore can be seen as a relic of aristocratic self-assurance and power. A stately pleasure palace filled with the hierarchical symbols of the Old World, complete with cathedral-like ceiling vaults and Italian fresco work, the Biltmore looks, and feels, like a royal residence that has only provisionally been turned over to the public, a temporary museum patiently awaiting the return of its aristocratic masters.

But if the Biltmore recalls the aristocratic values of the past, the Bonaventure appears to project the vision of a utopian future. Having done away with the painted ceilings and marble flagstones, the gilded scrollwork and glittering chandeliers of the Biltmore, the Bonaventure is all democratic steel and glass and concrete. In its rejection of the precious materials and elaborate ornamentation of the Biltmore's aristocratic style of architecture, the Bonaventure seems to reflect the egalitarian vision of the Modernist architects who first began building in glass and concrete. But while the Bonaventure owes much to the Modernist tradition, its semiotic significance is paradoxically at odds with what the Modernists were getting at.

For all practical purposes, we can say that Modern architecture, while anticipated by the Chicago School's Louis Sullivan, was born in 1919 with the founding of the Bauhaus School of design by Walter Gropius. Gropius had a dream: from the ashes of a Europe physically and morally destroyed by the four years of World War I, there would rise a new architecture stripped clean of every reminder of the past. As Tom Wolfe puts it in *From Bauhaus to Our House*, Gropius meant to "start from zero," to begin all over with a rationally efficient, geometrically pure architectural style suited to a century of industrial democracy. Envisioning a socialist future, the architects of the Bauhaus School set about creating a proletarian architecture purged of the ornamental detailing of feudal and bourgeois architectural design. No more vaulted ceilings, pitched roofs, masonry fronts, cornices, pillars, fancy colors, colonnades, or gables. The future was to be written in concrete, glass, and steel, painted white or gray, and shaped in pure, boxlike forms (recall Pruitt-Igoe). The interiors of the new buildings were to be ascetically bare: no moldings, wainscoting, mantelpieces, or cornices; just clean, unadorned lines and white walls. In short, the industrial age was to get an industrial architecture. Everything from the new workers' housing projects to office buildings and private homes would have the severely functional lines of a factory or boiler room.

But a funny thing happened on the way to the future. Rather than sweeping aside the forces of bourgeois capitalism, the Modern designs of the Bauhaus School became the favored patterns of capitalist contractors, who began to fill the cities of the world with Modernist office towers, housing projects, and hotel complexes with the same boxy structures built of glass and steel and concrete. Often referred to today as the International Style of architecture because of its worldwide ubiquity, Modernist design today is obliterating the architectural past on behalf of general utility, not progressive ideology. Ironically, while the founders of Modern architecture intended their designs to serve as a stimulus to the creation of a socialist society, they have proven to be more useful to corporate office builders, public housing directors, and luxury hotel designers than to proletarian revolutionaries.

The Bonaventure Hotel embodies this irony neatly. With its soaring elevators and unlimited vertical vistas, it would appear to be a symbol of unbounded opportunity, of an unfettered future for everyone. But that isn't its real meaning at all. With its breathtakingly expensive rooms and restaurants, its boutiques selling everything from luxury jewelry and perfumes to $1,000 stuffed animals, the Bonaventure is a space designed around the desires of a bourgeois plutocracy. Inside, everything may look like an urban utopia, but the appearance is possible only at the expense of the street, which must be blocked from view.

POSTMODERN REACTIONS

Despite its debt to Bauhaus Modernism, the Bonaventure Hotel is not a wholly Modern structure, however. With its four glass towers arranged symmetrically around a fifth cylinder at the core, the Bonaventure seems abstract enough to suit the Modernist's obsession with rational geometry, but this geometry is apparent only when you look at a blueprint or a scale model of the building. It all looks, and feels, quite different when you are actually inside.

Consider the view from the ground floor. In actuality, the floor plan of the Bonaventure constitutes a rectangular space centered on a cylindrical core, but the effect at ground level is that of a decentered circle. As you stroll from poolside café to poolside café around the perimeter of this confusing space, the central core is alternately concealed and revealed by the intricately planned landscaping, promoting the illusion of a shifting center by constantly varying your visual perspective. You feel that you are walking in a circle, but it is a circle that has been inscribed within a square. This is not only disorienting; it also has something of the symbolic effect of King Arthur's Round Table because here no space can claim priority of place over another. As opposed to the hierarchically arranged spaces of the Biltmore —which are deployed around the centrally dominant linear sweep of the Galeria Real, a marble-flagged hallway that extends the entire width of the building—space in the Bonaventure is not clearly broken up into distinct units at all. Inside the six-story lobby, for instance, everything soars and thrusts with few walls or ceilings to block the way: a void into which the eye peers as into an illusion of limitless space.

With its twelve bubblelike elevators and eleven cascading escalators, the lobby of the Bonaventure also resembles an American amusement park. One almost expects to be asked for a ticket before entering an elevator, and the escalators have no obvious destinations. All these people-movers appear to be here for the sake of amusement rather than function. Rather than a place of work, the building presents itself as a space for the recreational pleasure of its wealthy patrons.

While the sort of public architecture represented by the Bonaventure Hotel (variously called "Postmodern" or "Late-Modern," depending upon the writer) has retained many of the architectural values of the Modernists, particularly in its allegiance to technological innovation and glass-and-steel construction, it also seeks to revive the sensual ornamentation of pre-Modern design. Architects do this by adding features like mirrored glass, color, striping, structural "crowns," curvilinear profiles, anything to break up the severe asceticism of Modern construction. The Portland, a building in the city of that name in Oregon, for example, combines a fundamentally Modern box-like shape with ancient Egyptian and classical architectural effects, not to mention a little bit of Las Vegas thrown in for good measure. Prompting a good deal of outrage within the Modernist camp when it was designed in 1980, the Portland has proven to be quite popular with the people of Portland. Ordinary people evidently do not share the Modernists' distrust of "the traditional subjects of art and ornament—that is, institutional dignity, individual esthetic pleasure and transcendental meaning," as Charles Jencks puts it. Rejecting the cold pragmatism of industrial design, Postmodern architects are now grafting postindustrial values, including the tastes of a consumer rather than a producer culture, on essentially Modern patterns.

The Postmodern sensuality of the Bonaventure completes its

ironic reversal of the ideological spirit of the Modernists. Reflecting the values of a postindustrial culture in which services constitute America's leading commodity, the Bonaventure's partly Modern, partly Postmodern design presents itself as pure entertainment. Its confusing and illusive geometry is not supposed to make sense; it's only there to *be sensed*, to be consumed and enjoyed.

Is there any semiotic connection between the design of a public space like the Bonaventure Hotel and the private space of a contemporary home? I believe that there is. For in many of the upscale house designs of the late 1980s, the plans call for grandiose living rooms with towering atrium ceilings. Coupled with the elaborately equipped master bedrooms that such houses also commonly contain, the private pleasure domes of the eighties can be read as signs of a rather hedonistic culture eager to enjoy whatever pleasures it can grab. Ours is not a particularly self-sacrificing era, and we are inscribing our values into the walls of both our public and private architectural habitats. Does this make us much different from Wemmick? Probably not. After all, private castles are very much in style today.

CHAPTER 7

Reading the Tube:
The Semiotics of Television

Entertainer, painkiller, vast wasteland, companion to the lonely, white noise, thief of time. . . . What is this thing, this network of social relations, called television?

Todd Gitlin

For Marshall McLuhan, television's leap onto the center stage of Western culture signaled the beginning of the end of the Gutenberg galaxy, the electronic eclipse of an epoch of print and text. For Newton Minow, a former chairman of the Federal Communications Commission (FCC), it's little better than a "vast wasteland" that threatens to engulf the nation in a morass of mediocrity. For most Americans, it is just television, their major source of entertainment, information, and sheer time-consumption.

No matter how you look at it, in the scant space of some forty years, television has revolutionized our lives. First introduced as a novelty alternative to radio, television has rapidly evolved into the most profound invention of the age. Nothing is immune from its influence. Politicians play for the cameras, and so do international terrorists. Physicians call news conferences, and judges host courtroom dramas. Television, through its hyping of the Olympic Games, has transformed sport into politics and politics into sport, treating everything from presidential elections to military conflicts as prime-time entertainment. What is not televised is hardly thought of at all in a world in which television creates reality as much as it records it.

For the semiotician, there can be no richer subject for analysis than modern television. Every prime-time program, mini-series, news broadcast, sports contest, documentary, advertisement, and "special" constitutes a galaxy of signs whose significance lies at the heart of our culture. Deeper still, television is itself one vast sign in which we can read a fundamental lesson about human nature.

We can begin with a few fundamental semiotic questions: What accounts for television's extraordinary success? Why has it fascinated us so from the very beginning? How has it been able to transcend traditional barriers of nationality, race, religion, language, class, age, and gender to unite us all in its universal embrace? In virtually every nation on earth, human beings circle around their TV sets like moths, as if compelled by some mysterious force. Why?

At the most primitive, universal level of human behavior, we are attracted to our TV sets by something that evolution has lodged in our genes. Though divided along national, racial, and cultural lines, all human beings belong to a species that owes its success to its ability to respond to rapid environmental changes, to adapt to varying ecological conditions. We can live in the arctic or on the equator, in the plains and in the mountains. We have colonized the sky and may someday settle on the moon. We could not have succeeded in adapting ourselves to so many different environments, however, without an inborn restlessness, without a genetic propensity for variety, without an insatiable curiosity about what might lie over the next hill. Our craving for variety, in other words, is nature's way of providing us with an evolutionary edge in the struggle for survival in a constantly changing world. Because we are born with a predilection for change, we are able to respond to it positively and creatively when it occurs. The dinosaurs wouldn't have had much use for television. They liked things to remain as they were.

Television, with its constant changes of scene, its rapid pacing, and almost infinite variety, is uniquely suited to satisfy our restless craving for sensory stimulation and change. It's almost as if we evolved to watch TV. A cat is content to sleep all day, but even the most exhausted human being will prefer turning on the TV to simply staring into empty space. In minutes, even seconds, our television sets can take us on journeys that it took our prehistoric ancestors thousands of years to complete. We can visit Hawaii, China, Australia, and Europe all in the course of an evening, or just see what's going on downtown. Television takes us to arctic ice fields and to equatorial rain forests, to the summit of Everest and to the bottom of the sea. It has even taken us to the moon.

But human beings are not only curious about environments; they are also curious about other human beings. We are social animals and have evolved to feel a keen interest in the activities of other people. Before television, our social knowledge was generally limited to those closest to us: our families, our friends, our fellow workers. Gossip gave us glimpses into other lives, as did newspapers and books, but the view was always incomplete and speculative. Television, on the other hand, puts us on intimate terms with make-believe Dallas millionaires and invites us to the weddings of real-life princes and princesses. It puts us face to face with the agony of a just-tripped Mary Decker during the 1984 Olympics, and it allows us to glimpse, over and over, the smiling faces of the space shuttle *Challenger* crew minutes before their fiery deaths. It brings the elite and powerful into our living rooms and makes them appear close to us. In a certain sense, TV is the ultimate form of gossip.

In societies like our own, television counters the desensitizing force of modern life by giving us the color and texture of a world that we can't see from our windows. No wonder TV has risen to such social prominence in such a short time: it is our compensation for the monotony of modern times, providing us with the sensory stimulation that we miss in our real experience.

Then why are there so many complaints about it? Denouncing "the media," from both left-wing and right-wing perspectives, has become something of a cottage industry in cultural criticism. In its early days, TV was expected to enrich American culture, not impoverish it, but it is the intellectual poverty of television that is most striking today. What went wrong?

Everyone has a favorite culprit. From the political right, we hear denunciations of the immorality of modern television, of its corruption by "secular humanism." From the left comes a chorus of antibusiness complaints, blaming the profit motive of corporate capitalism for the low cultural level of commercial broadcasting. But while I'm inclined to agree that commercial television is concerned more with drawing the largest possible audience for its corporate sponsors than with providing quality programming, I do not think that we can simply blame corporate capitalism for TV mediocrity. Commercial television places a premium on entertainment value because that is what most Americans want. Public television, which was originally known as "educational TV," has a notoriously small audience. If its audience were to grow to Nielsen proportions, we should soon see a change in commercial programming. The high road simply doesn't pay, and the fault lies with us, not with those who provide the money for television programming.

Our general predilection for entertaining rather than educational television can be traced to the very causes of TV's extraordinary success. Entertaining television tends to be fast-paced, gossipy, and sensually stimulating—just the sort of thing that appeals to our inborn craving for sensory stimulation and social intimacy. Educational TV tends to be intellectually rather than sensually stimulating, and while it can show us many different types of human beings, it does not try to create an illusion of intimacy. There's a lot of talk on educational TV, while entertaining TV presents action and emotion. The bulk of the TV viewing audience in America regards television as a means of escaping from the need to think, not as a stimulus to thought.

For this reason, the most successful programs on commercial TV stick to social stereotypes and clichés, telling stories that never challenge their audiences to think critically about their world. Commercial television presents images of American life that are framed by the most common—and even trite—of cultural myths. Occasionally, a commercial program comes along that attempts to make us think about such myths and in so doing provides striking semiotic insights into American culture. But you've got to catch such programs early, because they rarely last long, generally disappearing at mid-season to be replaced by more conventional programming. In the sections to follow, I'll look at two such programs that appeared as off-again, on-again shows in the late 1980s—"The Days and Nights of Molly Dodd" and "Max Headroom"—both of which attempted to challenge television orthodoxy while adhering to commercial TV's imperative to entertain. The strain, as we shall see, was too much, causing each show to fail (at least in relative terms) both commercially and aesthetically, but they were still among the most semiotically interesting programs of their time.

The Rise and Fall of "Molly Dodd"

When I began to write this chapter, NBC's "The Days and Nights of Molly Dodd" was the newest and fastest-rising program on American TV. Since then, it has fallen victim to the fickle world of A. C. Nielsen, having been once cancelled and once rescheduled in the course of a few months. Whether it will survive its second life is hard to tell, but whether it succeeds or not, the semiotic significance of "Molly Dodd" remains the same, for few shows have so consciously attempted to challenge the myths and stereotypes of American television while still operating within them.

Few myths are as enduring in the world of television as the myths of gender that frame our perceptions of the sexes. The classic sitcoms of the fifties and sixties—"I Love Lucy," "Father Knows Best," "Life with Father," "The Ozzie and Harriet Show," and "Leave It to Beaver"—all reflected without comment or criticism a patriarchal mythology of paternal authority. The shows' titles alone say a great deal about the mythology behind them: "father knows best," not mother; "life with father" (mother, apparently, goes without saying); "I love Lucy," where "I" refers to Lucy's forgiving husband, Ricky, who sets up the show's framework by seeing Lucy's antics from an indulgent but always male perspective.

Similarly, television in the 1950s and 1960s frequently dramatized the struggles of single fathers but never of single mothers. We had "Bonanza," "Bachelor Father," and "My Three Sons"—programs featuring widowers and bachelors successfully raising children—but no "Bachelor Mother." Of course, there were plenty of single mothers in America at the time, but the myth held that women were not competent to raise a child alone, and so TV stayed away from them. Widowers were all right on TV—in fact, they were desirable because they offered the opportunity for new love interests each week—but widows were rare, reflecting the patriarchal myth that there is something morbid or unseemly about a woman living without a man. Even the independent-minded widow in "The Ghost and Mrs. Muir" was hooked up with a dead sea captain to soften her widowhood. Ben Cartwright needed no such solace.

"The Days and Nights of Molly Dodd" challenged the patriarchal mythology by showing a divorced woman living without a man. Of course, it was not the first show to do so. Mary Tyler Moore pioneered the role of the independent woman in "The Mary Tyler Moore Show," which was soon followed by a host of programs, from "Wonder Woman" to "Cagney and Lacey," that challenged the patriarchal myths of TV. But where "Mary Tyler Moore," "Wonder Woman," and "Cagney and Lacey" portrayed strong, independent women, "Molly Dodd" was a little different. Mary Richards may have been disappointed in love before arriving in Minneapolis to produce the news broadcast, but she was always chipper enough. Molly, on the other hand, is a divorcée on the verge of a nervous breakdown. If "The Mary Tyler Moore Show" represented a cheerful rejection of the social mythology behind Mary's housewifely role in "The Dick Van Dyke Show," "Molly Dodd" insisted on representing the dark side of the myth of the "new woman."

What set the program apart from the other working-women shows was its representation of a woman who was not succeeding either professionally or socially, a woman who was only barely coping in an often lonely world. Unlike her rather dopey sister, who is smugly satisfied with her life in the suburbs with a protective dentist for a husband, Molly takes risks, and she usually loses. So why did NBC create such a character?

The explicit message of the show was that, unlike the general run of TV sitcoms, "Molly Dodd" tells it like it is, showing life in all its messiness and irresolution. Most TV shows make no genuine attempt at realism, relying instead on television's grand illusion that whatever problems afflict us as frail human beings, they can usually be worked out in a thirty-to-sixty-minute framework. In real life, for example, legal cases are both messy and uncertain: Has justice been done? Have we gotten the right man? There is no such uncertainty in "Perry Mason." The lawyer not only wins all his cases, but he also gets at the truth, forcing a courtroom confession out of the real culprit.

Similarly, in the traditional family sitcom—from "Ozzie and Harriet" to "The Cosby Show"—Mom and Dad are always able to resolve their children's difficulties. Even "All in the Family" moved from conflict to resolution to a sense of harmony after a storm. Mary Richards had her crises, but she always ended up with a smile. Molly Dodd was different. The show characteristically ended with a sense of ambiguity and ambivalence. Open-ended rather than closed and resolved, each episode left us with a queasy feeling that the problem Molly had encountered has not gone away.

In an early episode of the show, for example, a depressed Molly consults a psychiatrist. In an ordinary sitcom, you'd expect two probable outcomes. Either the doctor will turn out to be a stereotypical shrink with a heavy Viennese accent and a buffoon-ish manner, ending in Molly's realization that she's not crazy after all, the shrink is. Or she would show all sorts of apprehension about her first visit only to discover how kind and helpful the doctor really is, the episode closing with a happily cured Molly and a fine, uplifting resolution.

But what actually happened in the episode was much more complicated. Molly *is* as apprehensive as a sitcom heroine should be before her first meeting with her psychiatrist, but the doctor turns out to be a disconcertingly bland woman who simply asks Molly to tell her what's troubling her. When Molly insists on psychoanalyzing herself in classic Freudian terms, her analyst interrupts her by taking a series of personal telephone calls that seem to establish her as a typically selfish Manhattan shrink who cares only for her fee. Frustrated by this apparent callousness, Molly angrily leaves the office and bursts into tears. Then she realizes how she has refused to discuss what's really hurting her —her still-painful divorce—and returns to the office where she begins to open her heart. Her analyst then reveals that the tele-phone has been disconnected the entire time and that she has taken the faked "calls" in order to shock Molly into opening up. And there it ends, with Molly's pain finally coming into the open, expressed but not resolved.

By avoiding the conventional stereotypes and artificially preordained conclusions of the ordinary sitcom, the creators of "Molly Dodd" attempted to re-create the unexpected rhythms, the accidents and irresolutions, of real life—or so we were meant to think. But while this was the program's major strength, it was also the major weakness. For once you set out to represent life as it really is, you'd better get it right, and the writers of "Molly Dodd" were constrained by their very medium to get it wrong. A television program that faithfully reproduced the actual speech and experience of real life wouldn't last very long. Real life is just too tedious to have to watch for half an hour. TV's major experiment in *cinema verité*—"An American Family"—ended up a failure not only for the network but for the real-life family it focused on as well. Life, in the persons of the Loud family, began to imitate art, as these ordinary Americans began to play out their lives for the camera, becoming just as melodramatic as the most strained soap opera.

The writers of "Molly Dodd" didn't attempt this sort of total realism, creating instead an illusion of realism. The illusion was sustained by dramatizing the experiences of a sometimes unhappy woman in her thirties who lives in a small Manhattan apartment and has the sort of job- and man-troubles you'd expect her to have. The narrative line of the show as a whole thus created a reality *effect*, but it could not present a raw, unmediated reality.

There were a number of signs that gave away the illusion behind the effect. First, there's the way Molly talks. While she generally avoids the artificial banter of the rest of the sitcom world, she delivers far too many set speeches and lectures of the sort that no one would ever put up with for very long. Then there's Molly's nosy family. Her sister is little more than a two-dimensional caricature of the Compleat Suburban Wife, a marginal character who seems to have been tossed in just to make Molly look more unconventional. Although Molly's mother does have her moments, she is easily recognizable as a standard-form Jewish Mother—though of Irish-Catholic origins in this case—kindly but intrusive, well-meaning but abrasive. Molly's deadpanning Irish elevator man could only be found working network television, while her wardrobe—three or four Saks Fifth Avenue changes per episode—could only spring from the imagination of a Hollywood scriptwriter.

The show's plots had the same problem. Though they appeared to flaunt industry stereotypes on behalf of "real-life" situations, they were finally as artificial as anything else on TV. For example, in one episode Molly takes on the average sitcom's assumption that every red-blooded American female is just waiting for some blond, blue-eyed hunk to come and sweep her off her feet. Molly's silly suburban sister tries to set her up with such a hunk—a blond, blue-eyed dentist in practice with her husband —who calls Molly at all hours of the day to leave aggressively suggestive messages on her answering machine. Breaking with TV tradition, Molly refuses to be swept off her feet by the seductively manipulative voice of the WASP dentist but responds to a phone message left by a refreshingly straightforward masculine voice—but is that a Yiddish inflection?—belonging to a candid young man in search of a piano teacher. Molly dolls herself up for her pupil's first lesson only to discover (and the discovery is straight situation comedy) that her pupil is a thirtyish Hasidic Jew in full religious regalia. Of course Molly falls for him, and they almost—almost!—go to bed together. But of course he breaks the affair off just in time, gently declaring that he must never see her again. The episode ends with Molly dreaming that they've consummated their affection after all in a peculiar song-and-dance sequence that at once borrows from the dream choreographies in *Fiddler on the Roof* and *Oklahoma!*.

What undermines the reality effect here is that such a man as Molly's Hasid would never have crossed her threshold in the first place, much less have kissed her. The writers have also gotten his appearance wrong. Yes, he does have earlocks, as he should, but he also has longish hair and a beard that looks about three days old. In reality, a thirty-five-year-old Hasid would have short hair and a beard at least fifteen years old. The plot has the unexpected zaniness of real life, perhaps, but little plausibility.

The semiotic key to our reading is contradiction. A show that pretends to display real life ends up contradicting itself in a series of unrealistic characters, plot lines, props, costumes, and so on.

And there's our sign, bearing the simple but culturally profound message that American television is so far gone into illusion and artifice that it can't find its way out, no matter how hard it tries. This is no accident, because commercial TV is not in the business of representing reality: its job is pushing products. And the best way to push them, American television has assumed almost from its inception, is to substitute a televised reality for a lived one, to turn the entire world into one big TV show, filled with potential consumers who, like Molly Dodd, must have three changes of clothing per day.

So who were the consumers that the creators of "Molly Dodd" had in mind? It's not a hard question: the intended audience was to include people like Molly herself: urban men and women—yuppies, if you will—who have discovered the stresses and strains of yuppie life. The fact that "Molly Dodd" was created for such an audience constitutes the implicit message of the show. Flush with cash and eager to spend, yuppies are a coveted market of corporate America. The program's creators and sponsors sought to reach this market by appealing to the tastes of a sophisticated audience that had grown up with TV and that was consequently savvy to its illusions. The show's producers clearly hoped that such viewers would respond positively to a program that seemed to substitute gritty realism for comic fantasy.

The telltale signs of "Molly Dodd's" yuppie appeal lay both in the unconventional plot lines of the show, which represented a sophisticated version of urban life, and in the way the program was framed. For example, before watching a single episode of the show I was struck by the semiotic suggestiveness of its title. Where had I heard a title like that before? I'll tell you where: in the 1970s PBS aired a peculiar, sometimes brilliant, English situation comedy called "The Fall and Rise of Reginald Perrin." The series concerned the usually comic, but eventually tragic, adventures of one Reginald Perrin, a middle-level executive in an English firm specializing in ice cream treats. Over the course of many episodes, the somewhat eccentric Perrin suffers a nervous breakdown; fakes a suicide to live a lonely, impoverished life for a while; gives this up to rejoin his wife and married daughter; founds the Grot Shop, a store that will sell anything as long as it's absolutely awful and absolutely overpriced; watches in horror as the Grot Shop, which was intended to fail, becomes a smash success; tries to destroy the monster he's created by sabotaging its top management; drops out again; organizes a retreat for harassed business executives; and finally commits suicide by swimming off like a lemming into the North Sea.

"Reginald Perrin" was a weird and wacky comedy with a lot to say about the quiet desperation of the middle class—something English television has always been more sensitive to than has American TV—and that violated every rule in the book about situation comedies. Until recently, American social taboos prevented television from subverting the most sacred myth of all in American life: the myth of the middle class. Most sitcoms poke fun at middle-class life, but they don't attack its most sacred cows: prosperity, security, happiness, success. "Reginald Perrin" was able to attack such middle-class ideals because it was created in a country with a vital working-class tradition with different ideas about society.

Lacking an influential working-class tradition of its own, American culture has been slow to question its middle-class mythology, but the men and women who make up the ranks of yuppiedom commonly did question the values of their middle-class parents in the 1960s. Though they grew up to join the establishment after all, they often harbor a nostalgia for social criticism, and "Molly Dodd" offered them an opportunity to think critically about American society.

Even before I watched my first episode, then, I felt that someone was trying to tell me something by the choice of the title alone. I asked myself, What sort of writer would create such a title, and why? Well, someone (I guess) who watched and admired Reggie Perrin's comic-tragic adventures, and who believed that American commercial television needed a Reggie Perrin of its own—a "highbrow," in other words, who wanted to create a different sort of sitcom that would question the sacred values of the middle class. I thought I'd better watch "Molly Dodd."

"Molly Dodd" was one of the first yuppie sitcoms. Shows such as "St. Elsewhere" and "L.A. Law" provide dramatic programming for young professionals, reflecting the career-centered consciousness of their audiences. But what kind of sitcom will work for young professionals? Not the sort of blue-collar comedies that vaulted ABC to the top of the Nielsens in the seventies. Programs such as "Happy Days," "Taxi," and "Laverne and Shirley," which all went into reruns in the eighties, have fallen behind the trends of popular culture. Although blue-collar heroes, from truckers to country singers to peanut-farming presidents, were fashionable in the seventies, the eighties brought a new cultural mood that was definitely not working class.

If the seventies was the decade of the trucker and the Nashville star, the popular imagination of the eighties has been obsessed with glitz, glamour, power, and the iconography of Wall Street. "L. A. Law" is one reflection of the new trend, and "Molly Dodd" is another. Let's compare Molly to Laverne and Shirley. Molly is a middle-class working woman, not a working-class one. She has worked in an ad agency, not a factory. Though she is out of work, she lives in a small but fashionable Manhattan apartment that is as bright and shiny as anything in *Better Homes and Gardens*, a lodging that contrasts sharply with the dingy interiors of working-class sitcoms. She is always expensively and fashionably dressed, and her accent and interests all reflect a high level of culture and sophistication. Shirley goes bowling, Molly writes poetry.

Still, in spite of its intended appeal to upscale viewers, "Molly Dodd" did not attract a large audience. Viewers instead turned to cheerier yuppie sitcoms like "thirtysomething." The show's initial failure suggests that it was just a little too depressingly offbeat even for its sophisticated target audience. Even yuppies like entertaining illusions.

M-m-max H-h-headroom!

It is commonplace among cultural critics that television exists solely to sell things, that its values are wholly commercial, and that whatever aesthetic potential it may have will always be sacrificed to the requirements of corporate sponsors intent on transforming us all into docile consumers. For my own part, I sometimes find this critical baying at the heels of commercial television just a little shrill—after all, no one forces us to watch TV—but I must concede that after watching the first episode of "Max Headroom" I've begun to feel that maybe the critics are right: television is dominated by an extremely sly bunch of corporate manipulators. For when we read it carefully, "Max Headroom" constitutes an even more potent sign than does "Molly Dodd" of just how futile a thing it is for television to attempt to transcend its commercially artificial nature.

In "Max's" inaugural episode, the setting is a futuristic dis-topia that resembles the nightmarish cities of *Blade Runner* and *Escape from New York*. It is a typically postmodern vision of the future: an anarchic urban wasteland where the streets have been turned over to punklike thugs and mutants while everyone else huddles glued to his or her television screen in cluttered, ill-lit high-rise apartment buildings (shades of Pruitt-Igoe).

Enter intrepid television reporter Edison Carter, who, against the orders of his superiors at Channel 23, investigates the mysterious death of one of the dwellers in those nightmarish high rises. Despite various attempts to stop him, Carter discovers that Channel 23 has developed a top-secret ad campaign to increase its revenues. A teenaged computer genius has developed an advertisement that prevents viewers from switching channels during commercial breaks. These ads, called "blipverts," bombard viewers with an electronic barrage of images, a dizzying montage that glues them to their seats. Blipverts have one nasty side effect, however: they can short out the bioelectrical circuitry in an especially fat and sedentary viewer, causing him to explode. This has already happened enough to worry Channel 23 executives, but the slickly evil chairman of the board elects to continue with the campaign and cover up the deaths.

In trying to escape the Channel 23 villains, Carter crashes into a parking gate and is captured before he can get the story out. While probing Carter's memory to discover what he knows, the teen computer whiz (who later becomes a good guy in an unconvincing manner) finds that he has created an entirely simulated computer personality based on Carter's memory. The first thing this "computer-man" remembers is that parking gate, which had "max. headroom" written on it, and so he is simply called Max Headroom. Eventually, Carter is rescued, the evil chairman of the board is exposed, and Max has entered every television screen in the anarchic city, preening, grinning, and stuttering to a growing audience.

Now, spot the contradiction. On the surface, "Max Headroom" presents itself as a sophisticated condemnation of the corporate domination of television, satirizing the corporate obsession with ratings and profits at the expense of human values and even lives. There's a good deal of the movie *Network* here, but the fact that *Network* was a movie and not a TV series is highly significant. For *Network*—scripted by Paddy Chayefsky, a writer from the early days of television who remembered the promise the medium once held to become a force for cultural enrichment—made its point in a medium other than TV. Its satirical portrait of corporate television managers who deliberately blur the line between the screen and reality on behalf of ratings is relatively independent of the world that it exposes. Like *Network*, "Max Headroom" exposes the ways in which television attempts to substitute itself for reality. Indeed, its real hero, the computer-man Max himself, doesn't exist apart from a TV screen. Who needs Dan Rather, the show ironically insinuates, when you can have Max Headroom, the ultimate TV personality?

But the satire is just a little hollow, considering that "Max Headroom" appears on commercial television, and even as we feel that we are detecting the machinations of corporate TV, we are already being subjected to them. The contradiction is that we've got to watch the program on the very terms that it attacks. As we watch "Max Headroom," we, too, are bombarded with advertisements that try to keep us from switching channels. And Max himself has become a spokesman for Coca-Cola, whose own electric-montage advertisements very much resemble blipverts, skipping images at us so quickly that it's hard to get up and make them go away. Finally, Max, in the ultimate logic of TV's dissolution of the illusion/reality line, has become a well-known celebrity much admired and imitated by adolescent viewers who are apparently in some danger of developing permanent stutters.

These are the contradictions. Essentially, they tell us that like a sophisticated commercial, "Max Headroom" appeals to our distrust of TV while appearing on TV. But it too is a creature of the corporation, and it wouldn't have made it to the airwaves without sponsors. So even as we feel good about ourselves for spotting the Machiavellian ways of television along with the intrepid crew at Channel 23, we are caught in the trap we thought we were avoiding. We're seeing blipverts after all.

The "Max Headroom" show was an awfully clever way to lure a sophisticated audience that grew up with television and thus feels that it knows all its tricks. And this is why I think that maybe the critics are right. The people who sponsor commercial television have hired a host of bright, creative people whose jobs, like the job of the whiz kid at Channel 23, are to make sure that there's always an audience for the ads that make TV tick. Some of these people write the shows; others, the ads; and the whole point is that the ads and the shows must be indistinguishable.

The blurring of ad and program is a relatively recent feature in the short but active history of television. It was easier to tell the difference between a Gleem commercial and "Leave It to Beaver" than it is to see the difference between a spot for Coca-

Cola featuring Max Headroom and the program itself. The implications here are disturbing; for in the blurring of the lines between product pitches and program drama we can see a reflection of a society that has become so saturated with commercialized illusions that it can't tell the difference anymore. The United States is becoming one big television show, with actor-presidents and performing executives (note how often Lee Iacocca appears in Chrysler commercials) all underwritten by corporate contributions.

If "Max Headroom" really had the courage of its convictions, it would have developed its ultimate implication to a logical conclusion: that a world controlled by television executives will finally have the appearance of one long, inescapable TV program. No way out. Wherever you look, Max is on a TV screen, a billboard, or a bus stop bench pushing Coca-Cola. Pat Robertson's potent campaign for the presidency in 1988 raised television's stake in the country one notch higher: televangelist for president! Who's next, Spuds MacKenzie?

Had "Max Headroom" told it like it was, the evil chairman of the board would have won. But true to TV's myth of closure and resolution, the good guys win the day. Intrepid television employees expose the villains at the top—though there is one benevolent pipe-smoking executive with a conscience who permits the exposure at last—even though the top brass seems to control the police as well as their own security patrols. A truly chilling episode would have had the intrepid team murdered as planned and Max smoothly incorporated into the chairman of the board's general plan. You can't escape the power of Channel 23: this is what the show implies but refuses to admit. That would be just a bit too scary, and the program's corporate sponsors had a vested interest in being sure that the show's viewers felt they could, with a little grit and gumption, happily escape the corporate net.

In the 1960s there was a program that accepted its own premises. "The Prisoner" was a show that from the start won critical acclaim, a small but loyal audience, and a short television life. "The Prisoner" was not explicitly about the corporate web; rather, it concerned a surrealistic colony of retired spies who have been rounded up to prevent them from revealing the masses of classified information they have acquired over the years. They are, in effect, prisoners of an international consortium of governments who have banded together, East and West, to tie up the loose ends of their own intelligence agencies. Patrick McGoohan played one prisoner who wanted to escape from his Disneyland-like prison. In each episode, he attempts once more to find Number 1, the mysterious prisoner who seems to run the place, but Number 1 can never be found. McGoohan at one point learns that he himself is Number 2, but he has no power. No individual seems to have any power. The prison is decentered and self-regulating. To please its viewers, "The Prisoner" did conclude with McGoohan's escape back to England, although one feels that he hasn't really escaped at all, that the whole thing has been staged, and he's still in prison.

It's a nightmarish vision, and a particularly postmodern one: a picture of life in an endless labyrinth with neither center nor exit (see chapter 11 for more on the postmodern worldview). Each episode tempted its audience to believe that the hero would finally find Number 1 and win his escape. But the lesson each time was that there really is no Number 1. No one's in charge. No one's responsible. As in the world of Franz Kafka, you can't find anyone to explain what's going on. Even the prisoner's final escape leaves him with no answers and an uneasy freedom.

In many ways this is the situation with us as we watch "Max Headroom," but the show didn't make this explicit. The program gave us an identifiable corporate villain whose fall is bravely arranged by the show's heroes. They even get applauded by all of Channel 23's employees at the end. Yet they're all still inside the vast tower of the station's corporate headquarters. They're all still inside the labyrinth. Just as we're inside too, being offered clichés about wicked businessmen by clever businessmen who know that this is a good way of selling a program.

Reading Bill Cosby

If "Max Headroom" didn't entirely break free of the corporate labyrinth, however, it did dramatize its existence. The show pointed out the dangers of seeing everything as TV sees it, of becoming lost in the illusions of the electronic medium. But it was not a commercial success in the end. So the question becomes, what *were* Americans watching during the "birth" and "death" of "Max Headroom"? The answer is easy: They were watching "The Cosby Show."

Throughout the 1980s, Bill Cosby has emerged as something of an American institution. The subject of a *Time* magazine cover story (September 28, 1987), Cosby looms as the most successful entertainer of his generation, black or white. There are a number of reasons for Cosby's success. First, as one of his early comedy albums puts it, he is a very funny man. More importantly, perhaps, Cosby has succeeded in restoring to television the image of the "strong father" after years of paternal buffoonery. Shows like "All in the Family" and "The Jeffersons" featured weak and foolish fathers who presented a contrast to the dignified fathers of the fifties. The undercutting of the seventies' TV father was deliberate: it reflected the iconoclastic mood of a country suspicious, for the moment, of authority. But with the advent of the new decade, paternal authority—symbolized for many by Ronald Reagan's paternalistic presidency—came back into popular fashion. Once more, American audiences were looking for TV father figures, men who were sensitive, nurturing, yet authoritative and masculine. Cosby fit the role perfectly, quickly emerging as America's favorite father.

Bill Cosby is not only America's favorite father, he is America's favorite symbol of the American dream, one that his success seems to establish as color blind. Cosby has embraced this symbolic interpretation of his career and incorporated it into his show, which has been self-consciously designed to project an image of black success, a black version of the American dream. But behind the image lurks a concealed semiotic reality.

The explicit symbolism of "The Cosby Show" is something that Cosby himself has done much to promote in the press. The Huxtables, he insists, are "an *American* family," an exemplary model of "the American way of life." Cosby continues: "If you want to live like they do, and you're willing to work, the opportunity is there." Cosby is defending himself against the common criticism that his show is an unrealistic representation of what life is really like for most black Americans in the 1980s. His defense—that he isn't trying to represent what life is like for most black families but is only trying to present a model family that all Americans can aspire toward—is perfectly justified. There's always room for the presentation of admirable examples, of positive images for others to imitate. Cosby seems to be succeeding in this very nicely, if we can judge from recent matriculation surveys at UCLA that indicate a high proportion of minority freshmen plan to become pediatricians and lawyers.

The semiotic question, then, is not whether "The Cosby Show" is a realistic picture of black American life. The question is, what does the creation and presentation of the Huxtable family image say about America in the 1980s? Consider how "The Cosby Show" resembles the "Father Knows Best"–style sitcoms of the fifties. True, the skin color is different, and Mom has a career of her own, but in "Cosby," as in its predecessors, it is the family home that constitutes the focus of everyone's attention. Dad's a pediatrician, Mom's a lawyer, the kids all have outside interests and activities, but the psychic and moral center of the family is the living room. There, child meets with father—who, like Ozzie Nelson, always seems to find time away from his job to lounge around the house—to settle his or her little problems. Dad is funny, often adorably self-mocking, but he's always there and his advice always works.

What is striking about this is not so much the similarity between "Cosby" and the family sitcoms of the fifties and sixties but the astonishing success of the program among audiences who are well aware of the artificiality of the mode. Americans are nostalgic not for "Father Knows Best" but for the family-centered mythology that show reflected. "Cosby" only adds a new layer of mythology to the old mythology, presenting a black family in the place of the white originals. Viewers of the show are thus doubly reassured on the one hand by images of a tightly knit family group even as the real nuclear family continues to come apart in American life, and on the other hand by the iconic representation of a successful black family at a time when black America is falling further behind white America. For black Americans, "Cosby" is a sign of promise, of economic desires that *can* be fulfilled. For white Americans, it is a sign of progress, of social desires that *have* been fulfilled. And for all the Americans who faithfully watch it week after week, it is a sign of continuity, of the continuing desirability of a close-knit family home.

But the fact that, semiotically speaking, these signs signify the state of American *desires* in the 1980s more than they do American *realities* is the most significant sign of all. College freshmen may want to become pediatricians, but few will make it, especially when financial aid resources for college tuition are shrinking. We may still want families in which the home is the center of activity, but for the kinds of families that the Huxtables represent, the focus of parental interest tends to be the career that got them their money, not their kids, who are being raised by professional surrogates, from nannies to day-care workers and school teachers.

"The Cosby Show," one could say, realistically represents our desires for a world that is practically the inverse of the one in which we actually live. It is perfectly true at the level of desire, but is desire a substitute for the real thing?

SEEING IS BELIEVING

Television appeals to the sense that we most rely on in our interaction with our environment; our eyesight. Dogs smell out their worlds, bats use radar, insects have antennas, but people *see*.

We also hear, smell, taste, and touch, of course, but we trust no other sense as we do our eyesight. Above all, we want to see something before we will believe in it. Words can lie, but you can trust what you see—can't you?

The dominant sign of television is the icon, the pictorial image that stands in the place of the things that it represents. Television images are so real looking that they lull us into thinking that they *are* real, that they aren't iconic signs at all but realities. Since we *see* them we trust them, often failing to realize that, like all signs, they have been constructed with a certain interest behind them.

Consider the images on the nightly news. Each picture we see purports to be an unconstructed view of real events and persons, but in reality they are images created by editorial decisions. The construction of a news image may be as simple and relatively innocuous as a decision to delete a camera shot of Ronald Reagan's aging jowls or to include one of Mikhail Gorbachev's bald head complete with birthmark, but it may also be far more profound.

The most influentially constructed news images of our time were those that came out of the Vietnam War. For the first time in history, noncombatants were offered a close-up view of military combat. But the view was not unmediated. The first images of the war to appear on American television screens tended to stress the *advisory* role of American forces. One saw images of individual American soldiers "advising" companies of South Vietnamese troops, not groups of Americans arriving together in Saigon. This imagery was calculated to suggest that America was not involved in a land war in Asia but was only advising its allies, a message that very much suited Washington's strategy in the early sixties.

But as the war dragged on, the American strategy changed, and once again what we saw on the news reflected a careful construction of the situation rather than an impartial reflection. For now we saw American soldiers fighting what looked like an

American war. Whatever military engagements the South Vietnamese army was involved in were not broadcast. Here too the imagery of the news reflected Washington's military strategy, which was at this point to frighten North Vietnam into submission by demonstrating that it was up against the full might of the United States. North Vietnam, of course, didn't submit, and the truth of the situation—that it was South Vietnam's war in the end—only appeared in the images of 1975, when the last Americans helicoptered out of Saigon, leaving the city to its fate.

But by then the television news had long since ceased constructing images of the war that matched Washington's vision of it. The break came in 1968 with the Tet Offensive. If the Pentagon had been managing the news, it would have broadcast images of American victory, emphasizing the fact that Tet ended with a Vietcong defeat. But the television news stressed instead the nearness of *American* defeat, the moments of apparent chaos at the beginning of the onslaught, presenting the same events in a wholly different framework. These broadcasts signified a disillusionment with the war, an impatience with Pentagon promises, and they conveyed the imagery of military futility. We could have been shown images of communist capitulation and slaughter. What we remember are scenes of American G.I.'s huddling under fire in the streets of Hue.

Television news often packages an image for its sheer entertainment value. Violence is particularly attractive to television audiences, and so film crews eagerly seek out violent events without troubling to put them in their political contexts. Lively images of Irish or Palestinian teenagers throwing rocks at English or Israeli soldiers make for good television ratings, but they don't inform you of the political circumstances behind the scenes. All you get is a picture framed as show business, not as genuine information, a violent surface without intellectual depth.

By packaging violence as entertainment, the television news expresses its own interest: to attract audiences and increase advertising profits. This interest was satirized in *Network*, where an ambitious television executive hires a band of terrorists to pull off the greatest ratings success in TV history: the on-air murder of a troublesome anchorman. It was supposed to be satire, but it was uncomfortably close to the truth. Television executives may not actually hire international terrorists, but they exist in a peculiarly symbiotic relationship with them: terrorists provide the nightly news with arresting images, and the news provides terrorists with a platform. Indeed, the capture of the American embassy in Tehran in 1979 led to the creation of a television news show, ABC's "Nightline," that broadcast images of chanting Iranians (who stopped chanting once the cameras were shut off) night after night to fascinated late-night-news junkies.

What we call "the news," then, is really "the news in a frame." The nature of the frame determines the import of the news. We don't see that frame when we watch the news, however; we only see pictures, nice trustworthy pictures. But pictures, too, semiotics reminds us, are signs, the products of ideology and interest. They do not simply show you the news: they construct it while pretending to do otherwise. In the end, it is this ability of television to frame and manipulate the news for its own purposes that constitutes its greatest power—and its greatest threat. By turning realities into entertaining illusions, television threatens to blur the line between the real and the unreal. Slowly but surely the world is becoming like one big television program, everything set up for the cameras. But in the real world that television has so successfully invaded, you can't just change the channel when you don't like what you see.

CHAPTER 8

You Are What You Eat: The Languages of Food

Real men don't eat quiche.
Bruce Feirstein

I magine that you have been invited over for supper by your firm's new vice president for marketing, a woman who, word has it, is quite a gourmet cook on the side. Sitting down for the first course, you find yourself confronting a plateful of nasturtiums, pansies, roses, and zucchini blossoms. Now, what do you do? Do you (a) return the flowers to the floral centerpiece where they belong? (b) Bravely clean your plate by depositing each blossom discreetly into your pocket? Or (c), dig right in, while politely informing your hostess between mouthfuls that zucchini blossoms went out last year according to a recent *Gourmet Magazine* poll?

If you chose option (a) or option (b), you belong to the majority of American consumers for whom garden flowers are still considered "inedible" foodstuffs. If you chose (c), on the other hand, you are a gourmet, for whom the pleasures of food are augmented by the possibilities for experimentation that food presents, by the way that adventurous diners can redraw the lines between the "edible" and the "inedible." Ask option (a) or (b) people why they think flowers are inedible and they'll tell you that they simply are, that human beings weren't made to eat such things. Ask option (c) people why they like to eat flowers and they'll tell you that it's fun, adding—probably with a little defensiveness—that flowers are a perfectly natural thing to eat, no different really from eating the leaves that we call lettuce or spinach, and just as nutritious. Besides, flowers are a lot prettier than lettuce leaves and make a more flavorful garnish than parsley.

Whether you choose to eat your hostess's plateful of flowers or not, their semiotic significance remains the same: the lines we draw between the edible and the inedible reflect personal and cultural tastes as much as they do the limits of nature. We can't live on grass or tree bark or straw, of course, but what about lizards, grubs, grasshoppers, and ants? Somewhere in the world people eat such things, though we in America would classify them as manifestly inedible. The difference between the edible and the inedible, in other words, is often a cultural decision. The only purely natural thing about eating is its necessity; after that, culture takes over, defining for us just which things are proper to eat and which are not, how to prepare and serve our foods, and even the times of day when we may eat them.

Consider the homely potato. It is easy for us today to take its palatability for granted, but as recently as the eighteenth century it was regarded as animal feed by European peasants who, even in the face of famine, vigorously resisted its transformation into human food. Originally imported from the New World, the potato appeared "unclean" to Europeans because it was of foreign origin, fit perhaps for South American Indians but not for good European farmers. (We've come a long way here, from pig swill to Pringle's.) The Japanese, in a similar fashion, once regarded the carrot as a food fit only for horses—and Koreans—while the

French taste for frog's legs has won for that nation the less than flattering sobriquet of "frogs" among non–frog-eating Anglo-Americans.

The distinctions we make between the edible and the inedible, then, are often analogous to the differences we perceive between the domestic and the foreign, between "us" and "them." We tend to feel that there is something barbaric about other people's food preferences, something "unnatural." Until recently, for instance, the Japanese taste for raw fish was regarded with horror in America, taken as a sign of the superiority of American to Japanese customs. The sushi fad in the United States has reversed this attitude, of course, but it hasn't changed the basic logic of the situation. Raw fish is still viewed as "foreign" food, but its foreignness has become what makes it attractive, because it is associated with a people whose business success has become an object of world envy and admiration.

To put this another way, a sushi bar is not simply an expensively exotic restaurant: semiotically speaking, it is a sign whose "language" is encountered not in words or symbols but in foods, in the things that we eat or choose not to eat. Though we are not always aware of it, we eat not only out of biological necessity but to communicate with one another, declaring by our food preferences such cultural information as our social status, national identity, and ethnic heritage. Our hypothetical hostess's flowery salad, for example, communicates high-status dining because of the high cost of its ingredients and its association with upscale gourmet trends.

More commonly, specific staple foods serve as icons of ethnic culture. Spaghetti is the identifying emblem of the Italian family; matzo-ball soup and gefilte fish signify Jewish cookery; tacos and enchiladas are Mexican icons; and stir-fry identifies Oriental cuisine. Of late, Spanish tapas (a form of gourmet Spanish dining) and Japanese sushi have transcended their national signification, communicating yuppie trendiness.

Like all languages, the language of food is "spoken" differ-

ently in different cultures, employing not only different "vocabu-
laries" (compare Asia's rice-based to Europe's wheat-based culinary codes, a distinction enforced by differing geographies) but
different ways of thinking as well. To read this language is to
interpret more than a menu; it is to delve into a culture's entire
way of being, its manner of apprehending the world.

Consider the list of dishes served up in "The Banquet of
Trimalchionis," a feast depicted in Petronius's *Satyricon*. Trimalchionis, a former slave and current parvenu vulgarian, serves
his guests a series of courses that includes a boar filled with live
thrushes, a pig stuffed with sausages, and pastry eggs baked
around the bodies of small fig-pecker birds smeared with egg
yolks. Each dish presents itself to Trimalchionis's guests in an
elaborate disguise, pretending to be one thing on the surface
(boar, pig, or egg) while being quite another thing underneath
(thrush, sausage, or fig-pecker). In a similar fashion, Roman
cooks delighted in concealing the identity of the dishes they
served by disguising their true flavors in heavy sauces and chopping them up to prevent them from being recognized by their
natural shapes. The Roman chef Apicius—who could be called
the father of cookbook writers—accordingly concocted a recipe
for smelt pie, which involves chopping up anchovies and mixing them with pepper, rue, oil, raw eggs, and sea-nettles, all
with the promise that "nobody will be able to tell what he is
enjoying."

Such recipes reflect not only the decadent tastes of an empire
in decline but an entire worldview. As Lowell Edmunds, a classics
professor at Johns Hopkins University, explains in his article "De
Gustibus," the Romans believed that "outward appearance and
inner substance are different," that things never are what they
seem but forever conceal their true natures beneath a misleading
husk. The Romans thought that in order to understand something you had to dissect it, tear it apart, to see what it concealed.
For this reason, as Edmunds observes, Roman religion "was
obsessed with the examination of entrails. Priests scrutinized the

colors and shapes of each internal organ, seeking in the depths of the animal, clues to coming events in the outside world." Thus, the delight of discovering a sausage inside a pig was Rome's culinary equivalent to philosophy.

Glad you're not in Rome and have to do as the Romans do? Not so fast. Edmunds compares the recipes of Apicius to "an all-zucchini dinner prepared by Brooke Swenson of Westport, Connecticut" in 1983, a meal whose singular origin went undetected by everyone who participated in it. Edmunds's comparison may be significant. Americans have traditionally believed in the commonsense truth of surfaces. Things, for us, are what they appear to be. If you want to understand something, look at it. We're predisposed to believe in straightforwardness and candor, not deception and disguise. Indeed, our national hero is best known as the man who never told a lie.

Our traditional meals reflect our belief in the honesty of appearances. The turkey on the Thanksgiving table not only looks like a turkey but we may hang pictures of whole turkeys around the dining room as decorations to remind us of what we are eating. The good old American steak dinner, of course, doesn't resemble a steer, but its unsauced plainness makes it clear that we are eating the muscular flesh of an animal. The beef industry has even tried to capitalize on America's traditional penchant for unadorned and undisguised food through its "Beef: Real Food for Real People" campaign, showing us a manly James Garner cooking and eating real beef rather than some effeminate egg-and-flour farrago like quiche. Real Americans, the campaign insinuates, don't eat quiche.

A delight in mixed-up, disguised, and highly sauced food is often taken as a sign of cultural decadence, or at least of an epicene society. So is a delight in exotic foods. Rising Rome prided itself on the plainness of its cuisine; declining Rome was fond of trick dishes and edible rose blossoms. To the semiotician, a comparison seems inevitable: Are all-zucchini dinners and edible flowers similar marks of cultural decline? Or do they mark a trend toward a lighter, more humane vegetarian cuisine? That's possible too. After all, why *can't* real men eat quiche?

STRICTLY KOSHER

Few food systems more thoroughly embody the worldview of those who practice them than the Hebrew "kashruth." It would be difficult to imagine a more completely codified system of culinary do's and don't's, or a more complex set of distinctions drawn between the edible, or "clean," and the inedible, or "unclean." For one who practices the ritual of the kashruth, there's no need to probe its meaning, for its purpose is clearly outlined in the Torah. The kashruth simply signifies the will of God for his chosen people. But for those outside the system, its complex regulations often appear to be bewilderingly legalistic, an unnecessary, almost irrational burden. Reform Jews—who sympathize with the regimen but do not practice it—have tried to explain the kashruth as an ancient system of culinary hygiene, pointing out, for example, that the prohibition on pork is an effective way of preventing trichinosis, and that the ban on mixing meat with milk avoids curdling and spoilage. But such explanations don't really get to the heart of the matter; for ancient Hebrew thought is characterized less by modern standards of rationality than by a deep sense of mystery. It is highly unlikely that the ritualized measures of the dietary laws are simply designed for public health.

In an essay entitled "The Semiotics of Food in the Bible," Jean Soler pursues a semiotic approach to the kashruth, arguing that the dietary laws of the Hebrews ultimately reflect an entire worldview. Their complex system of dietary prohibitions and regulations, Soler suggests, rests on a simple fundamental principle. For the ancient Hebrews, the ideal order of the world was instituted at the Creation: in Eden all creatures were in harmony with one another, and none ate another for food. "Behold," God says to Adam, "I have given you every plant yielding seed which is upon the face of the earth, and every tree with seed in its fruit;

you shall have them for food," adding that "to every beast of the earth, and to every bird of the air, and to . . . everything that has the breath of life, I have given every green plant for food." Note that no provision is made here for meat eating, which begins only after the Fall. Since, as the ancient Hebrews believed, the peculiar task of God's chosen people is to imitate the perfect regime of Paradise as closely as possible, it would seem that Judaism would be a vegetarian religion.

But the Hebrews, Soler argues, were realists, recognizing that fallen humanity will eat meat no matter what ideals are held up to it. Thus, the consumption of meat was permitted but only under careful religious supervision. Jehovah grants his people the right to eat meat, but with the provision that it shall not be eaten "with its life, that is, its blood." The prohibition on the consumption of blood stemmed from the Hebrews' belief that blood contains the life of an animal. God's chosen are forbidden to consume the life of any animal, but He has left a loophole: a thoroughly bled animal no longer bears that life, and so the Law permits its consumption. For this reason, a kosher butcher, who is as much priest as butcher in the Jewish religion, must bleed an animal while slaughtering it, ritually offering the blood, or "life," to God, who alone can give or take life.

To re-create the conditions of Paradise as closely as possible while allowing for meat eating among a fallen humanity, the kashruth also carefully excludes the eating of any animal that itself eats flesh. The prohibition on eating cloven-hoofed animals that do not chew the cud, Soler explains, stems from the fact that pigs—who have cloven hoofs but are not cud-chewers—eat meat, while cloven-hoofed, cud-chewing ruminants do not. Thus, this most famous of Hebrew prohibitions is not the arbitrary product of an overly legalistic culture that it is often taken to be. It reflects the logic that to eat a carnivore—an animal who cannot perform the proper rituals before killing and eating—is to double the sin of eating meat. As Soler puts it, "Man's problem with meat eating is compounded when it involves eating ʔ

animal that has itself consumed meat. . . . Carnivorous animals are unclean. If man were to eat them, he would be doubly unclean." Hence, we find the origin of our Western taboo on the eating of carnivorous animals like cats and dogs—a prohibition that does not exist in the Far East, where, to the dismay of Westerners, dogs and cats are more commonly eaten.

We can take Soler's argument a step further. If the laws of the kashruth express the ancient Hebrews' desire to live as closely as possible according to the prelapsarian order of things, it also reflects the worldview of a people whose sense of destiny is rooted in the past rather than in the future. Within this view, human perfection is a thing of yesteryear, lodged in a lost Eden. Whatever perfection humanity can achieve comes from a careful attention to tradition, to the laws and customs that have been passed down through the generations in order to guide a fallen world back to the paths from which it has strayed.

More importantly, the laws of the kashruth reflect the needs of a people in exile. To maintain their identity under the conditions of the Diaspora, the Jews have clung to the traditions of the past, traditions inaugurated in the days when they had their own nation to bind them together. When the political institutions of that nation were destroyed, Jewish society held itself together through its rituals. The kashruth, then, is not only a set of culinary rules: it is a fundamental example of the way that food operates to bind societies together.

SOCIAL BONDING AND FOOD

Food not only reflects social realities, it creates them, forming the very foundation of social life. Human societies have gotten along perfectly well without much clothing or elaborate shelter, but no society can survive without food. One could say that the entire evolution of human society has been centered on the need to produce and distribute the foodstuffs that are so necessary for survival. Bread, in other words, is not only the staff of life, it is the hub of social existence.

Food must be produced before it can be distributed, of course, and we have always felt a special veneration for the forces that we believe to be responsible for our daily bread. Haunting images of great bison and wild horses painted on the cave walls of Altamira and Lascaux testify to the reverence of ancient hunters for the spirits of the animals they pursued. Early agriculturalists worshipped the gods and goddesses of the harvest, while the ancient Egyptians deified their pharaohs by investing in them the power to control the annual flooding of the Nile that inaugurated the agricultural year. And even in an age of scientific farming, when chemicals, pesticides, and antibiotics form the stock-in-trade of modern agribusiness, the mythic figure of the humble family farmer continues to hold its place in the pantheon of American belief.

Food is so important to us that we offer prayers to our gods before eating it. Christians say grace before meals, while Jews have special prayers for their wine and bread. Food assumes such symbolic importance in the ritual of the Catholic Mass that it is consubstantially identified with the body and blood of Christ. In the most solemn ritual of the Catholic Church, the communion between God and humanity is enacted in a humble meal of bread and wine.

If our religions sanctify the production of food, our social organizations see to its distribution. No social group of animals can long survive without procedures for the sharing of food. We cannot live without nourishment and we'll fight for it if it isn't provided. By sharing food, social animals both avoid conflict and ritualize the structures of their societies. After bringing down their prey, for example, wolves line up to feed at the site of the kill in the order of their relative place within the dominance hierarchy of the pack. Social bonding is ensured through the sharing of the kill, while pack harmony is maintained by the hierarchical order of eating.

Human societies are no different, they're just a lot more complex. As the French sociologist Marcel Mauss pointed out at the turn of the century, the human social order is stitched together by elaborate rituals of food sharing and reciprocity. By giving and receiving food, human beings, like wolves, maintain social harmony and equilibrium.

The rituals of human food sharing can differ widely from culture to culture depending on the way they determine social dominance. Consider the dominance patterns enacted in a simple family meal. Who sits at the head of the table? Who is served first? Who last? Who serves? Asking such questions can help you decode the hierarchical structure of the society to which the family belongs. In traditional Chinese society, for example, social dominance is determined by age. The extended families of the Chinese household, which can include three or more generations living in the same home, accordingly serve their meals in relays: the eldest eat first, then the next generation, on down to the youngest, who eat last. In Eskimo families, on the other hand, where children are especially highly valued, parents will go without food to ensure that their young will have something to eat in times of famine.

The culinary economy of the !Kung Bushmen of the Kalahari Desert—a hunter-gatherer culture from South-West Africa—represents the structure of a collectivist society where social dominance is organized strictly on sexual lines. Every day, the women of a !Kung group go out together to gather vegetable foodstuffs. The roots, berries, and nuts they find are taken home to be consumed by their individual families. But when the men, who are the hunters, return with meat (a fairly rare occurrence), this food is shared with all the members of the band. By sharing the kill, the !Kung ritually reinforce the collective identity of the group while at the same time reinforcing the privileged position of the men, who alone are permitted to hunt. It is therefore in no hunter's interest to keep his kill to himself or to his immediate family, because the meat he shares is less food than symbol, a sign of his prowess as a man and of his importance to the band as a whole.

In contemporary American society, men traditionally bring home the bacon and keep it there. This is a sign of a patriarchal society centered on the institution of the nuclear family: that is, Mom, Dad, and the kids, with Dad sitting at the head of the table and served by Mom. The fact that *Dad* ritually carves reenacts the privilege of the male "hunter." Thus, the rituals of the American table reinforce the structure of a society based on male dominance and interfamilial competition. Unlike the collectivist society of the !Kung bushmen, American capitalism treats the nuclear family as a nucleus of private consumption. Rather than sharing goods equally across society, American culture stimulates competing families to accumulate as many goods as they can in their own private hoards. With the exception of special charity dinners and public soup kitchens, eating in America is a matter for the individual and his or her immediate family. Its rituals are concerned with holding the nuclear family together on behalf of competitive consumption.

But while eating in America is a relatively private affair, we too have our rituals of food sharing outside the nuclear family, of hosting meals and receiving them in reciprocation. We invite our friends to dinner, our parents and in-laws, and our co-workers. When the boss invites us to dinner, we go into a cold sweat and are sure to attend. For each kind of meal there is a subtle list of rules. The meals we serve to our parents are designed to show that we have successfully left the nest and are coping on our own as adults. In-law meals more self-consciously try to convince our spouses' parents that their son or daughter didn't make a mistake—which can cause a good deal of anxiety for a daughter-in-law who fears that she can't live up to Mom's home cooking. Meals with our social superiors are especially anxious affairs in which we feel obliged to impress our guests. Only meals with intimate friends are relatively anxiety-free, because we feel that we have less need to communicate or "prove" anything through our menus.

The subtle etiquette of meal sharing is especially visible when its rules are broken. Our annoyance at the frequent guest who never offers a meal in return reflects our expectations that invitations to meals are to be reciprocated. The host who serves food that his guests cannot eat—for reasons of religion or health—violates the etiquette of hospitality. The guest who fails to turn up on time or refuses a dish for socially inadequate reasons ("Oh, I never eat iceberg lettuce with Wish-Bone dressing!") violates his or her side of the bargain, which is to appear at the hour specified and to accept whatever is served so long as it is reasonable. How often have you told your host or hostess that the meal was "delicious" when you were just barely able to eat it? Such is the power of the rules of meal sharing, rules that are designed not only for the sake of politeness but for the sake of social cohesion as well.

The Kwakiutl Indians of the Pacific Northwest have a particularly rigorous ritual designed to reinforce the social harmony—and hierarchy—of the tribe. At certain intervals, the richest members of the community throw a "potlatch," or gigantic gift-giving shindig, in which they may give away everything they own. Lavish feasts, mountains of blankets, tools, ornaments, canoes . . . everything is given—almost flung—away with what seems a reckless abandon. But the potlatch is not as self-sacrificing as it appears, because only the richest of the Kwakiutl can afford to give away so much, and each time they do so they reinforce bonds of obligation between themselves and those who receive their gifts. In social terms, it is indeed better to give than to receive, because giving confers power to the giver through the sense of indebtedness that gift-giving creates.

Things are not really so very different in American society. We too know about the obligation that comes with a gift, the requirement of something in return: either in kind, as in the return of a dinner invitation, or in the form of loyalty or service. And though we don't exactly throw potlatch parties, the rich and powerful tend to host extravagant entertainments to impress their guests with their power. For while wealth is not exactly equivalent to power—as Fitzgerald's Gatsby learns at the end of *The Great Gatsby*—it is usually a sign of power, because only socially powerful individuals can accumulate sufficient wealth to give it away lavishly.

There is one ritual meal in American life that does not ordinarily confer a sense of obligation: the Thanksgiving feast. Even more than the Christmas meal, which can blend in with the corporate rituals of the Christmas season and thus become part of a cycle of competitive party-giving, Thanksgiving is a clear symbol of a social harmony created and reinforced by the sharing of food. Like other traditional harvest festivals in which people for thousands of years have given thanks to their gods for the harvest, Thanksgiving in America has become less of a religious festival than a national one. Indeed, most of us are given the impression as children that America invented Thanksgiving, that the whole idea originated with the Pilgrims. In truth, the Pilgrim Thanksgiving was modeled on existing English models; only the turkey was new. But by treating Thanksgiving as an exclusively American meal, we reinforce our sense of ourselves as an especially blessed people, a prosperous paragon among nations. By sharing the Thanksgiving feast, Americans feel closer to other Americans. It is the one meal of the year in which the nuclear family is not in competition with all the rest.

Perhaps this is why Thanksgiving seems to be the most harmonious of our ritual meals. Everyone belongs at the Thanksgiving table: there are no religious restrictions as there are in the Christmas or Easter or Passover feasts. Indeed, part of the myth of the American Thanksgiving includes the relaxation of racial prejudices. The first Pilgrim Thanksgiving, as legend has it, included Amerindians as well as Europeans. Since the Thanksgiving meal is particularly associated with the sharing of food, it tends not to carry the sort of obligation that other dinner invitations may bear. It also doesn't suffer from the high expectations that have ruined so many Christmas feasts, causing family feuds and anxieties that may last a lifetime. Children often wish that every day could be Christmas: we'd probably be much better off with a perpetual Thanksgiving.

EATING IN THE FAST LANE

Thanksgiving, Christmas, Easter, Passover . . . all of these are prominent ritual feasts based on the calendar and centuries of religious observance. The symbolic meaning of the foodstuffs at such feasts is quite conservative, maintaining the same values over many years. For generations, the matzo, the bitter herbs, and the burnt lamb shank of the Jewish Seder have symbolized the Hebrews' suffering and redemption in ancient Egypt. The Seder also includes a ritual egg, but its meaning—like the meaning of Easter eggs and Easter bunnies—is even older, taking us all the way back to pagan fertility rites in which eggs and rabbits were symbols of spring rebirth and growth. The Thanksgiving turkey continues to signify "American-ness" and is the bird of choice for Thanksgiving dinners around the nation. But what about ordinary meals like the American breakfast, lunch, and dinner? What significance does the semiotician find in them?

Let's look at three fairly typical American breakfasts. The first includes bacon and eggs, toast and hashbrowns, oatmeal and coffee. The whole family participates: Mom, Dad, and the kids all seated around the home breakfast table. The second breakfast is far less crowded. Seated alone, a woman dressed in office clothes gulps at a glass of Carnation Instant Breakfast while clearing away the cereal bowls of her children, who have already departed for school. In our third breakfast, a young man and woman, both clad in business suits, share an Egg McMuffin breakfast with each other at McDonald's. They are not in any particular hurry and appear to be regulars in the restaurant. Now, what are these three breakfasts semiotic signs of?

First, ask yourself who would be most likely to be eating the kind of breakfast we see in breakfast number one. There's a lot of cooking to do here, and someone had to get up very early to do it. Also note how the whole family is together. In these days of long suburban commutes, when commuters must leave their homes early to arrive at work on time, it is no longer common for the family father to share the morning meal. Only a father who works close to home can be on hand for breakfast: someone like a farmer, or blacksmith, or rancher. And if Mom is to have time to cook this breakfast, she can't work outside the home herself. She could be an ordinary house-wife, but it's more likely that she's a farmer's wife, and indeed, my first example is intended to exemplify a typical farm break-fast, once the standard for American breakfasting but now a vanishing form of the meal.

The traditional farm breakfast is a vanishing meal largely because the economy on which it was based is vanishing (its high fat and cholesterol content has also contributed to its demise: the traditional farm breakfast simply isn't very good for you). Less than 5 percent of the American population lives on the land today —a fraction that is rapidly shrinking as giant agribusinesses drive family farmers off their farms—and the patterns of life that went with farming are going with it. Modern industrial and postindus-trial life has altered our ways of earning a living and reshaped the structures of the nuclear family, including the way that they eat their meals.

Breakfasts two and three are signs of the social and techno-logical changes that have transformed American life in the last century. Suburban fathers commuting by train or automobile to urban workplaces do not have the time in the morning to sit around with the family at breakfast. I remember how my father always got up first in the morning, drank a cup of coffee, and then headed off to his job, where, after a long drive, he would have a bite to eat in a cafeteria attached to his place of work. Then my mother got up, prepared her own breakfast, cleared it, and set out hot chocolate and toast for me. She headed off to her job while I headed off to school, and I wouldn't see either parent until dinnertime.

In semiotic terms, this symbolizes the new realities of the American household which began to emerge in the sixties and seventies. An historically unprecedented number of women entered into the permanent work force during this period, and the traditional nuclear family breakfast was modified accordingly. With far less time for the preparation of breakfast, America's working moms turned to convenience foods like Carnation Instant Breakfast, which reduced breakfast preparation time to the few seconds it takes to mix a packet of powder in a glass of milk. My second breakfast, accordingly, shows Mom drinking her liquid meal before setting off for work. Her children may have had the same breakfast, if Mom's not very sentimental, but if she is, modern technology has provided her with frozen waffles, instant eggs, and microwavable sausages that give the appearance of a traditional farm breakfast in a fraction of the time.

In the 1980s, breakfast left the home altogether for many Americans, especially for childless professional couples who commute to work together. In this third phase of the American breakfast, we find a culture that is increasingly turning to the workplace for its emotional satisfaction. Centering their lives on the office rather than on the home, many modern couples no longer have much use for the ritual of the home breakfast. Hence, breakfast number three, which shows two young professionals adopting a new breakfast ritual: the fast-food meal.

Once a source of quick lunches and snacks, today's fast-food restaurants have branched out to supply breakfast and dinner as well. No longer must we choose between hamburgers and cheeseburgers at fast-food outlets. Now salad bars and fancy entrées compete for our attention. Fast-food joints like McDonald's, Burger King, Wendy's, and Jack-In-The-Box have all begun to turn themselves into restaurants. Where it once appeared that fast food would fall victim to the natural-foods fad, it is now bigger than ever on the American scene.

Semiotically, the rise of fast food reflects sweeping changes in America's economic order. First, it is emblematic of a shift from a mixed agricultural and industrial economy to a predominantly service-oriented one. Every year, fewer and fewer Americans produce the things they use or the food they eat, while more and more of us earn our livings by serving one another. Breakfast at McDonald's is iconic: rather than producing our own breakfasts, we go out to be served.

More significantly, the trend toward fast-food dining reflects a breakdown of the traditional American social unit: the nuclear family. The family dining table was once an icon of familial integration. At breakfast, lunch, and especially at dinner, the American family gathers not only to eat but to engage in the central ritual of family life. At the dinner table, families talk about their days, make plans for the future, and generally communicate with one another. It is the one place where the entire family gathers together.

Fast food represents the ultimate decentering of the family meal. Though advertisements try to convince us that fast-food restaurants are great family dining sites, they are really scenes of social disintegration, places for lonely and hurried consumers to grab a quick meal. Formica booths and tables cannot assume the symbolic value of the family dining table. They do not hold the family together, they pull it apart.

What this will finally mean for the shape of American society is not yet clear, but there are some signs on the horizon. We have traditionally relied on the nuclear family to enforce our system of moral values, and the breakdown of that institution may well have a connection to our current social dilemmas. It seems that when meals go unshared, values go unshared as well. America's children are supposed to learn their values from their parents. Their knowledge of their history and culture is not only the responsibility of the schools. As the basic unit of American society, the nuclear family—centered on the homey dinner table— has traditionally borne the burden of holding that society together, and it cannot be superseded without threatening the social whole.

THE COMMERCIAL CORNUCOPIA

In the place of the traditional nuclear family, American society today is substituting the antisocial figure of the private consumer. "You *can* have it all," Michelob promises its customers, thus implying that having and consuming is much more desirable than sharing in the current American scene. Beneath the surface, this ad symbolizes the way we are becoming a society geared to product development and marketing rather than to social integration. Consumption is a lonely business carried on by individuals interested only in self-gratification. It is just the opposite of the rituals of food sharing.

We can read this message in the explosion of consumer products that the food industry has presented to us in the last few years. Let's start with a semiotic interpretation of a simple box of cereal. Kellogg's Just Right is just right for the purpose. Just Right is a lightly sweetened mixture of rolled oats, wheat flakes, almond slivers, and bits of fruit. It is also a sign. Here's how you can interpret it. First, ask yourself about the system in which it appears—that is, the place it holds within the world of commercially prepared breakfast cereals. It's a pretty small place, isn't it, given the enormous numbers of cereals that line the grocery shelves of America. Now ask yourself, has it always been this way? Not at all. Until the late nineteenth century, American mothers woke early to fire the stove and cook dishes of oatmeal, hasty pudding, gruel, or good old mush. Then W. K. Kellogg came along and invented the cornflake, the first ready-to-eat cold cereal. It was the first major blow against one of America's food traditions, an innovation that eventually liberated the housewife from her need to cook the morning meal.

Cold flaked cereal is, in the first place, a sign of American innovation, of impatience with tradition, of a desire to do things more quickly and more efficiently. But the fact that we have now added to Kellogg's original box of cornflakes boxes and boxes of Shredded Wheat, Crunch Berries, Cocoa Puffs, Cap'n Crunch— the list gets longer every year—testifies, semiotically, to the existence of another American trait: an insatiable desire for new products, and a capitalist will to stimulate that desire. Here's where Just Right cereal becomes particularly interesting. It first appeared as one of Kellogg's many contributions to the adult cereal market, a market that burgeoned through the 1980s as yesterday's cold cereal–fed baby boomers matured into today's adult consumers. Just Right competed with Kellogg's own Nutri-Grain line as well as with General Mills' Raisin Nut Bran, Post's Fruit & Fiber, and a great many other new, "adult" cereals. The very name of the new cereal tries to assure its adult market that here, at last, is a cereal that fits all desires: it's nutritious, has plenty of fiber (reflecting here the American obsession with fiber in the wake of Ronald Reagan's much-publicized brushes with colon cancer), and tastes good without being too sweet.

At first, Just Right was aimed at yuppie consumers, as you can tell from the models chosen for its first run of television commercials. Bright young men and women, dressed in preppie clothes and seated in gleaming kitchens, spoon down the cereal all by themselves, with no children—the traditional target of breakfast cereal ads—in sight. But such advertisements limited the market for the cereal. Seeking to broaden its consumer horizons, Kellogg's ran some new versions of the Just Right ads, featuring in one ad two elderly women arguing over which box of Just Right could really claim to be "just right," and in another, two college boys arguing over the sense of calling two slightly different cereals by the same name.

But no cereal in America's highly competitive breakfast food market will ever be just right. Kellogg's will introduce more and more cereals to compete both with its own existing lines and with the lines of all the other companies that have followed W. K. Kellogg's lead over the years. No cereal can be "just right" because that would imply that the cereal industry no longer needs to research and develop new cereals. In a capitalist economy fueled by consumer research and development, this would spell the end of the show.

We find the same message not only on the cereal shelves of our supermarkets but on the cookie, cracker, snack, and soft drink shelves as well. Root beer and Coca-Cola, the traditional American soft drinks, now share space with countless competitors: caffeinated and decaffeinated colas (diet or regular), citrus sodas, seltzers (flavored and unflavored), carbonated fruit drinks . . . there are just too many to keep track of. There is even one soft drink, Jolt Cola, that has exploited the ever-versatile ability of Americans to create product fads through the inversion of current fads. Jolt boasts of having twice the caffeine and all the sugar of a regular cola at a time when its competitors are taking out the caffeine and reducing calories. The appeal of a product like Jolt is similar to what we find in the anti-bumper-sticker trade. The "I don't care what you love," "I don't care what you'd rather be doing," or the "I don't care what your other car is" stickers apparently appeal to consumers who are tired of other people's bumpers. In America, it seems, you can sell anything.

The same story is being told in the cookie and cracker industry. Once there were saltines, and only saltines; then Nabisco introduced Ritz Crackers to jazz up the market. By now, there are so many flavors and varieties of snack crackers that supermarkets can't begin to stock them all. The "soft cookie" phenomenon tells a similar tale. Seeking to cash in on the explosive popularity of such gourmet cookie shops as Mrs. Fields and Famous Amos, Nabisco, Keebler, Duncan Hines, and Sunshine all rushed to market with upscale soft-cookie lines intended—once again!— for the ubiquitous yuppie market. The new cookies were intended to taste fresh-baked—thus appealing to a sophisticated adult taste for "personalized" cookies—but didn't quite make that standard. As I write, all of these soft-cookie lines are still selling at prices far below the intended market price, as their producers struggle to keep them moving. Maybe you can't sell just anything in America.

Such stories are waiting for you every day on your supermarket shelves, and they all bear a similar semiotic message about our country. Think of the energy that we put into the creation of new food products! All these cookies, crackers, soft drinks, and cereals have sprung from the feverish imaginations of some of the best and the brightest minds in today's corporate world. America is putting an inordinate proportion of its creative energy today into the development of consumer products, and *that* is perhaps the most sobering message of all that we can read in the sign language of the retail food market. Sheer consumption is taking the place of the traditional values of American society. If this means we are coming to prefer the private gratification of personal consumption to the social satisfaction of shared behavior, then we may well eventually lose our society itself in the bargain.

CHAPTER 9

Dress for Success: Meditations on the Dress Code

We know but few men, a great many clothes and breeches. Dress a scarecrow in your last shift, you standing shiftless by, who would not soonest salute the scarecrow?

Henry David Thoreau

In the mid-1970s there was a saying in the Boston State House that if you wanted to know how a legislator was going to vote you only needed to look at his shoes. Gucci-shod politicians, it was said, swung to the right; the L. L. Bean crowd leaned to the left. Similarly, when John Connally sought the Republican presidential nomination in 1980, his frequent campaign appearances in pin-striped three-piece business suits were understood to signify his allegiance to the business vote, while Jimmy Carter's cardigan sweaters were interpreted as a sign of his identification with the "common folk." Indeed, the whole election campaign that year could have been described as a contest of wardrobes, with Ronald Reagan taking the prize by donning several different costumes, each one calculated to appeal to a different constituency. Like

Connally, Reagan often sported the navy blue pinstripes of corporate America, but he also appeared in vaguely ill-fitting suits, like those worn in the Carter campaign—a uniform preferred by Middle American voters suspicious of the sharply tailored Ivy League look of the Kennedy clan. Not to neglect the Western vote, Reagan also made cowboy clothing a regular part of his campaign wardrobe, often appearing in boots, a Stetson, a checked shirt, and a range jacket.

A suit of clothes, any politician can tell you, is more than a mere covering: it is a signaling system, a language with which we communicate to one another our feelings, our political beliefs, and, perhaps most importantly of all, our sense of group identity. Of all the signaling systems that surround us, none is more readily understood, and readily "spoken," than the language of our clothes, a language whose vocabulary extends all the way from the distinctive tartan of a Scottish clan to the Mao jackets and caps of China's Cultural Revolution, from the chadors of Islamic fundamentalism to the black leather of a motorcycle outlaw. But though the language of clothes is spoken in every nation on earth, it is nowhere as dynamic and complex as it is in America.

The complexity of the dress code in America, the astonishing range of styles that are available to us in our choice of clothing signs, directly reflects the cultural diversity of our country. Americans are differentiated by ethnic, regional, religious, and racial differences that are all expressed in the clothing they wear. Age differences, political differences, class differences, and differences in personal taste further divide us into finer and finer subcultures that maintain, and even assert, their sense of distinct identity through their characteristic clothing. From the severe black suits of the Amish to the safety-pinned T-shirts and chains of punk culture, Americans tell one another who they are through the articles of their dress.

There is something almost totemic in the way we use our clothing to communicate our sense of group identity. By simply donning the appropriate totems, we can announce who we are and with whom we identify. Long hair, patched jeans, and colorful beads, for example, were among the totemic emblems of the flower children of the 1960s, while Sperry Top-siders, polo shirts, and the Izod alligator became the official totems of preppiedom in the 1970s. And in the 1980s, the buttoned-down totems of such corporate giants as IBM—dark blue suits, white shirts, and conservative ties—have become the clothing icons of a nation of anxious job seekers, each one signaling his or her eagerness to enter into the corporate world by wearing the proper uniform.

The totemic power of our clothing is so strong that we will often trust someone merely because he or she is wearing the clothing of our own particular group. When a person's appearance corresponds to our own, we feel that he or she shares our values and belongs to a kind of extended family whose emblems are codified in their clothes. When we say that someone has dressed appropriately or well, we usually mean that he or she has dressed in a way that reflects *our beliefs* and values. Dress, in other words, can often be a kind of mirror in which we look for our own reflection, and if we don't find it there we tend to reject the wearer.

Our tendency to judge a person's character and values by his or her dress can backfire, of course. Unwary investors will put their life's savings into the hands of a glib-talking con artist in a three-piece suit simply because he "looks" trustworthy. On the other hand, there's always the legend of Apple Computer's Steven Jobs, who was refused financial backing by his employers at Atari because he just didn't look the part of an entrepreneurial tycoon. The top brass took one look at his long hair, beard, and sandals and sent him packing.

It's easy to send deceptive signals with your dress, or to be deceived by someone's appearance, because clothing, like verbal language, doesn't have to tell the truth. In principle, anyone can counterfeit membership in a group simply by adopting its clothing. In the past, societies have attempted to *make* clothing tell the truth by passing regulations—called "sumptuary laws"—that strictly defined just which fashions were permissible to which rank of society. In ancient Rome, for example, purple was the totemic color of aristocratic clothing, so no one below the royal level was permitted to wear purple. The wearing of long hair was an aristocratic privilege in the Middle Ages, and so medieval peasants were required to wear their hair cut short. When clothes really made the man, to dress in the styles reserved for another rank was a serious offense.

The fact that we have no sumptuary laws in America reflects a very different social and ideological order. Believing in the sanctity of social opportunity and mobility, democratic cultures like our own not only allow their citizens to wear the dress of ranks higher than those they are born in but may even encourage them to do so, because the adoption of high-status dress can signify one's desire to move up the social ladder. A poor man who looks for a job dressed in a business suit is not generally sneered at: his clothing is read as a sign of his serious—and legitimate—desire to enter the corporate world. In bourgeois societies, the low-status individual asks not "what must I wear to express my present place in society?" but "what must I wear to improve my place?" And so, in place of sumptuary laws, America has substituted libraries full of "Dress for Success" books, instruction guides designed to initiate their readers into the intricacies of the corporate dress code—and, by extension, into the secrets of corporate America itself.

The fact that the "Dress for Success" industry is almost exclusively concerned with the required dress for corporate success is itself a sign of the power that the corporation holds in American life. Other professions—medicine, law, academia—have their own dress codes, but even they look to corporate dress as their model. Established university professors, for example, can pretty well wear what they like, but graduate students seeking their first academic position tend to play it safe by dressing up in corporate pinstripes and three-piece suits for their job interviews. As Calvin Coolidge once said, the business of America is business, and (for better or for worse) business calls the shots when it comes to the working standards of white-collar American dress.

Corporate America takes its power and prerogatives very seriously and so is especially self-conscious about the dress of those who belong to its ranks. There are even gradations within the system designed to express one's precise place in the corporation. Entry-level job seekers, male and female alike, are encouraged to dress more conservatively—in the corporate sense—than those who have already arrived. In the January 1988 issue of *Glamour*, for example, Joyce Grillo—who is the president of her own corporate consulting firm, Impression Management—notes that while a navy blazer suit may say "take me seriously" when worn by a management trainee, "it can make an experienced manager look insecure, too wet behind the ears for her high-powered position." *Glamour* accordingly suggests bold, double-breasted pantsuits for the experienced manager, topped off by print blouses worn open at the neck over a turtleneck jersey.

The fact that fashion magazines like *Glamour* now contain the same sort of advice that has traditionally been given to young men eager to succeed in business is a clear sign of the changes in the work force that have taken place over the past twenty years. Women are entering the workplace in unprecedented numbers, and the corporate dress code has responded by modifying its precepts just enough to accommodate women. But not much: corporate women, especially those just beginning their careers, pretty much have to dress like corporate men. Their suits, blouses, and "ties"—the ubiquitous red foulard—are all feminine versions of existing masculine standards. The dress code for the corporate woman tells her that she must at once be feminine, but not too feminine (where "feminine" means sexy or frilly), and masculine, but not too masculine (that is, aggressive or threatening). Such restrictions signal the uneasy compromise the traditionally male bastion of the corporate world has made with the would-be businesswoman: she must neither threaten nor tantalize the men she will work with, and while she must appear to be like one of the guys, she must not forget that she's a woman.

Yet *Glamour*'s differing recommendations, one for the novice and another for the veteran executive, signify a certain self-consciousness in the corporate world about the rigidity of its prescriptions. It appears that one of the privileges of success in the corporate world is the right to a little freedom and variety in one's dress. But you have to earn such privileges, and to do that you have to pass through a sort of initiation, symbolized by a dutiful acceptance of a severely conservative corporate uniform. Once you have proven your willingness to conform, to be a team player, you can then hope to rise to a position in which your clothes can be more personally expressive. But to get to that level, you must first learn what is required of the initiate.

Semiotically, "Dress for Success" books are an indicator of a hidden cultural bias. The chapter titles of John T. Molloy's *The Women's Dress for Success Book*— "Instant Clothing Power for the Business Woman," "The Success Suit," and "Packaging Yourself"—clearly reveal the importance that "wardrobe engineers" place on self-marketing as the ticket to corporate power and success. "You are what you wear" is the message of such books, and you can be whatever you want to be just by choosing the right clothes—choices that have been made for you by wardrobe consultants who have interviewed hundreds of corporate personnel officers and executives to see which styles succeed and which fail.

But while every "Dress for Success" book will tell you what colors work and what colors don't, which blouses project authority and which make a woman look like a sex object, and even which kind of raincoat to wear and which to save for weekends, they do not tell you *why* these styles and not others have come to assume the authority they bear. Such books aren't concerned with your knowing the semiotics of the corporate dress code: they only tell you how to conform to it, treating its prescriptions as if they were the inevitable styles of the corporate animal, as "natural" as a tiger's stripes or a lion's mane.

If you accept the prescriptions of the corporate dress code as both "natural" and inevitable, then you have been taken in by them. Remember the unwritten law of semiotics: thou shalt not be hoodwinked. The corporate dress code is not natural; it has a long history behind it that conceals an ideological system that precedes the birth of the corporation. To discover that ideology, we have to explore its history.

THE IDEOLOGY OF CORPORATE DRESS

The first question a semiotician would want to ask a "wardrobe engineer," then, is not "what colors work best in the office?" but "why do business people always seem to prefer blue, black, or gray suits, white shirts or blouses, and neatly trimmed hair?" "Why do they avoid bright colors?" To answer that question, we have to go back to seventeenth-century England to look at a social conflict whose outcome has had profound implications for our country's economic history, as well as for the clothing that we wear to the office.

This conflict was a battle of styles, one in which two major forces fought for the political, religious, and cultural control of England. These forces were the Royalist "Cavaliers," who favored King Charles I, and the Puritans, who controlled the House of Commons and were led by Oliver Cromwell. The Cavaliers were high-living aristocrats who followed the relatively mild moral teachings of the Anglican Church. They were flamboyant dressers who enjoyed the latest Parisian fashions—brightly colored clothing, feathered hats, and long flowing hair. Their Puritan opponents, known as the "Roundheads" because of their closely cropped hair, were severe Calvinists whose religious beliefs forbade all frivolous pleasures, including colorful and ornamental clothing. Puritan dress was plain and sober, restricted to dark suits and dresses and white shirts and collars.

The Cavaliers dominated England politically through the 1620s and 1630s, which prompted many Puritans to immigrate to the northern colonies of America, especially Massachusetts. But in the 1640s, the Puritans began a civil war with the Cavaliers, and by 1649 the Puritan leader, Oliver Cromwell, had routed the royalist forces and had executed the king. The king's son, eventually to become Charles II, fled to France to set up a court in exile, while many other Cavaliers immigrated to the

New World, particularly to the southern colonies where they were far from the strict-living Puritans. For ten years, England was ruled by Calvinistic leaders who frowned on all forms of pleasure and entertainment—Cromwell closed England's theaters —and set a sober tone for the nation.

But though they won the war, the Puritans fell quickly from power after Cromwell's death in 1658 because they lacked popular support. Cromwell's Calvinistic rule was just too severe for merry old England, and in 1660 the nation rejected the Puritan regime and invited Charles II back to rule, thereby launching a cultural celebration known as the Restoration, a period of some twenty-five years characterized by the spiciness of its literature, social behavior, and fashions. Long hair, brightly colored suits and dresses, low-cut necklines, and luxurious fabrics came back into fashion, as the sober-clad Puritans went into social and political decline. For almost two hundred years, English Puritans were treated as second-class citizens, excluded from holding public office or attending a university, but they maintained their culture and their beliefs—including their severe dress code.

Eventually, the Puritans had their revenge. For the Puritans' belief in thrift and industry—often referred to as the "Protestant Work Ethic"—as well as their habits of temperance and self-denial enabled them to take advantage of the opportunities for economic advancement that came with the Industrial Revolution in the late eighteenth century. Both in America and England, the thrifty descendants of the Puritans built the foundations of modern corporate capitalism while the descendants of the Cavaliers looked on without quite realizing what was happening. By the middle of the nineteenth century, the heirs of Cromwell had turned the tables in England by becoming richer than their hereditary opponents through industry and trade. Ever since, England has been a bourgeois, rather than an aristocratic, nation, a country whose lingering royalty are only figureheads.

This political and economic victory was also a victory of *style*. When the descendants of the Puritans came to control the economic life of England and America (a victory in the United States that was underscored by the industrial North's defeat of the Cavalier South in our Civil War), they brought with them their old customs and beliefs—even if they no longer held to the strict Calvinistic ideology of their ancestors. Indeed, the Protestant Work Ethic, which began as an expression of the Puritans' belief that hard work and spiritual grace were intimately related, had by the nineteenth century become a belief in the more materialistic precept that hard work leads to worldly wealth and not only to otherworldly salvation. But the sober dress of the Calvinists remained the norm for the corporate capitalist because it was the sort of dress to which the founders of English and American capitalism were accustomed. Black broadcloth became the badge of the Victorian businessman.

We have inherited from the nineteenth century our basic sense of proper businesswear. The plainly cut blues, browns, and grays of the corporate dress code have been institutionalized by what is by now an unconsciously Calvinistic scorn for color and ornament. Pinstripes, red suspenders, single- or double-breasted jacket alternatives, colored dress shirts . . . all these variations in the code that appear from time to time always revolve around a fundamental axis of seriousness and sobriety. The time when gentlemen could wear colorful suits and feathered hats is now, like the Cavalier society celebrated in Margaret Mitchell's famous novel, gone with the wind.

THE RISE AND FALL OF PETER MAX

American men—and now women as well—have been dominated by the concealed ideology of the corporate dress code throughout this century. "The man in the gray flannel suit" became, in fact, something of a cultural icon in the 1950s. But in the late 1960s and early 1970s, American men—led, to a certain extent, by their children and by Peter Max—launched a fashion rebellion and appear to have torn down the bastions of traditional business dress, if only briefly. In reaction against the standard-issue brown, gray, or navy, and wool, cotton, or flannel suits they had always worn, American men began to experiment, albeit cautiously, with the sorts of colors, fabrics, and styles that the young were wearing. Whereas narrow detailing dominated the Ivy League dress code of the 1950s, wide lapels, broad, flowing ties, and bell-bottom trousers became increasingly common features of male fashion by the early 1970s. (It is worth noting that the Ivy League, and the style that derives from it, has its center at Harvard and Yale universities, schools that were founded in the seventeenth century to train Calvinist ministers.) White shoes and belts appeared as alternatives to traditional brogues, while polyester knits in a rainbow of light blues, greens, and beiges began to compete with the gray flannel orthodoxy. Hair became a little longer, sideburns common. And, for a short time, it appeared that the tie might lose the literal and figurative hold that it has traditionally had on American men, when turtleneck shirts and sweaters made a brief bid for control of the well-dressed neck.

In its time this was all rather revolutionary stuff. While staunch sartorial conservatives like my grandfather held firm against all such departures from tradition, their sons didn't. I was a little surprised when, in the early 1970s, my own father abandoned his traditional black and gray suits for some blue "double-knit" trousers and jackets, bought white shoes and wide ties, and grew a set of sideburns. But I now realize that his new clothes signified a desire in American men to free themselves from the tyranny of the corporate dress code, to try something different. And though the most extreme experiments during this period—like the notorious Nehru jacket and medallion—failed spectacularly, the general trend toward color and variety spread across the nation. What we might call watered-down Peter Max became a Rotarian standard, a staple of men's dress.

The fashion experiments of the 1960s and '70s were possible because of the declining prestige of the corporate world during the so-called "greening of America." "Uptight" dress signified an uptight mind in an era when middle-class Americans began to explore more liberated, even spiritual, lifestyles. The fact that

Americans in the 1980s have been obsessed with *conforming* to the severest dictates of the orthodox corporate dress code is a sign, then, of the resurgent popular prestige of the corporation in Ronald Reagan's America. The decade came in with a recession that put a halt to the loose-spending, loose-living 1970s and led to a new pro-business climate that welcomed a return to the most conservative elements of corporate dress. American men and women now even seem to enjoy a corporate clothing regime that would have been seen as tyrannous just ten years ago.

Since the corporate world values aggressiveness and acquisitiveness over social concern or spiritual development, we hear a great deal about "power suits" today. Whereas the notorious Nehru jackets of the sixties reflected an American desire to try on Indian spiritualism along with Indian fashions, all the talk about "power suits" signifies an enthusiastic if often unconscious acceptance of corporate materialism.

VIVE LA DIFFERENCE

By probing into the ideological history behind a particular system like the corporate dress code, we can answer the semiotic question "Where did this system come from?" But semioticians also ask other questions when they look at a fashion system. For example, how do we know whether an article of clothing is fashionable or not fashionable? The question is not so simple as it sounds. The fact that a suit is blue, for example, doesn't necessarily make it a fashionable business suit. You can don a blue polyester business suit with a rayon tie and look like a business yokel. We might say that the broad strokes are correct in such an outfit, but the details are wrong. So we must use a finer, more microscopic focus when we interpret the relative fashionableness or unfashionableness of an article of clothing.

In his pioneering book *Système de la Mode* (*The Fashion System*) Roland Barthes explores the precise procedures with which we determine the fashion status of a garment. Barthes analyzes the captions printed beneath the photographic displays featured in two leading French women's magazines from the early 1960s, *Elle* and *Jardin des Modes*. Rather than concentrating on the dresses as they appear in the photographs, however, Barthes scrutinizes the particular features of each dress that the captions call to our attention—for example, "Prints win at the races" or "Slim piping is striking." By focusing his attention on the details emphasized in the captions—"prints," "piping"—Barthes demonstrates that the overall structure of a garment, the fact that it is a dress or a jacket or a shirt or whatever, is less significant in the world of fashion than the little ways in which dresses, jackets, shirts, and so on can differ at the level of detail. What makes a dress fashionable in a given year, for instance, is not the fact that it is a dress but that it has slim piping. Because the basic forms of the garments we wear are relatively conservative—twentieth-century menswear is really not very different from that of the nineteenth century, for instance—fashion must look to relatively subtle differences to determine what is going to be fashionable this year and what is not.

Barthes's point is that a fashion system is entirely arbitrary. To find out what is fashionable and what is not, you just have to read the magazines in which the lords of fashion publish their pronouncements. If *short* skirts are in, a *long* skirt may be out. If *natural* fabrics—wool, silk, cotton—are called for this year, then a *synthetic* garment will signal "unfashionable." No fashion detail, in other words, means anything in itself. Fashion details only signify with respect to their relative presence or absence in a garment. Of course, the situation is complicated because one garment contains a number of different details, such as fabric, cut, and color. But the point is that the fundamental elements of the fashion code, the details that make the fashion message, are essentially meaningless in themselves. Instead, they build their meanings by virtue of their differences from other fashion alternatives.

Barthes's account of the semiotic workings of the fashion system is not a complete one, however, for Barthes does not establish the connection between fashion and culture. The fact, for instance, that the fashions he analyzes in *The Fashion System* are arbitrarily cut off from any functional requirements (for example, the print on one's dress has no effect on its usefulness) signifies a social message that Barthes misses: namely, that the women who wear them are considered as ornamental rather than functional members of their society. In other words, changes in women's fashions can be entirely arbitrary when women aren't expected to be anything more than fashion plates, and this itself is a cultural sign.

But in a society in which women are a major part of the work force, the design of their clothes does matter. Looking again at the January 1988 issue of *Glamour* magazine, we can find, for example, a spread on the "10 Best Fashion Moves to Make Now," all of which are addressed to working women to whom the details of their clothes are functionally important. The functional significance of the clothes featured is implicitly announced by the copy with which the spread begins: "Here, ten pages of the best moves going—fresh, flattering clothes that offer value through versatility. The constants you'll see: day-into-night shapes, building-block pieces that mix beautifully with the clothes you already own, transseasonal fabrics that will tempt you to reach for these clothes well into summer (and again next September)."

Now, the fact that *Glamour* stresses a "fresh" and "flattering" rather than a "traditional" look for their recommended styles sends the familiar message that women are expected to wear new designs each year (a man can get away with the same suit for quite some time so long as it's neat and clean) and that their clothes are supposed to show them off (again, men are not required to wear flattering clothing, though they may, as magazines like *Gentleman's Quarterly* insist). But that these clothes are also said to offer "value" and "versatility" sends a different sort of message, one suited to single working women who have to make a few dollars go a long way in their clothing budgets. Versatile as well as flattering, *Glamour*'s ten best fashion moves incorporate function with ornament to answer the needs of a growing market of businesswomen.

Fashion, then, does reflect social realities. Styles are not necessarily arbitrary and, as in the case of *Glamour*'s recommendations, may well respond to the needs of those who buy them. Styles that "mix beautifully with clothes you already own" and "put a premium on comfort" reflect the functional needs of career women. Even magazines like *Cosmopolitan*, traditionally a magazine for women whose identity is largely sexual, can reflect the changing roles available to women in American society.

Open an issue of *Cosmopolitan* from the 1950s or 1960s, and you'll see reflected an era before women commonly pursued careers. We find in the December 1966 issue an article on "The Young Male Executive," but the closest a woman comes to the working world in this issue is summed up in the essay "Why Be a Maid? Hire One Instead." In this feature, housewives are encouraged to get their husbands to hire maids for them so they can have more time to "swing." And if her husband hasn't the money for a maid, the bored housewife is advised to "work—not full time necessarily, and certainly not at something you don't want to do," but solely for the money necessary to hire a domestic. There is no suggestion that a woman might find self-fulfillment in a career: only some petty cash. The rest of the issue is devoted to problems on the order of "What the Pill is Doing to Husbands" and to features like "Phyllis Diller's Housekeeping Hints" (she doesn't have a maid?). Perhaps the attitude in the 1960s toward women's work is best summed up in an article in the October 1966 *Cosmo*—"A Different Job Every Day?"—by a woman who leaves her regular job to become a Manpower, Inc., temporary so she can meet more men on the job. Women's work, such stories tell their readers, is sex; only men belong in the marketplace for its own sake.

Switch to *Cosmo* of the late 1980s, and you'll find the magazine governed by a changing set of social realities. The December 1987 and January 1988 issues, for example, still include articles on traditional subjects like "What Lovemaking Can Do for You" and "Sexual Guilt: When He Seduces and Doesn't Call Back."

But they also contain fashion features on a "Computer Analyst's Soft Wear" and advice for the laid off, "Good Girl, Good Job, Good-Bye: The Ordeal of Getting Fired." In such articles, *Cosmo*'s blithe spirit turns serious, responding to the pressures that women are now experiencing as they enter into what was once an all-male preserve. The spirit of the magazine has remained the same, but to stay competitive in the magazine industry, even *Cosmopolitan* has had to bow to the pressures of a changing fashion, and hidden social, code.

BEYOND THE BOARDROOM

Fashion, of course, does not live by bread alone. Beyond the conservative and monolithic codes of the corporate world, there are dress codes for sportswear and weekend wear, for high fashion and formal attire, and for children and teenagers. Noncorporate fashions, which appear to change from year to year at the mere whim of Parisian, Italian, Japanese, and American fashion designers, may appear devoid of any underlying cultural significance. Fashion designers usually see themselves as artists, not ideologues, with the human body as their canvas. But though they often appear to dictate to us what it is that we will wear this year or that, their commands are often merely *responses* to already-existing popular values and desires. Popular culture, in other words, calls the shots in the fashion world far more often than its apparent overlords would have it appear.

Take Ralph Lauren's and Calvin Klein's turns toward the "classics" in their 1970s and 1980s clothing lines. "Classic," in the fashion world, is often code for "British": the styles preferred by upper-class Englishmen and -women. Filling America's store shelves and racks with the khaki trousers, argyle sweaters, polo shirts, Fairisle sweaters, plaid kilt skirts, and venerable tweeds of the country gentleman and gentlewoman, Klein and Lauren have led an American fashion trend that has appropriated the style, tone, and imagery of exclusive English society. The designers of such clothes didn't hit on this trend by accident, however; they've been responding to a broad-based desire in America to possess the characteristic icons of English aristocrats.

America's desire to "go British" reflects a profound change in our cultural consciousness. In the 1950s, American casual clothing often sent a message that was at once democratic and suburban. The Bermuda shorts, Hawaiian-print shirts, clam-diggers, and capris of the era were the insignia of middle-class men and women enjoying the prosperity of a postwar economic boom. Such clothes expressed a democratic version of the American dream, a belief in the suburban standard of living that had been put within reach of an unprecedented number of Americans. A man wearing Bermuda shorts in his backyard is not trying to signal his desire for social superiority: he is saying, "Look, I wear a business suit all week so I can afford a place where my family and I can be comfortable and secure." Rather than sending competitive messages with their casual clothing, in other words, middle-class Americans in the fifties wanted to fit in with other suburbanites who were generally living the same sort of lives.

The suburban ideal, of course, survived into the 1960s (as it continues into the present), but it was challenged then by many of the children of the fifties, to whom the relatively modest desires of the suburbs began to appear elitist. So rather than dressing up, casual fashions in the sixties dressed down. Denim, the traditional cloth of proletarian dress, became an icon of middle-class attire. Blue jeans, boots, and work shirts went from the construction site to the classroom and, yes, occasionally the boardroom. By the end of the decade, you didn't have to be a member of the counterculture to wear Levi's.

But while it's important to recognize that little gets lost in the vocabulary of casual dress, and that Bermuda shorts and blue jeans are still essential "terms" in many American wardrobes, the dominant casual clothing trends of the late 1970s and the 1980s have been *upwardly* mobile, expressing a desire to climb to the very top of the social heap. Polo shirts sporting silhouettes of Prince Charles swinging at a ball, Hunt Club fashion lines that recall the spirit of fox-hunting aristocrats, and the adoption of English public school rep ties for American businesswear all adapt upper-class British icons to American middle-class desires.

The prestige and popularity of upper-class British fashions in the 1970s and 1980s reflect the economic pressures and uncertainties of the times. Continued inflation through the seventies squeezed the middle class, making it more difficult to enter its ranks from below and much easier to fall out of it. The recession of the early eighties drove the lower end of the middle class into the under classes, while the stock market boom drove the upper end into the stratosphere. The good old American middle class split in two, essentially, a center that even now barely holds.

It is during such times that people most want to express their status, or their desired status, through their clothing. When the middle class was economically secure, as in the 1960s, dressing down expressed a certain moral uneasiness about middle-class affluence. It's easy to affect poverty when you're in no real danger of falling into it. But now it's all too easy to fall into the under class, so it has become much more important to put up a good front. Wealth is more valued when it is concentrated in fewer hands, so many of the same middle-class Americans who dressed down in the 1960s to express their solidarity with the working classes are now dressing up to enhance their competitive edge in a cutthroat economy.

PUNK AND NEW WAVE

Side by side with the resurgence of classic styles in the 1970s and 1980s, there has been a simultaneous borrowing of quite a different set of clothing icons from across the Atlantic: the emblems of the so-called "punk" movement. Though now a popular, if fading, look among suburban teens, punk originated in the slums of London as a protest against the English establishment. Like millions of teens before them, punks turned to rock music as a way of expressing themselves and rebelling against parental authority, but unlike the rockers of the early 1960s who emerged from the slums of Liverpool and Manchester—the Beatles, the Rolling Stones, and the Who—the punks rebelled against the established rock world as well.

For by the early 1970s, the rebels of the 1960s had become a powerful establishment in their own right, the well-heeled overlords of multimillion-dollar empires. The punks rejected commercial rock music to develop a raw musical style of their own, complete with an anarchic fashion code that rejected everything that the rock 'n' rollers of the sixties had stood for. Dyed, spiked, and mohawked hair had something in it to offend everyone, but it was particularly challenging to the leaders of the rock world who had equated long hair with an "Aquarian" spirit of harmony in the 1960s. Punk rockers would have nothing of such peace-and-love tactics. "All You Need Is Love," the Beatles had said. "All you need is blood," the punks answered, getting into sadomasochistic getups to express exactly what they thought of the spirit of free love. Intensely cynical, disillusioned by a cycle of poverty that trapped the English working class throughout the 1970s, the punks sported bloodstained T-shirts, safety pins in their ears and noses, S & M leather, and chains to show how, in a violent world, they chose violence.

Punk came to America in the mid-1970s with such rock bands as Sid Vicious and the Sex Pistols, where it appealed to American teens who were also looking for a style of their own, a way to distinguish themselves from their older brothers and sisters. Garry Trudeau characterized the new generation's desire for self-identity in his cartoon strip *Doonesbury*, where he created a younger brother for Michael Doonesbury—that quintessential child of the sixties—who becomes a punk rocker much to the uncomprehending amazement of both his mother and older brother.

In rebellion against the "flower children" of the previous generation, American punks often adopted a style that made them look like *abused* children. I had a particularly good opportunity to witness the clash of the generations one night in Cambridge, Massachusetts, when I stopped by a coffeehouse dedicated to the folk music of the early 1960s. There I found an audience full of aging flower children, many of them balding and spreading at the waist, but all emanating the mellow vibes of their youth. In the midst of this celebration of times gone by, a fifteen-year-old kid appeared dressed in dirty shorts that were far too small, high-top sneakers, and horn-rimmed eyeglasses. With his short hair, tight, short-sleeved shirt (it was snowing outside), and snarling expression, he looked like a brutalized child with a chip on his shoulder. He was trying to get a rise out of everyone in the house by shouting violent slogans, but even *ex-* flower children don't fight. In the end, he just gave up and stomped out, having at least put in an appearance, waving the rising flag of punkdom among the relics of another age.

But if the punk look originally expressed the rage of working-class kids who felt left out by the rock establishment, it soon entered into the mainstream, where it evolved into a new style that came to be known as "New Wave." If punk rocker Sid Vicious went out in a blaze of sordid glory, his New Wave descendants—bands like Blondie, Talking Heads, and the Pretenders—were much more cautious, adopting punk's cynical toughness but not its uncompromising violence. New Wave artists like Cyndi Lauper took the punks' dyed hair and made it fashionable for middle-class girls who could buy commercially produced wash-away cellophane rinses that enabled them to be a little outrageous without burning their bridges. Lots of girls began wearing their underwear *over* their clothing, less to rebel against their parents than to imitate Madonna. Hard-core punks, in short, essentially disappeared in the 1980s, to be replaced by playful New Wave entertainers.

Whereas the punk movement represented a wholesale rejection of contemporary culture, its New Wave descendants are fascinated by its imagery, electing to parody rather than remake the imagery of an epoch dominated by television. Parody is the ironic imitation of something, a mocking impersonation that requires a keen interest in the imitated object, modified by a sense of distance. For example, Debbie Harry, former lead singer for Blondie, imitates Marilyn Monroe, not to make people think she is another Marilyn but to parody the way the media have transformed Monroe into a cultural fetish. Elvis Costello, with his pompadour haircut and heavy horn-rimmed eyeglasses, parodies Buddy Holly and Elvis Presley, at once imitating their style while putting himself at an ironic distance from it. New Wave composer and film maker David Byrne's movie *Stop Making Sense* parodies documentary television to show how superficial and fatuous the media age can be.

The whole point of New Wave, in other words, is to parody the popular images and values of mass culture by proclaiming that nothing, not even nihilism, is to be taken seriously. New Wave presents itself as an ironic commentary on a society dominated by television and the corporations that control it, but it makes no attempt to change that society. Although appearing cool, ironic, and detached on the surface, New Wave is, in fact, often the servant of the corporate world, providing it with styles that can both move and create products. The highly stylized, manneristic advertisements for Calvin Klein's Obsession, for example, are essentially New Wave mini-dramas peopled by figures who seem to recall the appearance and behavior of characters out of the lush world of F. Scott Fitzgerald. Teasing the audience with suggestions of incestuous infatuation, while at the same time being a staged put-on that you can't take too seriously, the Obsession commercials both parody and preserve the styles of aristocratic decadence (see chapter 11 for a discussion of the connections between New Wave and postmodern culture).

THE DESTINY OF THE AVANT-GARDE

The evolution of punk anarchism into the chic, commercially exploitable images of New Wave illustrates one of the paradoxes of avant-garde fashions: what begins life as an icon of rebellion eventually returns as the insignia of mainstream culture. To illustrate this point in the semiotics classes I teach at UCLA, I often present to my students the following verbal portrait. Imagine a man dressed in a pale blue polyester sports jacket with four-inch lapels, white slacks slightly belled, a wide-collared yellow shirt, and a broadly flowing acrylic tie. His hair creeps just over the tops of his ears and is complemented by sideburns that reach just to the bottom of his ear lobes. Now, I ask my students, what kind of person is he? What are his politics?

When I asked these questions in the early- to mid-1980s, my students almost invariably told me that my imaginary fashion dummy was probably a midwestern Republican—a bit backward, provincial, maybe even a member of the Moral Majority. They were on the right track, because my hypothetical fashion dummy is modeled after a photograph of the charismatic Pentecostal preacher Jim Bakker taken in 1977, and through the early 1980s, such dress was standard evangelical fare. But if I had described the same fashion dummy in 1967, my students' response might have been far different. For in 1967, sideburns and bellbottoms, wide lapels, and brightly colored shirts and jackets were the emblems of the Beatles' "Sgt. Pepper" phase, and they signified a revolutionary departure from the traditional buttoned-down, narrow-cut, colorless suits that even the Beatles wore in their early years.

What was once a revolutionary fashion has thus become a common feature of mainstream, even reactionary, dress. Such is the fate of many an avant-garde style, which progresses by reacting against whatever is in fashion in the culture at large. When Middle American men in the mid-1970s adopted what were essentially Peter Max motifs—wide lapels and wide ties—avant-garde designers decreed pencil-thin ties and ultranarrow lapels. Politicians, who follow the mainstream, dumped their Ivy League suits—which are characteristically narrow in cut—and adopted the sort of loosely fitting, wide-lapeled suits that Gerald Ford and Jimmy Carter wore in the 1976 election. High fashion may have insisted on a return to narrowness, but a politician who follows high fashion will never win high office in this country.

Sometimes a new fashion fad can appear overnight. Consider the fuss over Oliver North during the Iranscam hearings, a popular infatuation that promised to produce its own "Ollie" look—complete with Marine Corps haircuts with a boyish curl over one brow and an olive-drab suit—until the whole thing fizzled once North completed his testimony and went out of the public eye. But though the "Olliemania" that swept the country for a few weeks in the summer of 1987 didn't go anywhere, it was a reflection of a larger cultural trend toward military fashions. For long before Oliver North entered the scene, Richard Gere had already popularized military haircuts in *An Officer and a Gentleman*. The thousands of teenaged boys in America who began to cut their hair in the early 1980s as if they were about to enter boot camp signified the Hollywood-style glamour that now surrounds the U.S. military. When memories of war were fresh, as in the aftermath of Vietnam, military styles were definitely out. Had an Oliver North shown up at the Watergate hearings, his gung-ho, anti-Communist demeanor would have provoked scorn, not a fashion flash in the pan. Americans remembering the scars of battle—whether at Khe San or Kent State—were not apt to glorify soldiers eager for war.

But that was fifteen years ago, and a long stretch of peace has prompted a militaristic nostalgia in the land, a belief that we can make ourselves supreme in the world again by rattling our sabers. Here the Pentagon embraces Hollywood, which compliantly produces films like *Top Gun* and *Red Dawn*, which in turn leads to further militaristic fashion fads. Marine Corps haircuts turn up on college freshmen who haven't the slightest intention of joining up. The college freshman may think only of how stylish he looks. A semiotician notices just how much we have forgotten.

If militarism bores or frightens you, don't despair, it will probably be out of fashion in a few years. As I write these words I hear that fashions of the 1960s are staging a comeback with kids who were born in the 1970s. Tie-dying—a joke for over ten years—is back in style among the young, as are torn blue jeans, miniskirts, and the Beatles. Just go to the Unique Clothing Warehouse in Manhattan—if it's still in business, or if the sixties-look is still in reruns.

Fashion moves with the times. Every year new fashions appear on the scene, as if by accident, but behind the "accidental" choices of fashion designers we can find an image of ourselves and of our culture. Where the fashion-conscious consumer sees on the department store racks only this year's styles, a semiotician sees the play of history. To read the message behind a suit of clothes is to tap in to the movement of your culture, a dynamic as fickle, as changeable, and as fascinating as a Paris fashion show.

CHAPTER 10

Gender and Culture:
The Semiotics of Sexuality

Give me chastity and continency,
but do not give it yet.
    St. Augustine,
    Confessions, book viii, ch. 12

A ny way you look at it, the November 1987 issue of *Playboy* was nothing short of extraordinary. In the weeks before its publication, word of its content spread like wildfire across newspaper columns, magazine pages, and television screens as the great American publicity machine cranked up public expectation one notch after another. What was *Playboy* up to? Another feature on the "girls of the Ivy League"? An incendiary interview with a presidential candidate? A centerfold of Helen of Troy? No, it was none of these things. Instead, *Playboy* promised its readers a 31-page exposé of a one-time evangelical church secretary whose single claim to fame had been established some seven years before in a murky sexual interlude with the founder of the PTL (Praise the Lord, or People That Love) televangelical ministry.

The name of that secretary is Jessica Hahn, and throughout

the summer of 1987 she made headlines as the woman whose tryst with Jim Bakker crippled a multimillion-dollar religious empire. Less than a year later, the scenario virtually repeated itself when, in the spring of 1988, Jimmy Swaggart was forced to resign from the Assemblies of God after it was revealed that he had had relations with a prostitute. The details were murky, but it appeared that Swaggart had hired the woman to pose for him in the nude. The media, of course, had a field day over both stories, but in spite of the pages and pages of commentary devoted to them, the fundamental semiotic significance of the two scandals was not discussed. Yet what is most striking about the two affairs is not what they reveal about the moral lapses of two televangelical stars but rather what they say about the division of labor in the economy of American sexual desire.

In analyzing the semiotic significance of the Bakker and Swaggart scandals, we can borrow the insights of feminist critics who use a semiotic approach to expose the ideological underpinnings of what may otherwise appear to be natural forms of sexual behavior. In fact, feminist semioticians have the most interesting things to say about the relationship between the sexes in the culture of contemporary America. Kate Millett, who helped launch the modern women's movement by dubbing this culture a "patriarchy" (from the Greek roots for "father" and "rule"), is not herself a semiotician, but many current feminists are. The titles of two leading feminist journals, *Signs* and *Semiotexte*, reveal the importance of semiotics to cultural critics who wish to change the sexual status quo by demonstrating that much of the sexual behavior that we regard as natural or inevitable has really been framed by the myths of a patriarchal order.

When examining the codes that govern our sexual behavior, semioticians distinguish between the biological category of *sex* and the cultural category of *gender*. Your sex is determined by nature, and the physiological and anatomical characteristics that accompany it are (barring surgery) largely beyond cultural control. Culture can't change the fact that women are born with a biological capacity for bearing children which men lack, or that men generally have larger and thus stronger muscles than do women. But culture does define the roles that men and women play in political and sexual society, and to this extent divides the two sexes into opposing genders whose behavioral codes reflect the mythologized beliefs of the societies in which they appear.

We all know many of the most common myths of gender in American society. Recall, for example, the belief that men are naturally aggressive while women are naturally passive; that a man's place is in the workplace, struggling for survival, while a woman's place is in the home, serving as a nurturing angel in the house to bear and care for children; or that men are less emotional and better suited for political leadership than are women. One really doesn't need to be a semiotician to be aware of such myths. But semiotics can underscore the fact that they *are* myths, and it can expose some of the subtler myths of gender that govern our beliefs about the relations between the sexes. In fact, it was two of the most important of these myths that made the Bakker–Hahn and Swaggart affairs "scandals" in the first place.

So let's take a semiotic look at these scandals, beginning with the Bakker–Hahn affair. What exactly happened? In Bakker's version, *he* was ensnared by an attractive woman working in collusion with some of his jealous colleagues, all with a goal of undermining his power and place in the PTL ministry. In Hahn's version, Bakker ensnared *her* by taking advantage of his power over an innocent and inexperienced employee. Despite their differences, both versions of the story share a common structure: in each case, the man's relation to the woman is defined in terms of *his* institutional power and sexual desire versus *her* institutional subservience and sexual desirability. In neither version is there any claim that the woman felt any sexual desire for the man. She is desired but not desiring. Whether Hahn used the lure of her sex as if she were a modern-day Delilah in the employ of religious Philistines, or whether Bakker came to Hahn as if he were an evangelical Zeus come down to earth to ravish a secretarial Leda, we can say that either way only the man is seen as holding the sexual initiative. Only the man desires. The woman's role is defined only in relation to his desire.

The story of Jim Bakker and Jessica Hahn thus repeats the pattern of some of the West's most enduring stories about sex and intimate relationships. If we cast Jessica Hahn as Delilah and Jim Bakker as Samson, we find the drama of a holy man who is undone by the machinations of an unfeeling woman working in concert with his enemies. If we prefer the myth of the rape of Leda, we may cast Jessica Hahn as a virginal innocent and Bakker as a lusting Zeus whose power is ultimately undone by that very innocence. Whichever way we look at it, the myths of the West hold feminine beauty responsible for the destruction of masculine power.

Of course, since within that mythology only men hold the real sexual initiative, one might think that they would get the blame for any trouble their lust might cause. But this is not the conclusion to which the myths lead. Instead, the blame is cast on the woman for being sexually attractive. Leda's daughter, after all, was Helen of Troy, whose running off with Paris led to the destruction of an empire. One way or another, women take the rap for what men do to possess them.

Women's own sexual desires, however, are repressed within the mythology of the West, because the very idea of female sexuality calls into question the assumption that men are in control. Those women who openly express their sexual desires traditionally have been cast in the role of harlot or witch, social outcasts who must be brought under control. Witches and whores have even attracted their own sexual iconography. The association of witches with cats, for example, stems from the mythic belief that cats are especially highly sexed creatures, and brothels are still commonly called "cat houses." This symbolic link between women, cats, and forbidden sexuality was once so close that in the Middle Ages many a witch was burned at the stake with her cat at her side.

To justify its stringent control of female sexuality, the old patriarchal order invented an entire mythology that shows the havoc that supposedly is wreaked by women who disobey patriarchal orders. From the myth of Pandora's box to the biblical story of the Fall, disobedient women are blamed for the ills of human life. Just think of the symbols involved in the story of the Fall: they particularly play on the sexual nature of Eve's actions. A phallic serpent causes Eve to tempt Adam with a forbidden fruit; and Adam takes Eve's offering much as a man today is said to take the "cherry" of a virgin. Instantly, both Adam and Eve become aware of their nakedness, and sin enters the world. Potiphar's wife, who attempts to seduce Joseph in Egypt, and Salomé, who demands the head of John the Baptist, are further biblical examples of women whose lack of sexual control threatens the social order. To counteract the disruptive power of the desiring woman, the West has developed the myth of the nondesiring woman, of the matriarch like Rebeckah or Rachel or the Virgin Mary: semidivine or divine women whose sexuality is denied or at least controlled by patriarchal forces. The TV mothers of the 1950s are modern versions of this asexual ideal.

The myth of the good woman without desire has led to the belief that women are born without sexual natures of their own. This belief has had some rather amusing consequences. The English, for example, once forbade male homosexuality but did not legislate against lesbian acts because they presumed that no woman could initiate a sexual contact with another woman. As the logic ran, with both parties lacking a sex drive, nothing could ever get started. In more modern terms, the belief in female asexuality is reflected in the controversy over the female orgasm. The stakes in this debate have less to do with the right of a woman to sexual pleasure than with her ability to have her own sexual identity independent of men.

A second major cultural myth unfolds in the Swaggart story. Here a man is overwhelmed by his desire to gaze upon female flesh, which he hires by the hour. The Swaggart affair exemplifies the common sexual myth that women are made to be looked at and that men are made to do the looking. Think of the myth of the Judgment of Paris, wherein the prince of Troy must judge among three Greek goddesses and choose the most beautiful one. The sexual ritual embodied in the myth is reenacted every year, of course, in the Miss America contest—and in countless lesser beauty pageants. These rituals reflect the cultural belief that women are born to endure the active gaze of men. The cultural, rather than natural, basis of this belief becomes quite apparent when one considers the marginal status of such male ogling contests as the Mr. America pageant. The fact that there *are* male beauty pageants reveals that the thing is possible; the fact that such shows attract relatively little attention—and even less in advertising revenues—reveals the cultural mythology behind the structure of male–female relationships in our society. For every Burt Reynolds discreetly posed in the centerfold of *Cosmopolitan* magazine, there are thousands, tens of thousands, of female nudes displayed for the masculine eye.

Both the Bakker–Hahn and Swaggart affairs are thus not simply tawdry tales drawn from the annals of popular history: to the semiotician they are true-life stories of mythic proportions. Each story reveals how our culture apportions its sexual division of labor. Within this asymmetrical system, men see and desire, while women are seen and desired without desiring for themselves. The media hoopla that surrounded the Bakker–Hahn affair simply repeated this mythic pattern. *Playgirl* didn't offer Jim Bakker $750,000 to pose in its pages, but *Playboy* could safely assume that American men would want to gaze upon the body of Jessica Hahn. Hahn, to be sure, accepted *Playboy*'s offer with the protestation that she was doing so not for the money but to build up her own sense of herself as a woman, but even if this were her real reason, it still reveals the asymmetrical nature of our sexual codes. The fact that an American woman can feel that the way to establish her own self-confidence is to pose in the pages of a national "skin" magazine simply reinforces the cultural mythology that defines female sexuality in terms of the active desire of the male gaze.

It would be foolish, I think, to attribute the reality of male desire wholly to cultural determinants, however. After all, the male of the species has been at least partly programmed by nature to respond to female appearances. There are just some hormones that culture can't entirely control. But the mythological belief that women neither desire to gaze upon the bodies of men nor harbor sexual desires of their own actually flies in the face of nature. The female of the species, too, has evolved to be attracted to a suitable mate.

The belief that women are naturally asexual or without desire is an example of a naturalized gender myth, a myth that has been created and lived out over centuries of male-dominated culture. The belief that women are made to be seen and men are made to do the seeing is another gender myth. Like many cultural myths, this belief is commonly dressed up in the guise of nature —for instance, "women are the beautiful sex"—but it really reflects subjective cultural values. Other cultures may feel differently. The ancient Greeks, for instance, expressed no particular preference for feminine over masculine beauty. In their art, they celebrated the physical potential of the *human* body by representing it in the form of both gods and goddesses. For every sculpted Athena and Aphrodite, the Greeks had their Apollo and Hermes.

To appreciate fully the difference between Greek attitudes toward the body and our own, consider how few male nudes exist in the tradition of European art. There's Michelangelo's *David*, of course, but that was sculpted in direct imitation of the Greeks. There are a lot of fig-leafed Adams, but those are intended as forms of sacred illustration. The figure of the female nude, on the other hand, is ubiquitous. We take it for granted that this should be the case, that male bodies aren't particularly interesting, but the distinction between male and female nudes is no aesthetic accident: it is a sign that directly reflects the interests at work in European culture.

To be naked is to be vulnerable, weak, defenseless. The only people who are ordinarily allowed to be naked in public are the most defenseless among us: babies. Clothing brings protection and even power. Thus, the great portraits of men in the tradition of European art tend to represent their subjects dressed up in gorgeous robes or shining armor. Such coverings signify the power of the man in the picture, who, while he may be identified as a real king, pope, or prince, symbolically represents the power of all men in the patriarchal order of European painting.

The female nude, by contrast, represents a usually anonymous female subject whose nakedness serves as a symbol of female powerlessness and passivity. Consider Ingres's *Odalisque*. The nude lies back and looks coyly at her observer, whose gaze will almost certainly be masculine. She seems to hope that her appearance will captivate, please, or perhaps appease him, for in her nakedness she is like a child who requires both attention and protection.

In her ability to captivate a man with her body, a woman, paradoxically enough, exercises what little power she has in the sexual economy of the patriarchy. She needn't even be naked to do so, because the very suggestion of female nakedness can be enough to overpower the gazing eyes of men. This is particularly true in cultures where women's bodies are customarily covered up in public. Islamic culture finds the bodies of women to be so inciting that it covers them up from head to toe, while the glimpse of a naked ankle among the well-covered Victorians could be enough to cause a scandal. In James Joyce's once-banned novel *Ulysses*, for instance, one of its characters, Leopold Bloom, actually experiences an ejaculation while visiting the beach and watching a teenaged girl's skirts rise above her ankles and knees as she gazes at a fireworks display. It's her garters that set him off, for in the post-Victorian culture in which the novel takes place, the concealed features of a woman's dress were read as sexually charged signs of the body parts that they touched. There's almost something quaint about this today, when a trip to the beach can be almost as revealing as a trip to the boudoir, but for our grandparents and great-grandparents the female body was so thoroughly covered in public that clothing drew especial attention to the nakedness that it concealed (of course, it still can today if it's a particularly tight sweater or skirt).

The ancient Greeks, by contrast, didn't wear much clothing, and they were not very much excited by intimate attire. If we may judge by their art, they also didn't get particularly steamed up by feminine appearances either. We all know the legend of Helen of Troy, for example, but nowhere is she physically described. Classical sculptures of the female form are almost sexless by modern standards. There just isn't much fuss about the female body in ancient Greek civilization.

There is plenty of fuss made about female bodies in contemporary American civilization, however, and they are not always seen as a source of social disruption. Anyone who has spent any time at all in front of a television set knows very well just how often the power of female flesh has been harnessed by commercial interests in order to attract the attention of consumers. From beer to automobiles to fast food, the body of the woman is dangled before a presumably masculine gaze, frequently converting products themselves into sexual fetishes. Perhaps the most bizarre example of this is the Anheuser-Busch campaign for Budweiser beer featuring Spuds MacKenzie. Spuds, a homely English bullterrier, has been cast in the role of "party animal" in a series of commercials otherwise filled with buxom women who are all in ecstasy over the dog. This ad campaign fits into our sexual mythology quite well, for Spuds (who is in fact a female dog but is presented as a male) is not sexually desirable in himself. The women around him are attracted to his wealth and power— Spuds has his own submarine and yacht—and his reputation for wildness, but they can hardly be attracted to his good looks. The audience of the commercials can hardly miss the girls in the ads, however, and the young men to whom these commercials are aimed are encouraged to cast themselves as Spuds. Drink Budweiser and you too will be surrounded by nymphs, the ad promises. The beer itself has disappeared behind the body of a woman.

What appears in the Budweiser commercials is repeated across the spectrum of American advertising. Consumer desire is framed as sexual desire, and the two are finally lumped together. But it is almost always male desire at the base. Even when commercials pretend to appeal to a feminine audience, they don't escape their patriarchal origins. There is a commercial for Chevrolet's Beretta, for example, in which a female test-car driver assesses the new car. Now, one would think that casting a woman as a test driver and showing her at a computer would be a sign of a feminist commercial. Normally, women are simply juxtaposed before a phallic automobile, so this ad seems to be a step in a new direction. But the ad gives itself away as the woman's voice-over says that she had doubted whether the Beretta could "drive" as well as it looks. Then we look at the woman: if she's not a fashion model, she looks like one, and we see the car "driving" as well as *she* looks. In the end, we're looking at the body of a beautiful woman again, not at a product.

THE WORD OF THE FATHER

By analyzing the sexually coded messages that lie beneath the surface of a scandal or an ad campaign, we can reveal the patriarchal structure of our political and commercial culture. But feminist semioticians are probing even more deeply to analyze the patriarchal structure of consciousness itself. For such semioticians, masculine control is exerted internally as well as externally, beginning with the very language we speak. We ordinarily do not think of language as having anything to do with either sex or gender, but for many semioticians, what we fondly call our "mother tongue" is really the voice of the patriarchal father.

The argument here blends psychoanalysis with semiotics. In essence, it says that language originates in the libido, and that the libido that expresses itself in every known language on earth is a masculine one. Since male desire, as the argument runs, is bound up with the faculty of sight, patriarchal language is necessarily pictorial in nature, a language of imagistic symbols. If I say the word "cat" in English, for instance, an image of a cat may appear in your mind. Similarly, since the male libido prizes its power over the world, the languages that spring from it name and classify all things in rational categories in order to bring them under conceptual control.

There are no matriarchal languages because every child must abandon the nonsymbolic language of the mother to learn the symbolic language of the father. In the feminist account, as an infant matures and learns how to talk, it moves away from its mother—whose communication with her child is conducted through her body, through her breast and womb—toward its father, whose language is made up of abstract symbols. As the child learns the language of the father, it absorbs the patriarchal concepts that constitute it. It is the language of the father, for example, that privileges the male gender by speaking of the human race as "mankind" and by commonly using "he" as a generic pronoun. It is the language of the father that speaks of a paternal God and that divides up the world into the species named by Adam *before* Eve's creation. In short, the language of the father is the language of history, or, as feminist writers sometimes write it, of his-story. It is the language of the deeds of men: of kings and presidents, warriors and scientists, priests and poets and philosophers. In Simone de Beauvoir's words, the role of women in "his-story" is accordingly that of a kind of "second sex," of minor players and spectators in a human drama whose leading characters are almost always men and whose script is written in a masculine tongue.

The language of the mother, on the other hand, is unconcerned with history. It is a language of touch and sensation, of the inarticulate communication between a nursing infant and its mother. Though a mother may speak to her child in full sentences, her words, according to the feminist theory, are not really her own. They belong to the language of the father, a language that she learned when she was herself a child. But her own language, the language of the mother, is a language of cooing, humming, soothing sounds that do not represent visual images and do not really "mean" anything. Neither rational nor logical, the language of the mother caresses where the word of the father classifies.

Feminist semioticians thus believe that a truly *feminine* language would be one motivated by the sense of touch rather than of sight, an illogical, or, more precisely, an *a*logical language based on feeling. If man finds pleasure in what he sees, a woman's pleasure lies in what she touches and what touches her. Her challenge is to develop a system of signs that would express her own libidinous desires.

A number of feminist semioticians, including such French writers as Julia Kristeva, Hélène Cixous, and Luce Irigaray, have attempted to design such a language. But it's a hard task. For the words in which they must write are symbols drawn from the masculine order. To read them you must see them on the page and picture their meanings in your mind. To transform such symbols into a new order of signs motivated by touch rather than by sight is a formidable task, and the few experiments that have been made in this direction are—understandably enough—almost unreadable, because they must break with the rational order of masculine language to play with irrational forms that must communicate beneath the level of understanding. In essence, such writings become almost "sense-less" cooings, words that do not attempt to "mean" or communicate anything but which would probably be best "understood" by a nursing infant.

Luce Irigaray's poetic essay "When Our Lips Speak Together" is a good example of an experimental discourse designed to express a feminine language. As Carolyn Burke describes Irigaray's essay:

> Her text is a process of discovery and an exploration, through language, of the connections between female

sexuality and the expression of meaning—in its own terms, between the senses and sense, as women know them. . . . Irigaray tries out a language of immediacy, which hovers between the written and the spoken and stresses the sense of touch in the here and now. A language of flux, it refuses rigid definitions and avoids images or metaphors that stabilize meaning in too permanent a manner.

So what does such a language sound like? Like two lovers, speaking together, thus:

If we continue to speak the same language to each other, we will reproduce the same story. Begin the same stories all over again. Don't you feel it? Listen: men and women around us all sound the same. Same arguments, same quarrels, same scenes. . . .
     If we continue to speak this sameness, if we speak to each other as men have spoken for centuries, as they taught us to speak, we will fail each other. Again. . . . Words will pass through our bodies, above our heads, disappear, make us disappear. Far. Above. Absent from ourselves, we become machines that are spoken. Machines that speak.

Irigaray explains why such a language is necessary for women in the words that I have cited. "If we speak to each other as men have spoken for centuries, as they taught us to speak," she writes, "we will fail each other." The failure Irigaray refers to here is the failure of women to realize themselves *as women*, independent of the patriarchal order. To so fail is to remain in submission to a conquering power. For if you, as a woman, believe that the language that you speak is alien to you, coming from a gender that you do not share, then your own speech will appear to you like the speech of a foreign country. Like a conquered people who must speak the language of their conquerors, feminist semioticians find themselves divided between the language of their fathers and the forgotten language of their mothers. Males do not suffer this division, because when they cease to nurse and learn the symbolic language of their fathers, they are simply coming into their patrimony, joining in the patriarchal order. But when a female infant leaves her mother to enter into the world of masculine discourse, she leaves something of herself behind. She is split. The desire for a language of her own is thus a desire for wholeness in an independent realm ungoverned by masculine discourse.

The search for an alogical discourse is not limited to feminist semioticians. Avant-garde writers in the postmodern tradition are also developing new languages that dispense with the values of traditional discourse in favor of irrational modes of representation (see chapter 11). Luce Irigaray herself is a postmodern philosopher and psychoanalyst and shares the postmodern distrust of the rationality of the philosophical tradition. In a certain sense, feminist semiotics could be classified as a subset of the larger domain of postmodern culture. But to so classify such work is to reduce it back to the language of the father, to master it by placing a purposefully illogical discourse in a logical context. From the perspective of a feminist semiotician, my very attempt to explain feminist semiotics is an attempt to corral it in the forms of patriarchal discourse. Paradoxically, a truly matriarchal discourse cannot be described in familiar—that is, in patriarchal—terms. Deliberately violating the norms of ordinary language because the "norm" has been defined by the patriarchy, the language of the mother has to be heard with a new kind of ear, an ear that no man, perhaps, can ever have.

On the other hand, the belief that our ordinary languages— English, French, Russian, Chinese, and so on—spring from a patriarchal libido that excludes the libidinous desires of women may be purely theoretical. One could also argue that language is a *human* artifact that is unmarked by gender distinctions at the most essential level. But whether one agrees with the theory or not, whether it is true or not, the fact that it exists at all is itself a potent cultural sign, signifying to a semiotician the deep resentment that many women now feel against the established cultural order.

The feeling is one of intense cultural alienation. Feminist semioticians regard women not as one of two biological sexes but as the *different* sex, the sex that history has repressed, the sex that history has hidden away. Feminist semiotics seeks to bring women out of hiding not simply by denouncing the patriarchal order of things but by developing a matriarchal order complete with its own language, mythology, and mode of perception. That project is only beginning and its eventual success is unclear. But if it is ever completed, a totally different kind of semiotics would have to be written, one, perhaps, that could be read only by women.

WHAT DO WOMEN WANT?

In Geoffrey Chaucer's *The Canterbury Tales*, the Wife of Bath —a boisterous widow who has joined the poet's pilgrimage to Canterbury—tells a story that, at first reading, may appear to anticipate the matriarchal consciousness that feminist semioticians wish to foster. Her story concerns the adventures of a young knight in the court of King Arthur who rapes a young maiden. For this crime, he is sentenced to death, but the ladies of the court intercede to offer the knight one last chance for his life. He is given one year to wander the world in search of the answer to an ancient question: to wit, "What thing is it that women most desire?" Having little choice in the matter, the knight undertakes this quest, but though he seeks the answer everywhere he goes, he can find only conflicting responses. Some say that women want riches, others happiness, others a good time in bed; still other women tell the young knight that they want freedom, or flattery, or even the trust of their husbands. Despairing of ever finding the answer, the knight meets an old hag who promises to tell him exactly what women most desire if he will promise to marry her.

The knight promises and carries this answer to the court: what women most desire is mastery over their husbands and lovers. The ladies of the court agree, and the knight is spared.

It's important to recall that the "Wife of Bath's Tale" was written by a man, and that the answer to the question "What do women most desire?" reflects a patriarchal fear of a feminine challenge to the patriarchy. The very fact that this question is often asked is a sign of the division between men and women in our culture, a division that places man as the inquiring sex and woman as the mysterious one, as an object to be studied. Surely women are not mysterious to themselves, though men may be mysterious to them. But the question "What do men want?" rarely arises. Is this because everyone knows what men want, or because men, who have traditionally been empowered to ask most of the questions in our culture, have never bothered to ask? Probably something of both, but the fact that the question "What do women want?" is an ancient one in our culture, asked by such divergent writers as Chaucer and Freud, signifies an asymmetrical relation between the sexes, an assumption that women are a mystery to men but that it doesn't matter so much whether men are a mystery to women.

The traditional, masculine reading of the "Wife of Bath's Tale," then, focuses on the answer to the knight's question. But if we read Chaucer's story from the perspective of a matriarchal consciousness, we would see a very different story from the one I have told. We would note, primarily, that a man is spared the punishment for rape because of the intercession of *women*.

Rape is not a pleasant subject, and most of us (and that probably includes both men and women) prefer not to think about it. But it has become a crucial subject for feminist semioticians who wish to expose the patriarchal mythology surrounding it and—in some cases—to substitute a myth of their own. The patriarchal myth of rape equates it with sex and so blames the problem on women, who, as we have already seen, have traditionally been blamed for stimulating male desire. Women who have been raped are believed to have somehow invited it, to have sent a sexual signal to the desiring male. Because this belief is the dominant myth of rape in our culture, it has been built into our judicial system, in which it is incumbent upon a rape victim to demonstrate that she didn't invite her attack.

Related to the patriarchal myth of rape is the cultural belief that the body of a man's wife is, in a very real sense, his legal property. In the Middle Ages this belief was expressed most forcefully in the grotesque figure of the chastity belt—which, believe it or not, still exists—but now appears more commonly in a judicial disinclination to get involved in cases of domestic violence. Though a number of states—like Connecticut—are now passing stricter laws to protect women from their husbands or lovers, the history of domestic violence in this country has generally been one where courts looked the other way. If a woman belongs to her husband, she is his to do with as he pleases.

For some feminists, rape actually serves to reinforce the patriarchal control of women's bodies. Susan Brownmiller, for example, in a book entitled *Against Our Will: Men, Women, and Rape,* has proposed an antipatriarchal theory of rape which argues that rape, or the threat of it, is neither an accident nor a form of deviant behavior. For Brownmiller, history has been one long battle of the sexes, a battle that has been won by men through the systematic practice of rape. Kept in perpetual terror by the reality and possibility of rape, Brownmiller proposes, women throughout time have been forced to turn for protection to the very sex that threatens them. Rape, Brownmiller argues, is the product of a male conspiracy in which a minority of rapists serves the majority of men by forcing women to turn to their fathers, brothers, and husbands to protect them, thus ensuring their control over their daughters, sisters, and wives.

I personally find Brownmiller's myth rather extreme, and so did many feminists when it was published. Most people today would view rape as an act of violence, neither invited by the victim nor encouraged by society. But again, whether Brownmiller's myth is true or not is less important than the cultural signal it is sending. The fact that a woman can believe that men benefit from rape is yet another sign of intense sexual alienation. Shere Hite's published interviews and surveys of disaffected women are further signs of the alienation of the sexes. While Hite's books may not conform to the conventions of scientific sampling, the tremendous sales they enjoy signify an emotional need for a solid front against men that at least some women are feeling today.

This anger reflects the consciousness of women who believe that their culture has always told them what they want without ever consulting them. It has told them that their aspirations should be confined to the nurturing of their families, and that whatever power they may enjoy must be exercised within the confines of the home. It has taught them to be ashamed of their own sexual desires and to define themselves as passive objects to be gazed upon by men. To combat such naturalized cultural beliefs, feminist semioticians are seeking to undermine the entire structure of Western perception, beginning at the level of language and moving up to demystify the dominant sexual myths of our culture. So "what do women want?" As a man, I'm probably not in the best position to answer that question. But from the signs that we can read in the annals of feminist semiotics, what many women want is a new language and a new mythology: in short, a new semiotic that has yet to be born.

CHAPTER 11

Our Decentered Culture: The Postmodern Worldview

Stop making sense.
David Byrne

P ostmodernism. Or is it post-modernism? Or perhaps Post-Modernism? However you spell it, the word "postmodern" (the spelling I'll use in this chapter) is my candidate for the fastest-rising yet least well-defined semiotic adjective of the 1980s. A product of the media age most commonly encountered in pop culture and the arts, the postmodern spirit pervades everything from an Andy Warhol soup can to the music of Talking Heads. Thomas Pynchon is postmodern, and so is Laurie Anderson. Philip Glass and Brian Eno are postmodern. MTV has postmodern affiliations. Even "Miami Vice" has a postmodern look. Such a wide-ranging influence makes it difficult to pinpoint the precise essence of the postmodern spirit, however, and the task isn't made any easier by the fact that the term was coined in the 1970s by Charles Jencks to describe a specific school of architectural design (see chapter 6). For since its first appearance on the cultural scene, "postmodern" has come to signify something much bigger than a particular style of architecture. Postmodernism is not merely a style: it is a cultural attitude, an emerging worldview that is now changing the shape of American consciousness.

In its most general sense, postmodernism represents a new mode of perception fostered by an age of instant communication: by radio, cinema and, most importantly, by TV. Viewing the world as a television camera views it, the postmodern eye reduces the length and breadth of experience to a two-dimensional spectacle, to a carnival of arresting images and seductive surfaces. Like the nightly news, whose quick camera cuts can juxtapose images of international violence with pitches for fabric softeners and headache remedies, the postmodern experience is best described as a perceptual montage. Gazing upon the world as if it were one vast variety show, the postmodern eye perceives the course of human events as a narrativeless and nonsensical series of skits, as one long episode of "Monty Python."

The postmodern ear hears differently too. Words enter it, but only as noise, the cliché-strewn babble of a culture in which *what* you say is far less important than *how* you say it. It hears music, but not melody, giving us the electronic static of John Lennon's "Revolution #9" and the street noise of La Monte Young's "Poem for Tables, Chairs, Benches, etc.," a postmodern chamber piece in which tables, chairs, and benches are dragged about on a concert floor, an egg is fried, a lawn is mowed, music textbooks are read aloud, and tapes of two other Young compositions are played simultaneously, all while Beethoven is banged out on a piano.

The postmodern eye and ear have been shaped by the culture of contemporary industrial and postindustrial civilization. I can think of no better example of this than Godfrey Reggio's 1983 feature film *Koyaanisqatsi*. At once an illustration of postmodern aesthetic technique and a criticism of the culture that produced it, *Koyaanisqatsi* is a sign both of where we are going and where we have been. With its disconcertingly narrativeless flow and violent juxtapositions of discontinuous images, the film presents a postmodern parody of traditional film documentaries to show us just how senseless and disharmonious the modern world has become. Paradoxically enough, it's a postmodern denunciation of the culture of postmodernism.

If you didn't catch *Koyaanisqatsi* in the theater, you can still see it on PBS, where it plays a regular role in public television's avant-garde programming. If you've seen the film, you'll appreciate my difficulty in describing it. To begin with, it has no characters, no dialogue, no words, no subtitles, no narrative, nor anything recognizable as a plot. Without commentary or overview, the cameras simply juxtapose such violently contrasting images from the natural and the industrialized worlds as Indian hieroglyphics, a slow-motion rocket launch, time-lapse photography of cloud patterns, scenic aerial views of the American Southwest, atomic blasts, shots of the litter-filled streets of New York, endless replays of the demolition of a decaying housing complex, scenes from Las Vegas, and violently accelerated film clips of L.A. freeways, factory workers, television shows, and shoppers, in which people look like mindless automatons, and cars like a vision from an urban planner's nightmare.

As all of these images race before your eyes, the synthesized music of Philip Glass pulses in rhythmic correlation with the imagery, repeating over and over again, with only slight variations, the same orchestral themes, combined with what sounds like a demented choir of angels chanting in the background. Words and music blend into a cacophonous shout, a sheer wall of noise that neatly complements the unbalanced world presented on the screen.

Finally, after eighty-seven minutes of unrelieved sensory assault, *Koyaanisqatsi* grinds slowly to an end. The Indian hieroglyphs return and with them the film's only recognizable words, projected on the screen as if from a dictionary:

koyaanisqatsi (from the Hopi language) 1. crazy life,
2. life in turmoil, 3. life out of balance, 4. life
disintegrating, 5. a state of life that calls for another
way of living.

Koyaanisqatsi, clearly, is a film with a message. Through its
relentless display of the dehumanizing squalor of modern industrial civilization, the movie makes an eloquent, if unarticulated,
plea for "another way of living," for a return to preindustrial
harmonies. Denouncing the sterile repetitiveness of modern life,
it calls for a more organic approach to our world. But while this
is the moral message of the film its semiotic message is more
subtle. The *moral* of *Koyaanisqatsi* could just as easily have been
expressed in a Sierra Club newsletter, or in a traditional documentary format complete with interviews, statistics, and narrative
voice-over. For the semiotician, however, it is the distinctively
postmodern *medium* of *Koyaanisqatsi* that provides the deepest
insights into the state of contemporary American culture. Here
the medium, not the moral, is the message.

Let's start with *Koyaanisqatsi*'s lack of narrative structure.
We ordinarily expect a movie—or short story, or novel, or
play—to tell a story, to begin at the beginning and then carry
us through to a logical conclusion. Each character and event in
the story is related to the other through a *plot* that gives narrative shape and meaning to the experiences that the story represents. Where our unnarrated lives are often chaotic and
inexplicable, plagued by accidents, uncertainties, and unlooked-
for disasters, narratives quite literally "make sense" of the apparently senseless course of daily existence by framing it in
universally significant forms.

A narrative, then, is very much like a myth, taking the
disorganized stuff of experience and casting it in a meaningful
frame. As Aristotle put it in his *Poetics*, the West's first major
work of narrative analysis, the plot, or *mythos*, of a story is what
gives it its shape, endowing the particularity of human experience

with a universal significance. The unplotted events in the life of Oedipus, king of Thebes, for example, simply chronicle the violent experiences of a man who accidentally kills his father and unknowingly marries his mother. But when the Greek tragedian Sophocles framed this story in the form of a tragic plot, it was transformed into an expression of the tragic destiny of a man struggling with his own character and fate. Similarly, Arthur Miller's *Death of a Salesman* presents the moral failure of an ordinary salesman named Willy Loman (Low-Man = Everyman) as if it too expressed the universal struggle of a man with his destiny. Loman joins the ranks of Oedipus and King Lear, his fall endowed with a significance, even a grandeur, that the failure and suicide of a real-life salesman would lack.

In essence, that's what narratives have always been for: to create meaning in the face of meaninglessness, to make sense of the senselessness of the world in which we live and die. To make the chaotic flow of experience adhere to some rhyme or reason, we give it a shape, complete with a narrative beginning, middle, and end, because if a thing or experience is to have any meaning for us, we have to know where it came from and what it is for, its origins and ends. But human experience—or history, if you like—sometimes doesn't seem to have a beginning or an end. It just *is.* As they said in the Middle Ages, life sometimes appears to be just one damn thing after another—even in twentieth-century America. So in the face of our own meaninglessness as human beings, we have decided to tell a story, a narrative complete with a beginning, middle, and end, "written" by a divine Author who will make sense of our lives, tell us what we're here for.

For nearly two thousand years, the Judeo-Christian Bible has provided the West with a narrative that has created meaning out of chaos by framing history between the limits of a creative origin and an apocalyptic end. From Genesis' "In the beginning" to Revelation's vision of Judgment, the Bible makes sense of human experience by explaining where we came from, who made us, and why. At its center we find a divine Author who has created us as if we were all characters in a cosmic drama, endowing our births and deaths with a providential significance. In essence, that is the purpose of all sacred narratives: to center our lives around a creative origin and to give meaning thereby to our mortality. In semiotic terms, narrative itself is sacred, constituting our greatest—and perhaps only—weapon against death.

ALIVE FROM OFF CENTER

In the postmodern worldview, narrative has lost its sacred power. The semiotic significance of this loss is profound, for by rejecting the traditional narratives of the West, the postmodern myth has rejected the centering structures that have long given meaning to human history. At the postmodern center there is only a void, which is the same as saying that there is no center to the postmodern worldview. History has neither a beginning nor an end, neither a creative origin nor a purposive goal. Life is nothing more than a decentered, narrativeless course of waiting for death —or for a nonexistent God who never comes.

Samuel Beckett's postmodern anti-play *Waiting for Godot* (revived in 1988 with Steve Martin, Robin Williams, F. Murray Abraham, and Bill Irwin in the leading roles) dramatizes exactly what it's like to live in a universe without a narrative center. Written at about the same time as *Death of a Salesman* was (ca. 1948–1949), *Waiting for Godot* shows us two tramps, Vladimir and Estragon, waiting on a nearly empty stage for a mysterious figure named Godot to keep his appointment with them. For two long acts, virtually nothing happens. The second act almost repeats the meager actions of the first, as if the two tramps were doomed forever to repeat themselves in a kind of postmodern hell. As the hours creep by, Vladimir and Estragon try to kill time by engaging in senseless theological speculations, doing silly exercises, calling each other names, and wondering whether they shouldn't commit suicide and how best to do it. They reminisce about a past they cannot clearly remember and threaten to leave each other without ever really trying. A strange couple named Pozzo and Lucky appears, vanishes, reappears in the second act, and vanishes again. It's a cruel world. Pozzo whips Lucky, whom he treats like a cart horse. Lucky kicks Estragon when he comes too close. Vladimir and Estragon tackle Lucky to shut him up when he launches into a deranged parody of a philosophical lecture. Time and time again, Estragon tells Vladimir that they might as well give up and leave. But they can't leave, Vladimir reminds him, because they're waiting for Godot.

Godot never shows up, and the curtain falls on the second act with the clear implication that were it to rise again, our two tramps would still be onstage, quarreling with each other, waiting for a Godot who will never come. If Godot did come, then perhaps their waiting would have some meaning; but Godot—like the "God" his name resembles—refuses to keep his appointment. The center they are waiting for does not exist; their waiting is in vain. There is nothing to be done.

Waiting for Godot is one of the first works of Western art to reflect the postmodern loss of faith in the power of either sacred or secular narrative to make sense of human experience. Even the language of *Godot* makes little sense. In traditional literature, words are regarded as communicative instruments, as sounds that convey meanings; but in postmodern literature the lines of communication are definitely down. The result is static. Vladimir and Estragon exchange hundreds of words, Pozzo launches into a cliché-ridden speech about life, Lucky delivers a demented lecture on theology, but most of it is nonsense. There is a strong element of farce in the proceedings, but *Godot*'s message goes beyond farce in its dramatic demonstration of how both language and narrative no longer "make sense" in the postmodern worldview, because no sense can be made in a universe in which God does not come. Life is not a divine drama, it is just a course of meaningless accidents. Language isn't the breath of the Lord, it's just wind. Nothing is worth anymore than anything else when everything has been stripped of its meaning. Cruelty and love, nonsense and philosophy, curses and theology, all come down to the same thing in *Waiting for Godot*. Life goes on, but it isn't going anywhere.

Waiting for Godot was written by a perfectly healthy Nobel laureate, but it might almost have been composed by one of the brain-damaged patients described in Oliver Sacks's *The Man Who Mistook His Wife for a Hat*, a woman for whom, as Sacks writes, the "world had been voided of feeling and meaning." Describing her emotions—or lack of them—to her doctor, the patient complained that nothing "any longer felt 'real' (or 'unreal'). Everything was now equivalent or equal—the whole world reduced to a facetious insignificance . . . to anarchy and chaos. The end of such states," as Sacks puts it, "is an unfathomable 'silliness,' an abyss of superficiality, in which all is ungrounded and afloat and comes apart"—a world in which the center (God, meaning, human dignity, reason, what have you) will not hold.

Godot invites us into the abyss, reducing the high seriousness of tragedy to the facetious anarchy of farce. *Koyaanisqatsi* shows us where the abyss came from: not from the diseased imagination of a playwright but from a culture whose traditional values have been subordinated to the impersonal laws of supply and demand. Sacks's patient has seen her life drained of meaning by the destructive activity of a brain disease; *Koyaanisqatsi* dramatizes the disequilibrium of a world in which moral value and cash value are the same.

In the capitalist wasteland, we find the neon jungle of the Las Vegas Strip, sprawling shopping malls, freeways, strip mines, and smokestacks in the desert. *Koyaanisqatsi* spares us nothing. Mountains of garbage testify to the voraciousness of a consumer culture. Sprinklers running around the clock drain the Colorado River to keep the golf courses of Palm Springs green. Smog spills into the desert air. Shoppers scurry for goods as TV spurs them on to even more consumption, more garbage production, more need of nuclear power plants to keep the engines of a consumer culture humming.

What saves *Koyaanisqatsi* from becoming depressing is its

tremendous energy. There is something exhilarating in its kinetic montage of images, something comic in its fast-frame accelerations, its time-lapse sequences. What would be squalid or repellent to the naked eye becomes fascinating when transformed by the magic of video technology. *Koyaanisqatsi*'s cameras enable us see our world as we have never seen it before, slowing it down, speeding it up, soaring high into the sky, and swooping down into the streets. Ultimately, the sheer spectacle overwhelms the moral. Social criticism becomes postmodern art.

And that's the semiotic secret concealed by the overt moral message of *Koyaanisqatsi:* that the technological resources of the television age have souped up our apprehension of reality. We don't really care whether things make sense as long as they look interesting. Electrically powered and technology-wise, postmodern consciousness is *entertained* by what it sees. If the modern world's a wasteland, it's a very entertaining wasteland.

So while the postmodern eye and ear apprehend only senseless spectacle and noise in the modern world, they have learned to enjoy the show. When David Byrne took on the wasteland of modern culture in his postmodern pastiche *Stop Making Sense*, for example, he didn't denounce it, he laughed at it, or, more precisely, he laughed *with* it. A parody of television documentaries, the movie is neither more nor less zany than the culture it parodies. The title of the film is significant, because it not only refers to a culture that has stopped making sense, it equally commands us to "stop making sense"! It's not simply that Byrne is unable to make sense of the wasteland: his postmodern message is that our anxious desire for meaning is unnecessary. Just sit back and go with the flow.

Postmodernism, then, represents a certain intellectual adaptation to the conditions of modern life. An era dominated by technology can be expected to produce a technological consciousness. To better understand how American culture has come to such a point, then, we might look for a moment into the history of modern technology: when it began and what it all meant. The beginning of the modern age, of course, is impossible to pinpoint, but I like to think that it all began one quiet afternoon during a visit to the Great Paris Exposition of 1900.

THE DYNAMO AND THE ASSEMBLY LINE

Imagine a small, dramatically bald, rather elderly man standing before a display of electric generators and whirling dynamos: the latest technology that a brand-new century had to offer. The place is the "gallery of machines" at the Paris Exposition of 1900. The man is Henry Adams, aging grandson and great-grandson of two American presidents, "aching," as he puts it in his classic autobiography, *The Education of Henry Adams*, "to absorb knowledge," though feeling "helpless to find it." Adams was looking for a key to unlock the mysteries of the new century, a sign that would explain to him just what it was that set the then-emerging modern era off from the course of European history. He found his sign in the gallery of machines.

For there, in a hall filled with the latest advances in motors and electronic generators, Adams had an illumination. The engines glowed into life and meaning as he "began to feel the forty-foot dynamo as a moral force, much as the early Christians felt the Cross." Adams felt humbled. The new force was entirely outside his experience, but it was clearly the force of the future, like it or not. "Before the end," he remarks, "one began to pray to it; inherited instinct taught the natural expression of man before silent and infinite force. Among the thousand symbols of ultimate energy, the dynamo was not so human as some, but it was the most expressive."

In the humming, whirring figure of an electronic generator, Adams had found a sign for the new century. The Dynamo, Adams saw, was taking the place of the Virgin and the Cross, of the Christian faith that had formed the narrative center of European culture ever since the Emperor Constantine had declared Christianity to be the official religion of Rome in the year A.D. 313. Such a shift was astounding, signaling the end of an epoch more than fifteen hundred years old. For nearly two millennia, Christianity had provided Europe with a guiding narrative that had shaped the entire course of its history. During these years, everything that European culture had accomplished, from the building of an empire to the raising of a cathedral, had been done (at least in principle) in the name of Christ. But as Henry Adams saw in the gallery of machines, a new force unlike any other that had guided human history before was coming to power. The Cross was yielding to the Dynamo, the forces of religion were being replaced by the forces of science. The modern age, Adams foresaw, would be more an age of technology than of belief.

Adams was a historian, not an artist, and an elderly one at that. He could find no place for himself in the brave new world of modern technology. He simply records the advent of a new era and leaves it to a new generation to make sense of it. Like Moses, he resigns himself to being left behind.

The modern era quickly found its Joshuas, however, in artists like Italy's Filippo Marinetti, who wrote a Futurist manifesto in 1909 that called for a worldwide aesthetic response to the realities of the modern age. For the Futurists, the machine had glamour. Vladimir Mayakovski, a Futurist poet from the Soviet Union, shaved his head to resemble the clean austerity of an automaton and composed poems whose movement imitated the violent thrusting of a piston. Influenced by the Futurist fervor, Cubist painters abandoned the sacred Madonnas of the past and began to paint the human form as if it replicated the dynamic geometry of a machine. Art Deco designers produced industrially stream-lined patterns for the mass production of domestic goods—which explains why your grandmother's toaster resembles a diesel loco-motive—while such modernist architects as Le Corbusier and Walter Gropius designed office buildings and apartment blocks in the image of factories. The Dynamo had arrived indeed.

But as Adams foresaw, the arrival of the Dynamo would not be without cost, and the price paid was the price of history itself. For the Dynamo represented an absolute break with everything that had gone before. Adams could see no connection between the emerging age of the Dynamo and the declining era of the Cross and the Virgin. From now on, the modern world was on its own, free to determine its own destiny, but cut off from the traditions of the past.

In the heady years of early twentieth-century industrialization, this seemed to be a small price to pay. "History is bunk," Henry Ford was once heard to say, his eyes on the future. Handcraftsmanship was "history," the future belonged to the assembly line. Individualized production was inefficient and costly; the assembly line would introduce mechanical efficiency into the workplace. Mass production was the ticket. History was only a dead letter.

We are Henry Ford's future, but the future has not quite turned out as planned. Today the assembly line, far from representing progress and efficiency, has become a metaphor for the repetitive sterility of a mass-produced culture. The Dynamo is making us uneasy. As early as the 1930s, threatening images of the machine began to appear in such cultural icons as Charlie Chaplin's film *Modern Times*, which dramatized the plight of a humanity caught up in the cogs of industrial production. But in an era of cybernetics and robotics, the machine is now assuming a new iconic significance, one that is at once fascinating and fearsome—a semiotic significance dramatized in the postmodern movie *Blade Runner*.

Blade Runner represents the experiences of a kind of futuristic FBI operative, played by Harrison Ford, who's been ordered to destroy a gang of renegade androids who have escaped the control of the sinister corporate tycoon responsible for their creation. As in many postmodern scenarios, the scene is set in a vaguely postnuclear urban wasteland where the streets are commanded by punk mutants while a pathetic citizenry locks itself up in dehumanized apartment towers, glued to their TV sets. Ford himself lives in such a tower, and relies on a futuristic videotape player —complete with stop action and precision image-enhancers—to track his prey through the dark corridors of a nightmare city that has been abandoned to the forces of anarchy.

Ford tracks down his targets one by one, hampered by their exact resemblance to human beings. If anything, the androids are superhuman: stronger, more attractive, and more intelligent than any mere human on the scene. The semiotic implication here is profound: having created a dehumanized and dehumanizing civilization, modern humanity is losing faith in itself and beginning to dream of a new, unfallen, synthetic "humanity" that might take its place. Perhaps humanoid machines will succeed where we have failed, *Blade Runner* intimates. Indeed, as Edith Milton has written in her article "The Track of the Mutant," "Machines . . . are now the icons of all our best qualities. Freed from human needs and greeds . . . our logical computer-selves . . . can develop epic amounts of decency."

It is thus Ford who often appears indecent in *Blade Runner*, gunning down his victims one by one in cold blood. To succeed at all, he has to be aided by one of the androids themselves (can we call her a "woman"?) who has fallen in love with him (this is still Hollywood, after all). And he owes his survival to the clemency of the androids' leader, who spares Ford's life while delivering a speech that expresses the anguish of a dying "man" to whom "life" has been more precious than to any of the pathetically deformed real humans in the inhuman city.

The paradox of postmodernism, then, is that it has looked upon the dehumanizing effects of the age of the Dynamo and has decided that the machine has a greater moral potential than the fallible human beings who created it. R2-D2 and C-3PO are postmodern storybook heroes who are as lovable as Pinocchio, but unlike our reaction to that premodern mechanical child, we have no desire for them to become human. To the semiotician, the popular success of films like *Star Wars* and *Blade Runner* suggests that there is something fascinating for postmodern culture in the prospect of designing creatures that are superior to their creators: robots whose intelligence dwarfs our own, and whose robotic bodies are stronger, and sexier, than anything nature can produce. Indeed, Harrison Ford flies off into the sunset with the surviving android-woman at the end of *Blade Runner*. (In the movie *Making Mr. Right*, the roles are reversed: here, a woman pursues a mechanical lover!) It's Adam and Eve all over again, but this time there's a machine in the family tree.

If there is ever a successful sexual union between man and machine, their offspring might resemble the members of the New Wave rock band DEVO, whose performances were designed to resemble the movements of demented robots. DEVO's aesthetic credo represents the flip side of the postmodern vision of the machine: if our machines are evolving upward, humanity is devolving downward into a kind of mechanical dementia. A series of Federal Express TV commercials aired during the 1988 Olympics seemed semiotically to underscore this point by presenting groups of factory workers, international sales personnel, and business executives lurching around like robots as they produce, sell, and ship the objects that come off a stylized assembly line. The odd thing about the ads, however, was that it was difficult to tell whether they were meant to satirize the scenes they depicted or to glamorize them. In the postmodern equation, one can never be sure whether one loves the machine or hates it.

But love it or hate it, there's no leaving it. As Adams predicted, twentieth-century Western culture has cut its ties with the past. We can no more return to premodern ways of thinking than we can return to a hunting and gathering way of life. Tradition has become nostalgia, an empty desire for what has been forever left behind.

The final irony of the postmodern worldview, however, is that it doesn't hold much hope for the future, either. The postmodern vision of the future often sees only a nightmarish repetition of the present: the cluttered urban anti-utopias of *Blade Runner*, "Max Headroom," and *Escape from New York*. In the anarchic landscapes of the postmodern imagination we find only a distorted reflection of the modern world, of the world we already inhabit. Machines may be improving, but we're not. Nothing for us is getting better. Nothing is even really changing. Our lives are only getting, if anything, a little more disorganized. All we can do is repeat ourselves, repeat the same mistakes, run through the same ingrained bad habits that are making such a mess of our world.

Cut off from the past and dubious of the future, the postmodern imagination sentences itself to an eternal present of unceasing *repetition*. Within the postmodern myth, human life is not a drama of moral and cultural progress; it's just a set of more or less meaningless habits. We run through the same motions day after day, like factory assembly-line belts. Philip Glass's score for *Koyaanisqatsi* performs accordingly. As images of an assembly line flash before our eyes, the music repeats, over and over again, the same musical phrases. If you leave the room and come back a few minutes later, you won't feel that you've missed anything: the music is still running in place on an electronically synthesized treadmill. The effect is no accident. Glass's computer-programmed repetitions are a mass-produced sound for a mass-produced age.

FETISHIZING THE IMAGE

Postmodern artists have been fascinated by the cultural implications of mass production ever since Andy Warhol first began to paint disconcertingly accurate canvases of Campbell's soup cans back in the early 1960s. By investing a soup can with the aura of high art, Warhol challenged his audience to recognize the nature of modern industrial culture. Reflecting the commodity fetishism of an economy that mass produces consumer goods and then invests them with an aura of desire to ensure their consumption, Warhol's canvases parody the imagery of the American marketplace. "What America really believes in," Warhol was saying, "is mass production and mass consumption. If medieval artists painted the dominant icons of their culture—the Madonnas and Crucifixions that now line the walls of our art museums

—why shouldn't we paint our icons, such as consumer products, celebrities, and dollar bills, and stick them up in museums too?"

Behind Warhol's postmodern canvases, then, the semiotician can find an industrial and postindustrial culture dedicated to mechanical reproduction, to turning out millions of identical automobiles, microchips, stuffed animals, hamburgers, what have you. To sell all these goods and services, their producers turn to advertisers who transform them into "concepts," into icons of desire, and so keep the wheels of mass consumption in motion (see chapter 4). Warhol doesn't criticize this culture so much as make us see it. He even seems to find it rather entertaining. An age of commodity fetishism requires an *art* of commodity fetishism, an art of the soup can. The medium, once again, is the message.

The human equivalent of commodity fetishism is the cult of the celebrity, which might be called a kind of image fetishism. Just as advertising transforms products into desirable images, celebrity image-managers transform human beings into icons of desire. Celebrities are people with attractive surfaces, images that play to the cameras. They are like mirrors, reflecting back the dreams and desires of those who worship them. Whatever human reality lurks behind the image, whatever doesn't show up on camera, is irrelevant. In fact, in the postmodern age, one often gets the impression that there *is* nothing behind the image.

In the age of the Cross and the Virgin, one did not speak of one's "image." Rather, human beings were thought of as creatures with souls, or spirits, or characters that were fixed at birth. But in an age when the Dynamo has lent its electric energy to TV, human beings are being redefined. Today we think of ourselves as actors, as role players who can wear many different social masks, adopt any number of "looks" or images. Like TV heroes, we can change our roles by rewriting our own scripts, become someone else, exchange one image for another. Mask yields to mask. You pull away the veils of your social disguise and, as John Fowles suggests in *The Magus*, reveal . . . another disguise.

It's no accident that the postmodern ethos has emerged in the age of *People* magazine and the actor-president. The faces in *People* are designed solely for public consumption, images calculated to appeal to America's voracious appetite for media stars. Ronald Reagan, for his part, has given new meaning to the phrase "the making of the president," standing as our era's dominant media creation. Garry Trudeau has summed it all up by portraying Ronald Reagan as "Ron Headrest"—a sort of political Max Headroom—that is, as a celebrity image that exists not only *for* your TV screen but can't exist *outside* it.

In the postmodern worldview, there is no such thing as an essential "me," no centering self-identity, no inborn character. There are only roles, images we take up in imitation of other images. The careers of such postmodern pop celebrities as Madonna, David Bowie, and Michael Jackson are paradigmatic. Madonna began by playing the role of a "punk" rock star in her "Like a Virgin" phase and then redefined herself in the image of an even more potent TV-age icon, Marilyn Monroe. David Bowie has played every role from Ziggy Stardust to the title role in the film *The Man Who Fell to Earth*. Michael Jackson has gone from Motown to sadomasochistic black leather, allegedly altering his hair, facial features, and skin color in the process.

You can see it all happening every day on MTV, where the fetishized image reaches its pop cultural apotheosis. In an MTV video, the look is everything: character, the spirit that lives beneath the skin, is nothing. Images are put on and taken off at will, each new role unencumbered by the need for a coherent plot. As Pat Aufderheide writes in her essay "Music Videos: The Look of the Sound," "Music videos have no heroes, because they do not feature individuals in the sense that plot-driven entertainment does. Music video offers unadulterated celebrity. The human beings do not play characters, but bold and connotative icons." Rock-video stars play-act at being "sailors, thugs, gang members, and gangsters," Aufderheide observes, and as "prostitutes, nightclub performers, goddesses, temptresses, and servants," images "drawn not from life or even myth, but from old movies, ads, and other pop culture clichés."

So rather than creating original self-identities, postmodern rock stars like the B-52's, the Go-Go's, and the Bangles emulate the look and style of the early 1960s, while Elvis Costello pastiches Elvis Presley and Buddy Holly. David Byrne's "big suit" echoes the zoot suit craze, while Cyndi Lauper toys with the punk look—which, for its part, was a parody of sadomasochistic pornography. In the postmodern worldview, there can be no original image: there is only parody, a world of cultural clichés.

For all its ironic mockery of the iconography of mass culture, however, postmodernism has proven to be a profitable ally of corporate America. MTV videos, after all, sell records, and even *Koyaanisqatsi* has inspired a television advertisement for First Interstate Bank that takes us on its own cinematic odyssey from the great Southwest to the fast-frame world of Los Angeles. Coca-Cola commercials often resemble rock videos, creating a dizzying montage of celebrity and noncelebrity images that fosters an illusion of intimacy between the ad's viewers—who can see themselves in the noncelebrity frames—and the celebrities they glimpse drinking Coca-Cola. Indeed, the images flash by so quickly that the celebrity and noncelebrity frames blend together, making everyone a celebrity—if not for Warhol's fifteen minutes, at least for fifteen milliseconds.

I suppose it was inevitable. In a culture devoted to the transformation of products into images, one could hardly expect to see the postmodern flair for image production passed up. Nor has Madison Avenue ignored the distinctively narrativeless texture of the postmodern imagination. Traditional commercials often set up a narrative situation of some sort, which, though trivial, has a beginning, a middle, and an end—as when Mrs. Olson saves her young neighbors' marriage by introducing them to Folger's Coffee. But in Calvin Klein's postmodern campaign for Obsession perfume, it's virtually impossible to tell just what is going on. A tormented young woman seems to be torn between a young boy and an older man—or does the young boy represent a flashback to the older man's youth? Maybe it's her kid brother? Her son? She touches his face for an instant but refuses to be touched and glides away. Tears run down her glacial Art Deco face, but it isn't clear what she's crying about. She speaks a few words, but their meaning is obscure. A surrealistic dream vision rather than a coherent narrative, the Obsession commercial substitutes eccentric imagery for narrative significance. What matters is the "look," the inscrutable aura of postmodern chic.

Commercial TV has produced its own version of the postmodern antinarrative in the action thriller "Miami Vice." As Todd Gitlin observes in his essay "Car Commercials and 'Miami Vice,'" the show represents a world that is all surface, all cool pastel pinks and greens. The plots are usually negligible, because the point is not to tell a story but to display Crockett and Tubbs: their clothes, their cars, their blank imperturbability in the face of a world filled with danger and intrigue. The dialogue is often mumbled, Lieutenant Castillo's words bitten off as if they taste funny and his language reduced almost to silence in a violent world that words cannot describe. Language attempts to make sense of things by labeling and categorizing them, but labels are of little value in the Miami underworld, where narcotics detectives disguise themselves as drug dealers and drug dealers disguise themselves as legitimate businessmen. Your own partner may be on the take, so it's better not to give yourself away. Emotional commitment is dangerous in such a world, so just wear your mask and be cool.

Staying cool in the face of an increasingly chaotic world is the essence of the postmodern attitude. Though it may appear to some as an expression of cultural exhaustion or even decadence, the postmodern pose is one way of maintaining psychic equilibrium. Better to be indifferent than to burn out in the pressure cooker of modern life.

What began as an avant-garde rejection of the narrative of the West has thus become a general social attitude, a way of coping with the times. With its increasing connections to mainstream culture, postmodernism is no longer just a name for something that artists in Greenwich Village may be doing: it is the name of an era. For in its coolly ironic images, its repetitive surfaces and lack of historical depth, we may meet the future, and yes, Pogo, it is us.

Deconstructing the Temple of Semiotics: The Night Thoughts of an Anxious Semiotician

Is nothing sacred?
    Anguished proverb

T here's this old joke about the history of Jewish philosophy. "Maimonides," the joke begins, "said that the meaning of life was all in *here*"—and with this the joker points to his head. "Marx," the joker continues, "said that it was all in *here*"—now pointing to his stomach. "Freud," he mischievously adds, "said that it was all in *here*"—pointing to his groin. "And Einstein," the joker concludes triumphantly, "said that it was all relative."

As this semiotician contemplates the logical consequences of his own philosophy, the joke, it sometimes seems, is really on him. For if we insist that our perceptions, knowledge, and values depend on the languages that we speak and the cultures to which we belong, we must conclude that no perspective—even the semiotic one—is privileged and that our judgments are indeed relative in the end. But if that's true, what does it mean for the semiotician? That his interpretations, no matter how interesting and ingenious, can never be conclusive? Yes, it means that. But does it also mean that his very science has only a limited validity, that "semiotics" is just one more cultural myth among an irreducible supply of myths with no greater claim to explanatory superiority than any of the others? Alas yes, it could just mean that too.

All this can put semioticians in a somewhat false position if they're unwilling to face up to a few uncomfortable facts. First of all, they're going to have to learn to live with a certain probably irreconcilable contradiction: namely, that the central principles of their own "science" effectively prevent it from being a science—that is, something with universal validity. This did not occur to the founders of semiotics—C. S. Peirce and Ferdinand de Saussure—but it is one of the ironies of intellectual history that this most shattering of semiotic lessons first became apparent in the mid-1960s, just at the time that semiotics first began to command the attention of American intellectuals.

Here's what happened. In 1966, two literature professors at Johns Hopkins University—Richard Macksey and Eugenio Donato—organized an international colloquium with the intention of introducing to American intellectuals a broad array of European philosophers whose work pioneered a number of the semiotic principles that we've explored in this book. No one expected that one of these philosophers—a young Frenchman by the name of Jacques Derrida (pronounced DARE-e-da)—would effectively blow the lid off the semiotic treasure chest even before most Americans knew what was inside. But that's exactly what he did, and no semiotician has been able to sleep well at night ever since.

In a paper entitled "Structure, Sign, and Play in the Discourse of the Human Sciences," Derrida quite simply pointed out that if, as the semioticians insisted, all human knowledge is encoded in ideologically motivated systems of signs, then every attempt to crack the codes of human knowledge can only produce another code. To put this another way, to achieve a final interpretation of some cultural phenomenon, you'd have to be able to transcend the entire mythological system in which you dwell. And that, semiotics itself argues, is something you can't do. It's like trying to pull yourself up by your own bootstraps: no matter how hard you try, no matter what new interpretational method you come up with, you're not going to be able to escape the circle of signs. No one in the semiotic game, in other words, can get outside the game. There is no instant replay, no high commissioner, to decide controversial calls. Everyone, from the scientist to the theologian, must operate from within some mythological and ideological system.

Since 1966, Derrida has written an ever-growing number of books and articles—many of them almost obsessively complex— that attempt to take apart or, in his own word, to "deconstruct," the truth claims of all the human sciences. Every interpretation —of a culture, of a literary text, of an object, of nature itself— is not only essentially provisional but is unstable as well, according to Derrida, forever inviting further, often contradictory, interpretations. No field of knowledge, in other words, is sacred, immune to criticism and self-contradiction.

All this can be awfully unsettling if you've spent your life trying to establish the firm foundations of a science, and Derrida has been called a lot of names—from "nihilist" to "negative theologian"—by a lot of angry intellectuals. But he has also won an extraordinary number of converts. Indeed, since Derrida's first appearance on the American scene in 1966, a growing army of semioticians, sociologists, literary critics, philosophers of science, linguists, psychologists, even lawyers has taken up his challenge and has been zealously deconstructing the truth claims of their disciplines with a kind of joyful abandon. A deconstructively minded literary critic, for instance, doesn't interpret a text: he painstakingly describes why the text can't be properly reduced to any noncontradictory meaning. A lawyer who's read some Derrida will similarly point out that the law cannot rest on a firm foundation of "truth" or "justice," because these are just words whose meanings are relative to the cultures in which they are spoken. And deconstructing semioticians have to pull the rug out from under themselves every time they claim to have found the meaning of a cultural object.

You may well wonder how one goes about this. Some deconstructors—Derrida among them—simply make it very clear that they have no position of their own. At the end of an analysis, they may take back anything they said, or point out how their analysis can't be concluded until it too has been deconstructed, and then you've got to deconstruct the deconstruction, and so on, ad infinitum. I once heard a particularly good lecture on Shakespeare's *The Winter's Tale*, for example, in which the lecturer effectively argued that the play was really about the impossibility of interpreting anything properly, that you're always going to get something wrong. I suggested to the lecturer that if he was right, then he had successfully interpreted something after all. He looked a little uncomfortable, and then simply said, "but now you've got to deconstruct my interpretation."

It's a good deal like the old paradox of the lying Cretan. The ancient Greeks invented this one. Let's say that a man from Crete walks up to you and says "all Cretans are liars." The problem here is that you can never be sure of the truth of what you've been told. If all Cretans *are* liars, a Cretan isn't going to be able to tell you the truth about it. So if he's telling the truth, he must be lying; or is it the other way around: that is, if he's lying, he must be telling the truth? Philosophers have been giving themselves headaches over this one for more than two thousand years.

The trouble, as Douglas Hofstadter pointed out so effectively in his best-selling book *Gödel, Escher, Bach*, is that the world is coming to resemble an M. C. Escher drawing. We seem to be caught in the closed loops of our own knowledge, each one of our interpretations of the world ultimately referring back to the way in which we interpret that world rather than to anything outside the interpretational system. This is the ultimate implication of the semiotic judgment that a language system represents cultural points of view rather than natural realities. Nature, uninterpreted reality, it now seems, is beyond our grasp.

So have I led you down a blind alley after all, pulling the rug out from under you and deconstructing my own book, taking it all back even as I present it to you? I don't intend this. But I have to acknowledge that all is not well among the semioticians. As Marshall Blonsky points out in his introduction to an anthology of essays titled *On Signs*, there is a certain amount of melancholy in the semiotic world today. This is by no means universally the case, but those semioticians who are not at all excited by the deconstruction of semiotics—and I'm one of them —have been pressed into a bit of a corner. So what can I say in response? How can I justify semiotics to you when professional semioticians themselves have so complicated the field?

THE POWER OF THE SIGN

If I really felt that semiotics was hopelessly self-contradictory, I wouldn't have bothered writing this book. And I am not going to take it all back now and "deconstruct" the semiotic edifice I have built. Because in spite of its contradictions, semiotics is founded on a firm reality: the reality of power. That, finally, is what semiotics is all about: the power we have to define and enforce our own conceptions of reality. Because it is in the interest of those who hold power to conceal the fact that *they* have defined the "facts" of social reality, we need semiotics to unmask them. And herein lies the secure value of semiotics for all of us: it enables us to question authority, to challenge the status quo. This is why semiotics has proven so popular among those groups (such as women) who have traditionally been shut out of the corridors of power.

There is nothing inherently liberal or revolutionary about semiotics, however. When in late 1987, for example, the conservative jurist Robert Bork was turned down by the senate in his quest to become a Supreme Court justice, he was rejected by senators who objected to his belief that our constitutional rights are *granted* by the constitution rather than *protected* by it; that our freedoms are political in origin rather than natural. But this, ironically enough, is a perfectly sound semiotic position, simply reflecting the semiotic precept that society, not nature, is at the heart of human realities. Many of us would like to believe that we are born with certain inalienable human rights, but the fact that we are alienated from these rights all the time should make us know better. If we are fortunate enough to have any rights at all it is because we have instituted a political system that grants them to us. Bork, it seems, rather let the semiotic cat out of the bag, proving that even conservatives can be covert semioticians.

My point is that semiotics in itself serves neither a liberal nor a conservative interest; it neutrally exposes the interests behind all myths of culture. How you use the power of semiotics is very much up to you. As a practicing semiotician you'll meet resistance every step of the way, however, because people do not enjoy having their most cherished beliefs questioned and exposed. Still, irrational prejudices can only be disrupted by rational procedures, and at its best, semiotics is a rational science that enables us to get a better understanding of our own world and the interests that constitute it. If that understanding can never be a perfect one, there are still greater and lesser degrees of cultural blindness. Semiotics can lift the veils from our eyes, illuminating the hidden causes of our actions by reading the signs that express them. It can reveal the motives behind the behavior of others and the motives behind our own. The signs of our time are written everywhere around us. In the end, this book itself is a sign whose meaning fits into an entire cultural system. Now, what might that meaning be?

The following list includes the bibliographical information for works cited in my text, as well as general reference works and journals that will help you explore further the horizons of semiotics on your own.

Ardrey, Robert. *The Territorial Imperative* (New York: Atheneum, 1966). A controversial argument for the biological origins of human territoriality. Ardrey suggests that evolution has programmed us to define our own private spaces whose boundaries we will fight to defend.

Aufderheide, Pat. "Music Videos: The Look of the Sound," in *Watching Television*, ed. Todd Gitlin (New York: Pantheon, 1986). Aufderheide traces the history of American music videos while analyzing the relation between MTV and postmodern culture.

Barthes, Roland. *Mythologies*, trans. Annette Lavers (New York: Hill and Wang, 1972). A pioneering collection of essays by one of the founders of modern semiotics. Barthes analyzes the semiotic significance of everything from professional wrestling to plastic, from striptease to laundry detergent.

———. *Système de la Mode* (Paris: Seuil, 1967). Barthes analyzes the Paris fashion system, applying the fundamental principles of structural semiology.

Berger, John. *Ways of Seeing* (New York: Penguin, 1972). A Marxist art critic exposes the hidden relationship between painting and political culture. Based on a television series for the BBC, Berger's book is generously, and provocatively, illustrated.

Blonsky, Marshall. *On Signs* (Baltimore, Md.: Johns Hopkins Univ. Press, 1985). An enormous anthology of semiotic essays, including contributions from Umberto Eco and Jacques Derrida, as well as a cartoon contribution from the creator of *The Story of O*. Blonsky's introduction surveys the state of contemporary semiotics in the wake of Roland Barthes's untimely death.

Brownmiller, Susan. *Against Our Will: Men, Women, and Rape* (New York: Simon and Schuster, 1975). Brownmiller presents her radical-feminist argument that rape is a universal male conspiracy to keep women in subjection.

Derrida, Jacques. "Structure, Sign, and Play in the Discourse of the Human Sciences," in *The Structuralist Controversy*, ed. Eugenio Donato and Richard Macksey (Baltimore, Md.: Johns Hopkins Univ. Press, 1972). Derrida's ground-breaking essay, which effectively pulled the rug out from under semiotics by pointing out its internal contradictions. Not for the faint of heart.

Eco, Umberto. *A Theory of Semiotics* (Bloomington: Indiana Univ. Press, 1979). A monumental theory of code formation by the author of *The Name of the Rose*. Often technical in both style and content, Eco's book is nonetheless a classic in contemporary semiotic studies.

Edmunds, Lowell. "De Gustibus," in *Johns Hopkins Magazine*, vol. 39, no. 6 (December 1987), 14–19. An engaging article on Roman culture and cuisine. Worthwhile reading before preparing your next all-zucchini meal.

Eisenstein, Hester. *Contemporary Feminist Thought* (Boston: G. K. Hall, 1983). Eisenstein surveys the history of modern feminism, presenting clear expositions and critiques of many of the leading figures in feminist scholarship.

Engelhardt, Tom. "Children's Television: The Shortcake Strategy," in *Watching Television*, ed. Todd Gitlin (New York: Pantheon, 1986). An entertaining and thought-provoking essay on the relationship between children's television and the commercial interests that create and sponsor it. Read it before you buy the next He-Man doll for your kids.

Gibian, Peter. "The Art of Being Off Center: Shopping Center Spaces and Spectacles," in *Tabloid*, nos. 4–5 (1981). Gibian meditates on the history of the American shopping mall, finding surprising connections between mall design and avant-garde art.

Gitlin, Todd. "Car Commercials and 'Miami Vice,' " in *Watching Television*, ed. Todd Gitlin (New York: Pantheon, 1986). A lively analysis of the cultural significance of modern automobile advertising by one of America's leading critics of popular culture. Gitlin's analysis of "Miami Vice" supplements his interpretations of car commercials with useful insights into postmodern culture.

Goodnow, Jacqueline J. "The Nature of Intelligent Behavior: Questions Raised by Cross-Cultural Studies," in *The Nature of Intelligence*, ed. Lauren B. Resnik (Pittsburgh: Univ. of Pittsburgh Press, 1976). Explores the ways in which we define and measure intelligent behavior, revealing the cultural biases behind intelligence testing.

Greenbie, Barrie. *Spaces: Dimensions of the Human Landscape* (New Haven, Conn.: Yale Univ. Press, 1981). A lavishly illustrated exploration of the American architectural landscape. Greenbie's photographic odyssey takes him from city to suburb and beyond, while his clear and entertaining text interprets the human dimensions of the built environment. A delight whether you live in the city or the country.

Hawkes, Terence. *Structuralism and Semiotics* (Berkeley: Univ. of California Press, 1977). The clearest and most succinct account of literary semiotics that I can recommend. Provides useful summaries of the work of Ferdinand de Saussure and C. S. Peirce. I use it frequently in my own courses.

Hofstadter, Douglas. *Gödel, Escher, Bach: An Eternal Golden Braid* (New York: Random House, 1980). A masterful, best-selling introduction to the labyrinth of human perception. Hofstadter explores logic, music, and painting to show how we are forever locked into a circle of signs.

Huyssens, Andreas. *After the Great Divide: Modernism, Mass Culture, Postmodernism* (Bloomington: Indiana Univ. Press, 1986). One of a growing number of new books exploring the emergence of postmodern culture from out of the modern scene.

Irigaray, Luce. "When Our Lips Speak Together," trans. and with an introduction by Carolyn Burke, in *Signs: Journal of Women in Culture and Society*, vol. 6, no. 1 (1980), 66–79. An experimental poetic "essay" written in a feminist language divorced from the patriarchal conventions of ordinary discourse.

Jencks, Charles. *The Language of Post-Modern Architecture* (New York: Rizzoli, 1984). An illustrated tour of Postmodern architecture by the man who coined the term "post-modern." Jencks explains the difference between the Modern and the Postmodern tradition in international architecture.

Kaplan, Ann E. *Rocking Round the Clock: Music Television, Postmodernism, and Consumer Culture* (New York: Methuen, 1987). Explores the connections between the culture of consumption and the postmodern worldview, focusing on music videos.

Kowinski, William. *The Malling of America: An Inside Look at the Great Consumer Paradise* (New York: William Morrow, 1985). The personal odyssey of a man who spent seven years visiting shopping malls across America. Absolutely the last word on the history of the American shopping center. Was he born to shop?

Kron, Joan. *Home-Psych: The Social Psychology of Home and Decoration* (New York: Clarkson N. Potter, 1983). Everything you ever wanted to know about the high-powered world of interior decoration.

Kuhn, Thomas. *The Structure of Scientific Revolutions* (Chicago: Univ. of Chicago Press, 1962). A revolution in its own right, Kuhn's book startled the scientific world with its documentation of the cultural bases of scientific research. Arguing that what scientists look for is determined by the communal contexts in which they work, Kuhn undermines the myth of the absolutely objective and disinterested scientist. A classic.

Lévi-Strauss, Claude. *The Raw and the Cooked*, trans. John and Doreen Weightman (New York: Harper & Row, 1969). Lévi-Strauss's massive semiotic analysis of the cultural mythologies of such New World societies as the Bororo Indians of central Brazil. A classic of structural anthropology.

————. *The Savage Mind* (Chicago: Univ. of Chicago Press, 1970). Another anthropological classic. Here Lévi-Strauss analyzes the semiotic significance of nonscientific forms of natural classification. Defending native taxonomies like those of the Hopi Indians against the charge that they are inferior to scientific taxonomic systems, Lévi-Strauss explores the connection between culture and classification.

McLuhan, Marshall. *The Gutenberg Galaxy* (Toronto: Univ. of Toronto Press, 1962). McLuhan explores the impact of the printing press on Western consciousness and anticipates a new mode of consciousness emerging in the wake of the invention of the electronic media. A classic by the man who put the word "media" on the map of modern cultural criticism.

Maddock, Kenneth. *The Australian Aborigines* (Harmondsworth, England: Penguin, 1974). My source for the story of the Dalabon taxonomic system.

Mauss, Marcel. *The Gift: Forms and Function of Exchange in Archaic Societies*, trans. Ian Cunnison (New York: Norton, 1967). A pioneering sociological study of the role of gift-giving in binding societies together.

Millett, Kate. *Sexual Politics* (New York: Avon, 1970). One of the first manifestos of the women's movement, Millett's book made the word "patriarchy" a household term.

Milton, Edith. "The Track of the Mutant," in *Boston Review*, vol. 12, no. 6 (December 1987). An engaging overview of recent science fiction films and the messages they are sending about our changing relationship with the machine. A must if you're planning to make your own Mr. Right.

Molloy, John T. *The Woman's Dress for Success Book* (Chicago: Follett, 1977). A guide for the ambitious working woman by a successful wardrobe engineer.

Patterson, Francine G. "Conversations with a Gorilla," in *National Geographic*, vol. 154, no. 4 (1979), 438–465. Patterson documents her remarkable "conversations" with Koko, a gorilla she has taught to communicate in American Sign Language.

Peirce, Charles Sanders. *Collected Papers*, 8 volumes, ed. Charles Hartshorne and Paul Weiss (Cambridge: Cambridge Univ. Press, 1931–1966). The lectures, essays, and notes that started it all. A monumental compilation of the writings of the founder of modern semiotics.

Preziosi, Donald. *The Semiotics of the Built Environment: An Introduction to Architectonic Analysis* (Bloomington: Indiana Univ. Press, 1979). A technical study of architectural semiotics by a past president of the Semiotic Society of America. Preziosi's book is one of the first to investigate architecture from a semiotic perspective.

Sacks, Oliver. *The Man Who Mistook His Wife for a Hat and Other Clinical Tales* (New York: Harper & Row, 1987). Startling and bizarre case studies drawn from the files of America's best-known clinical neurologist.

Sale, Roger. *Fairy Tales and After: From Snow White to E. B. White* (Cambridge, Mass.: Harvard Univ. Press, 1978). A history of the fairy tale that explores the cultural significance of the stories we tell in the nursery. Sale examines the history of the era of life that we call "childhood" and points out how we have not always been conscious of it as a distinct stage of human growth.

Sapir, Edward. *Selected Writings in Language, Culture, and Personality*, ed. David G. Mandelbaum (Berkeley: Univ. of California Press, 1949). Classic papers from one of the pioneers of structural linguistics. Sapir describes the relation between language and perception, thus anticipating contemporary semiotic analyses.

Saussure, Ferdinand de. *Course in General Linguistics*, ed. Charles Bally and Albert Sechehage and trans. Roy Harris (London: Duckworth, 1983). The posthumously published lectures of the founder of structural linguistics and semiology. Along with Peirce's *Collected Papers*, this book presents the foundations for all semiotic study.

Sebeok, Thomas. "Smart Simians: The Self-Fulfilling Prophecy and Kindred Methodological Pitfalls," in *The Play of Musement* (Bloomington: Indiana Univ. Press, 1981). The founder of the Semiotic Society of America challenges Francine (Penny) Patterson's claims about Koko's linguistic abilities. According to Sebeok, human language is one thing and animal signs are another, making it impossible for anyone to really talk to the animals.

Silverman, Kaja. *The Subject of Semiotics* (New York: Oxford Univ. Press, 1983). A technical introduction to the psychoanalytic school of semiotic studies by a professor of Film and Women's Studies.

Soler, Jean. "The Semiotics of Food in the Bible," in *Food, Drink, and History*, ed. Robert Forster and Orest Ranum (Baltimore, Md.: Johns Hopkins Univ. Press, 1979). The most convincing semiotic explanation of the significance of the kashruth that I have found. Soler's essay charts the close relationship between the Jewish dietary laws and the worldview of ancient Jewish culture.

Sutton-Smith, Brian. *Toys As Culture* (New York: Gardner, 1986). An engaging history of the varying roles that toys have played in human society, Sutton-Smith's book demonstrates once and for all that there is nothing trivial about toys.

Wolfe, Tom. *From Bauhaus to Our House* (New York: Farrar Strauss Giroux, 1981). An iconoclastic history of modernist architecture by one of the founders of the "new journalism."

Wolfe's amusing and informative text probes the ideological origins of all those glass office towers that dot the modern urban landscape, as well as the thinking behind modern home design.

SEMIOTICS JOURNALS

Semiotica. An international journal of semiotic studies edited by Thomas Sebeok. Aimed at an academic readership, the essays in *Semiotica* can be very technical, but they cover the entire range of contemporary semiotic research.

American Journal of Semiotics. The official journal of the Semiotic Society of America, *AJS* publishes articles by many of the same semioticians who contribute to *Semiotica* but tends to specialize in literary semiotics.

Signs: Journal of Women in Culture and Society. An academic journal devoted to the study of women in society, *Signs* explores the entire range of gender studies, including both feminist theory and practice.

Semiotexte. An avant-garde review of modern culture.